Security and Privacy in Social Networks

Yaniv Altshuler • Yuval Elovici • Armin B. Cremers
Nadav Aharony • Alex Pentland
Editors

Security and Privacy in Social Networks

 Springer

Editors
Yaniv Altshuler
MIT Media Lab
Cambridge, MA, USA

Yuval Elovici
Telekom Innovation Lab
Information systems engineering
Ben-Gurion University
Beer-Sheva, Israel

Armin B. Cremers
Univresity of Bonn
Bonn, Germany

Nadav Aharony
MIT Media Lab
Cambridge, MA, USA

Alex Pentland
MIT Media Lab
Cambridge, MA, USA

The book is based in part of works initially presented at the Workshop on Security and Privacy in Social Networks that was held in conjugation with the IEEE Social Computing conference 2012, Cambridge, MA.

ISBN 978-1-4939-0122-7   ISBN 978-1-4614-4139-7 (eBook)
DOI 10.1007/978-1-4614-4139-7
Springer New York Heidelberg Dordrecht London

Printed on acid-free paper

Springer is part of Springer Science+Business Media (www.springer.com)

Contents

Introduction to Security and Privacy in Social Networks

Yuval Elovici and Yaniv Altshuler

As the area of online social networking develops and many online services add social features to their offerings, the definition of online social networking services broadens. Online social networking services range from social interaction-centered sites such as *Facebook* or *MySpace*, to information dissemination-centric services such as *Twitter* or *Google Buzz*, to social interaction features added to existing sites and services such as *Flickr* or *Amazon*. Each of these services has different characteristics of social interaction and different vulnerabilities to attack.

The value of online social networking sites stems from the fact that people spend large amounts of time on these networks updating their personal profiles, browsing for social or professional interactions, or taking part in social-oriented online applications and events. People nowadays have become immersed in their preferred online social environments, creating an exciting entanglement between their real and virtual identities [1]. However, this immersion also holds great peril for users, their friends, and their employers, and may even endanger national security.

There is much information in the patterns of communication between users and their peers. These patterns are affected by many relationship and context factors and can be used in a reverse direction to infer the relationship and context. Later on, these relationships can be further used to deduce additional private information which was intended to remain undisclosed. A recent study carried out at MIT is said to be able to reveal the sexual orientation of Internet users based on social network contacts. In this example, the users whose privacy was compromised did not place

Y. Elovici (✉)
Telekom Innovation Lab, Information systems engineering, Ben-Gurion University,
P.O.B. 653, Beer-Sheva, Israel
e-mail: elovici@bgu.ac.il

Y. Altshuler
Human Dynamic Group, MIT Media Lab, 77 Mass. Ave, Cambridge, MA 02139, USA
e-mail: yanival@media.mit.edu

Y. Altshuler et al. (eds.), *Security and Privacy in Social Networks*,
DOI 10.1007/978-1-4614-4139-7_1, © Springer Science+Business Media New York 2013

this information online, but rather disclosed their social interaction to users who apparently did disclose this information [2].

In other cases, this problem can become even worse due to the (false) assumption of users that information marked as "private" will remain private and will not be disclosed by the network. Indeed, although the operators of social networks rarely betray the confidence of their users, no security mechanism is perfect. Because these networks often use standard (and not necessarily updated) security methods, a determined attacker can sometimes gain access to such unauthorized information. The combination of sensitive private information managed by users who are not security-aware in an environment that is not hermetically sealed is a sure cause of frequent leaks of private information and identity thefts [3, 4].

This problem becomes even more threatening when viewed from the corporate (or even national) perspective. Users who possess sensitive commercial or security-related information are expected to be under strict control in their workplaces. However, while interacting virtually in social networks, these same people often tend to ignore precautions due to a false sense of intimacy and privacy, all the while being unaware of the damage their naive behavior may cause. Because it is hard (and sometimes illegal) to monitor the behavior of online social network users, these platforms constitute a significant threat to the safety and privacy of sensitive information. Hard to detect and almost impossible to prevent, leaks of business, military, or government data through social networks could become the security epidemic of the twenty-first century [5, 6].

This book aims to bring to the forefront innovative approaches for analyzing and enhancing the security and privacy dimensions of online social networks. To facilitate the transition of such methods from theory to practical mechanisms designed and deployed in existing online social networking services, we need to create a common language for use between researchers and practitioners in this new area, ranging from the theory of computational social sciences to conventional security and network engineering.

The rest of this book is divided into three parts covering three complementary themes and is structured as follows. The first part contains four studies that touch on fundamental aspects of security and privacy in social networks, raising and discussing topics such as the conceptual definition of identity in social networks and the interplay between ethics and crowdsourcing. The second part of the book is devoted to innovative mathematical models which link the social dimension of networks to existing privacy and network security issues. This section contains three studies which analyze different domains ranging from mobile networks to financial trading networks and demonstrating the essential differences between security issues in social and non-social environments. The third section focuses on specific case studies and presents an in-depth analysis of three unique examples of how "security-oriented research" is carried out in social domains and how it differs from similar efforts which do not take place in such environments.

Chapter "Introduction to Security and Privacy in Social Networks" introduces a multidimensional concept of privacy in social networks which delineates aspects of privacy along various legal, technical, and social dimensions. The privacy concept thus developed is then visualized using tripartite diagrams which provide a quick orientation to this paradigm's strengths and weaknesses as demonstrated in social networks. The chapter then investigates how these properties evolve from the fact that information in the physical word decays over time, while in the online world, information is in principle permanently available. Although this chapter focuses on a qualitative analysis of this topic, a more quantitative metric that would clearly enhance comparability of privacy issues in different social networks and the tracking of improvements over time is envisioned for future development.

A key aspect of social networks is the digital identity (or identities) adopted by users to characterize and recognize themselves and others. At first glance, it may appear that users of social networks treat and use digital identities similarly to their "real-world" identities. However, the absence of physical contact enables people to create several identities, some of which may be anonymous. Furthermore, users of social networks search and acknowledge each other based mainly on attributes that they exchange through the infrastructure of the social network (which in turn can be further used to disguise one's true identity). Chapter "Interdisciplinary Impact Analysis of Privacy in Social Networks" sheds light on the fascinating topic of digital identities by presenting a basic conceptual framework that analyzes fundamental aspects of the use of identities in social networks and recommends possible methods to improve the use of such identities. The chapter begins by presenting basic concepts related to the differences between digital and real identities, followed by a discussion on the challenges of the digital facet. Next, solutions for security and privacy challenges relating to digital identities are presented. The chapter discusses the perception of the identity of an entity as a notion existing in the minds of other entities. This gives rise to the possibility of multiple identities for a single entity in different contexts, a phenomenon which is called "pseudonymity" and which is possibly or potentially available in the online world more readily than in the real world.

Chapter "Recognizing Your Digital Friends" presents an overview of the requirements for and comparisons of encryption schemes for social networking services based on a peer-to-peer (p2p) infrastructure (as opposed to centralized server architectures) and describes the challenges of p2p social networking architectures and their high-level requirements. The chapter then discusses the criteria by which p2p encryption systems should be evaluated and compared: efficiency, functionality, and privacy. Four examples of existing p2p social networking architectures are then reviewed (*PeerSoN, Safebook, Diaspora*, and *Persona*), which focus on encryption as a means of ensuring data confidentiality. This is followed by a comparative analysis of these architectures against the evaluation criteria presented earlier. In addition, this chapter contains a parallel discussion of the differences between broadcast encryption and predicate encryption techniques in the context of the p2p encryption challenge.

The first part of the book concludes with chapter "Encryption for Peer-to-Peer Social Networks," which thoroughly investigates various ethical issues with respect to the expanding field of crowdsourcing. This highly disruptive field involves the partitioning of a mission into many small pieces, each given to ad hoc employees using an online platform. The rapid pace of this process enables fast completion of highly complex tasks at extremely low cost. Together with the anonymity of these platforms (which protects the identities of both the employers and the employee), this approach transforms crowdsourcing platforms into the equivalent of a super-computer network for a fraction of the cost. The number of potential applications is boundless, and several ethical questions arise. This chapter reviews recent developments in this area while examining some of these ethical challenges. In addition, chapter "Encryption for Peer-to-Peer Social Networks" studies the attitude of workers in crowdsourcing platforms (such as *MTurk*, *oDesk*, or *Elance*) towards performing unethical tasks and asserts that, although many workers in several crowdsourcing platforms studied expressed reluctance to perform unethical tasks, in practice, many workers were willing to accept unethical tasks (especially if they were well paid). Simple but unethical tasks may include breaking into someone else's email account and sending a fake email on behalf of that person, or faking a review of a commercial service. However, more elaborate large-scale uses may involve activities such as identification of demonstrators by police agencies or dictatorships. Interestingly, the results of an experiment detailed in the chapter hint that the anonymity provided by the crowdsourcing platform, the anticipated task consequence, and gender were not found to be influential. On the other hand, when the amount of monetary compensation offered increased, so did the willingness of workers to perform highly unethical tasks.

The second part of the book is introduced by chapter "Crowdsourcing and Ethics" and investigates how social networks influence the pricing of assets in the financial market. This influence is a result of the ongoing and unavoidable comparison of relative performance imposed on investors and traders because of the comprehensive integration of social networks into everyday life. Counterintuitively, this abundance of information may sometimes act to suppress of integrity in investment practice by pushing investors to adopt irrational investing strategies. For example, leading investors will in many cases be manipulated into buying risky assets knowingly at inflated prices. This chapter presents a mathematical model that studies these dynamics and suggests that the overpricing of risky assets that is often observed in the market is derived from these "social forces".

Chapter "The Effect of Social Status on Decision-Making and Prices in Financial Networks" predicts the existence of new kinds of malicious attacks on communications and on mobile infrastructures that are targeted at extracting, not password or credit card information, but information about the relationships in a real-world social network and characteristic information about the individuals in the network. The chapter discusses the expected features of such attacks and explains the differences between these attacks and traditional types of attacks against data privacy. The chapter then presents a mathematical model of such attacks and predicts that they would be impossible (or very unlikely) to detect using most of the network monitoring tools used today. This problem is caused by the surprising fact that the best strategy for attackers seeking social information and habits is, counterintuitively, a very slow and nonaggressive strategy (in contrast to most of the known malware threats).

Many online social network (OSN) owners regularly publish data collected from their users' online activities to third parties such as sociologists or commercial companies. These third parties further mine the data and extract knowledge to serve their diverse purposes. In the process of publishing data to these third parties, network owners face a nontrivial challenge: how to preserve users' privacy while keeping the information useful to third parties. Failure to protect users' privacy may result in severely undermining the popularity of OSNs as well as restricting the amount of data that the OSN owners are willing to share with third parties. Chapter "Stealing Reality: When Criminals Become Data Scientists (or Vice Versa)" discusses this problem while focusing on the use of classical privacy preservation models originally developed to protect tabular data privacy, such as k-anonymity and l-diversity, to preserve users' privacy in the publication of OSN data. The history of these methods is reviewed, and their applicability is demonstrated.

The third part of the book examines specific case studies regarding the unique features of security and privacy in social networks. This section opens with a discussion of innovative methods for using machine-learning techniques to reconstruct the structure of unknown social networks. Using this method, publicly available information may be used to reveal concealed information, which severely compromises the users' privacy, anonymity, and trust in the network. Chapter "Applications of k-Anonymity and ℓ-Diversity in Publishing Online Social Networks" presents the "link reconstruction attack," a method that is capable of inferring a user's connections to others with high accuracy. This attack may be used to detect connections that the user wanted to hide to preserve his privacy. We show that the concealment of one user's links is ineffective if it is not also done by others in the network and we present an analysis of the performance of various machine-learning algorithms for link predictions inside small communities.

In contrast to chapter "Applications of k-Anonymity and ℓ-Diversity in Publishing Online Social Networks" which demonstrated an attack that can be executed on social networks to steal private information, chapter "Links Reconstruction Attack" analyzes this topic from a different angle by studying the *Bitcoin* peer-to-peer monetary exchange system. The degree of anonymity in the *Bitcoin* system, an electronic analog of cash in the online world, is investigated using data from transactions which are publicly available to ensure the integrity of the *Bitcoin* system. Using mainstream methods from network theory, this chapter demonstrates how this anonymous (at least in theory) payment system can be partially de-anonymized. This technique is then used to track the "flow" of large amounts of stolen monetary credits, thus demonstrating how the identity of the users responsible for this theft can be disclosed using this network-based analysis method.

As discussed in previous chapters of this book, integration between several data sources may lead to compromised data privacy through the use of certain network-based analysis methods. Chapter "An Analysis of Anonymity in the Bitcoin System" is devoted to exploring the record linkage problem and presents a scheme for the maintenance of data privacy when data and records from multiple databases are combined in a way which still allows record-linking information verification services. The chapter begins by discussing two common modes of operation in this field, the de-identified and the fully trusted mode, and asserts that these approaches do not provide a definitive response to the needs of social data privacy. The chapter then reviews existing techniques and related work on record-linkage and privacy-preserving computations, pointing out the need for a new scheme for representing integrated data. The chapter contains a proposed model for a decoupled data architecture. The main technological concept studied in this chapter is the separation between identifying information and sensitive data, which needs to be protected. In this chapter, it is demonstrated how this decoupled data-access model can provide the same protection as de-identified data while at the same time being able to integrate data to support broad research in computational social sciences in a flexible manner. The study also tested the impact of different mechanisms for hindering inferences of identity when names are revealed for record-linkage purposes.

References

1. Onnela J-P, Reed-Tsochas F (2010) Spontaneous emergence of social influence in online systems. Proc Nat Acad Sci 107(4):18375–18380
2. Jernigan C, Mistree BFT (2009) Gaydar: Facebook friendships expose sexual orientation. First Monday 14(10)
3. Stana RM, Burton DR (2002) Identity theft: prevalence and cost appear to be growing. GAO-02-363. U.S. General Accounting Office, Washington, DC
4. Gross R, Acquisti A (2005) Information revelation and privacy in online social networks. In: Proceedings of the 2005 ACM workshop on privacy in the electronic society, Alexandria, pp 71–80
5. Brunner M, Hofinger H, Krauss C, Roblee C, Schoo P, Todt S (2010) Infiltrating critical infrastructures with next-generation attacks. Fraunhofer Institute for Secure Information Technology (SIT), Munich
6. Krishnamurthy B, Wills CE (2009) On the leakage of personally identifiable information via online social networks. In: Proceedings of the 2nd ACM workshop on online social networks, New York, pp 7–12

Interdisciplinary Impact Analysis of Privacy in Social Networks

Michael Netter, Sebastian Herbst, and Günther Pernul

Abstract The rise of the social web has traditionally been accompanied by privacy concerns. Research on social web privacy has been conducted from various viewpoints including legal, social, and the computer sciences. In this chapter, we propose an interdisciplinary approach to capture the multidimensional concept of privacy. For this purpose, we developed a three-layered framework to systematically analyze the privacy impact of various research directions. In addition, we conducted an interdisciplinary literature analysis, highlighting areas for improvement as well dependencies between different research directions.

1 Introduction

Over the last decade, the evolution of the World Wide Web led to the significant growth of Online Social Networks (OSNs), which are receiving much attention in the research community. While social networks have always been an important part of daily life, the advent of Web 2.0 and its easy-to-use services increasingly shift social life to their online counterparts. OSNs provide an infrastructure for communication, information, and self-expression, as well as for building and maintaining relationships with other users.

The increase in relevance and the quantity of social web services has been accompanied by privacy concerns. On one hand, these worries have arisen due to the prevalent oligopolistic social web landscape with only a few service providers possessing large databases with millions of user profiles. On the other hand, privacy concerns focus on the challenges of presenting different facets of the self to different audiences, and to keep those views consistent. While this bears a

M. Netter (✉) • S. Herbst • G. Pernul
Department of Information Systems, University of Regensburg, Regensburg D-93040, Germany
e-mail: michael.netter@wiwi.uni-regensburg.de; sebastian.herbst@wiwi.uni-regensburg.de;
guenther.pernul@wiwi.uni-regensburg.de

Y. Altshuler et al. (eds.), *Security and Privacy in Social Networks*,
DOI 10.1007/978-1-4614-4139-7_2, © Springer Science+Business Media New York 2013

resemblance to managing different appearances of the self in the real world, the inherent properties of mediated OSN communication (e.g., the permanency and searchability of personal information) places privacy at risk. Although privacy controls are in place to currently restrict access to personal data, users seem to be shortsighted with respect to future aspects of current behavior [1].

Both aforementioned areas of privacy have been studied extensively by researchers through various viewpoints such as law, the social sciences, and computer science. However, the ambiguous nature of privacy and the multiple definitions available impede a consistent view of the concept. Robert C. Post notes that privacy "... is a value so complex, so entangled in competing and contradictory dimensions, so engorged with various and distinct meanings, that I sometimes despair whether it can be usefully addressed at all." [2].

In this chapter, we stress the need to integrate insights from diverse areas of research on social web privacy. We contribute to this field by providing a framework with which to decompose social web privacy and systematically analyze the effects of different research directions. Subsequently, we applied the proposed framework to the body of research. Our results highlight areas for improvement as well as dependencies between different research directions, emphasizing the necessity to foster interdisciplinary research on social web privacy.

The remainder of this chapter is structured as follows. In Sect. 2, we give an overview of related work. In Sect. 3, we decompose social web privacy and transfer its components into a framework for analyzing the concept from different research directions. We apply our framework on the existing body of research, differentiating between privacy issues related to OSN users and OSN service providers in Sects. 4 and 5, respectively. Finally, in Sect. 6, we summarize our findings and highlight areas for future work.

2 Related Work

In this section, we present existing approaches that aim to integrate several research directions in order to create a holistic view of privacy. Approaches to particular aspects of privacy are discussed in our detailed impact analysis of the various privacy perspectives in Sects. 4 and 5.

Spiekermann and Cranor provide a framework with which to build privacy-friendly systems [3]. They distinguish between privacy-by-policy and privacy-by-architecture. The former is a legally-driven approach that focuses on notifying the user and obtaining consent prior to processing personal data. The latter is a technically-driven approach to minimize the collection of personal data without limiting functionality. However, their approach does not consider the social perspective of privacy and focuses on privacy in general, whereas our work examines social web privacy. The importance of social web privacy is acknowledged by the European Union, which is promoting several related research projects. For example, PADGETS[1] uses an interdisciplinary approach to strengthen users' privacy while harnessing social network data for policy making. Similarly, the European research project PrimeLife[2] has developed a framework with which to analyze privacy issues related to other OSN users [4]. Project results show that privacy issues arise when legal or social norms are disregarded or technical safeguards are circumvented. Depending on the owner's initial categorization of personal data (private, semi-public, or public), the PrimeLife framework allows an estimation of potential privacy risks. Unlike our approach, this work does not take privacy threats stemming from OSN service providers into account, but solely focuses on user-related privacy issues. PRESCIENT,[3] another EU-funded project, conducted an in-depth study of privacy conceptualizations [5]. It takes a legal, social, economic, and ethical perspective of privacy, highlighting similarities and interdependencies. This project's results provide useful insights to help understand the concept of privacy; however, the analyses do not follow a structured approach, as described in this chapter.

3 Proposed Three-Layered Framework

In this section, we give an overview of our proposed framework. The framework provides a general-purpose structure for social web privacy research domains. Subsequently, the concept of privacy is broken up into a set of characteristics that are used to conduct our impact analysis, as described in Sects. 4 and 5.

3.1 Overview

In their conceptualization of privacy in 1890 as "the right to be let alone," Warren and Brandeis were one of the first to recognize the multidimensionality of the privacy concept [6]. Until then, privacy threats were primarily related to potential physical harm [7]. The rise of the information age led to a large number of privacy conceptualizations from a variety of directions such as the social sciences, law, architecture, urban design, health sciences, and computer and information sciences. In their work to structure the concept of privacy, Patil and Kobsa introduce three main perspectives from which to describe and analyze privacy [8]:

- *Legal*: This aspect focuses on laws and policies that protect the individual from corporations, governments, and other individuals. For example, the European

---

[1] http://www.padgets.eu/

[2] http://www.primelife.eu/

[3] http://www.prescient-project.eu/

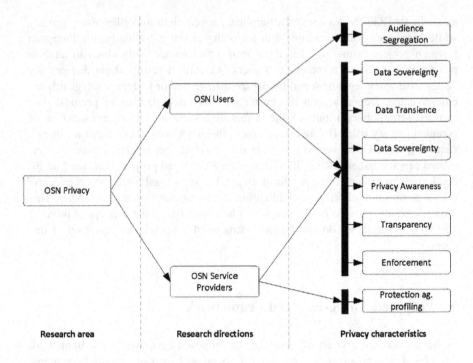

Fig. 1 Classification of OSN privacy research

Data Protection Framework promotes informational self-determination that emphases an individual's rights to control the collection and use of personal data [9].

- *Technical*: This aspect translates norms and regulations into technical specifications. The Platform for Privacy Preferences Project (P3P) is a popular example of enhancing the individual's ability to control information disclosure by technical means [10].
- *Social*: This aspect concentrates on managing social relationships and the boundaries between private and public life. For instance, Nissenbaum describes privacy as contextual integrity, arguing that personal information is published within a well-defined social context [11]. Privacy is breached if personal information is available outside its intended context.

In this study, we adapt this three-layered view and extend it to cover privacy risks in online social networks. Typically, two distinct areas of research can be observed [12, 13] as depicted in Fig. 1:

- *OSN Service Providers*: Research in this direction includes the means to legally bind service providers to comply with current legislation, to increase end-user trust in service providers, and to provide technical safeguards; e.g., by crypto-graphic or steganographic means [14].

Table 1 Proposed three-layered framework for analyzing social web privacy

	Privacy issues related to	
	OSN users	OSN service providers
Legal	International standards (Organisation for Economic Co-operation and Development (OECD) privacy principles, EU data protection framework), national laws	International standards (OECD privacy principles, EU data protection framework), national laws, privacy policies
Technical	Cryptography and steganography, privacy agents, fine-grained access control models, visualization of personal data	Cryptography and steganography, privacy agents
Social	Peer-group pressure, trust relationships, tie strength, privacy awareness	Privacy awareness, pressure of the media

- *OSN Users*: This research aims to recreate the different social contexts of the real world; e.g., by supporting an individual to segment social streams for specific audiences, and by providing the means to have different digital identities [15].

The two aforementioned research directions are combined with the three perspectives on privacy (legal, technical, and social), resulting in our proposed framework. The framework is shown in Table 1, with the cells containing concepts that become relevant for their respective dimension. Note that the three dimensions are not mutually exclusive – they are interdependent. In Sect. 3.2, the two research directions (OSN service providers and OSN users) are further decomposed into a set of privacy characteristics.

3.2 Characteristics Used to Analyze Social Web Privacy

This section outlines fundamental characteristics of privacy derived from a literature review. These privacy characteristics are not exhaustive; rather, they aim to provide a solid foundation for analyzing the impact of the three perspectives on privacy. The characteristics are described in detail as follows.

3.2.1 Data Sovereignty

Data sovereignty describes the extent to which an individual is able to control the processing of his personal data [16]; i.e., his informational self-determination. Personal data in an OSN is typically available in a structured manner and can easily be copied, linked, aggregated, and transferred [4]. Consequently, it is difficult for an OSN user to control the flow of personal information, and thus privacy is placed at risk. The problem increases because the OSN typically lacks the spatial, social, and temporal boundaries of the real world, which limits the flow of personal information by default [17].

3.2.2 Data Transience

Data transience relates to the loss of personal information over time, which can be considered a typical characteristic of real-world communication [4]. In contrast, the mediated communication of OSNs results in permanent storage of personal information. As Mayer-Schönberger noted, "Since the beginning of time, for us humans, forgetting has been the norm and remembering the exception. [...] Today, with the help of widespread technology, forgetting has become the exception, and remembering the default." [18]. In addition, this permanency of personal information poses a great challenge to privacy, since we are no longer free to construct our future identities because contradictory information may be available online [19].

3.2.3 Protection Against Profiling

Protection against profiling subsumes an individual's ability to prevent an adversary from collecting, aggregating, and linking personal data in order to create a digital dossier [20]. Such profiling threats are increased if secondary data such as location (e.g. from mobile phones) and connection logs are linked to existing OSN profiles [21]. The relevance of these threats is underlined by sophisticated attacks such as stealing-reality attacks [22]. The current landscape of social web service providers, with their targeted advertising-centered business models and large identity silos, adds to this threat.

3.2.4 Audience Segregation

Originally developed by Goffman [23], audience segregation states that each individual performs multiple and possibly conflicting roles in everyday life, and it needs to segregate the audiences for each role in a way that people from one audience cannot witness a role performance intended for another audience, thereby keeping a consistent self-image and maintaining privacy [24]. In current OSNs, contacts are typically classified as "friends," making it difficult to selectively share personal information with a specific group of people. As a result, privacy is threatened because a large audience might have access to personal information.

3.2.5 Privacy Awareness

Privacy awareness encompasses the attention, perception, and cognition of the personal information others have received and how this information is or may be processed [25]. An individual's awareness of privacy risk is a prerequisite for privacy-preserving behavior.

3.2.6 Transparency

With regard to OSN service providers, transparency describes the user's ability to be informed of processing and dissemination practices [26]. Taking a social point of view, transparency implies the ability of an individual to understand the flow of personal information within an OSN and to recognize contextual boundaries, which is important for contextual integrity [11].

3.2.7 Enforcement

Enforcement is an individual's means to bring his privacy preferences into force. With regard to OSN service providers and OSN users, it describes the extent to which an individual can control adherence to privacy settings and limitations [27].

3.2.8 Summary

Figure 1 provides a summary of the presented characteristics of privacy. Most properties apply to privacy issues related to social web users and service providers; audience segregation only applies to the former, and protection against profiling only applies to the latter.

3.3 Classification Scheme

The analysis of each privacy characteristic is based on a structured scheme. First, legal aspects are analyzed, highlighting their impact on privacy issues related to OSN users and OSN service providers. Second, the effects of existing technical approaches for enhancing social web privacy are discussed. Finally, the implications of social norms on strengthening privacy in a given scenario are examined.

Additionally, for each privacy characteristic, a visualization of the classification and the effect is provided. A tripartite diagram is used to represent the legal, technical and social dimensions. In this diagram, a colored circle represents the impact (dark blue indicates a major impact, mid-blue a medium impact, and light blue a minor impact).

4 Privacy Issues Related to Social Web Users

In this section, we describe an impact analysis of privacy issues related to OSN users. The results are summarized in Sect. 4.7.

4.1 Data Sovereignty

From a legal point of view, laws and policies applicable to governing the exchange and flow of personal information between people are typically not available. Thus, the legal dimension does not contribute to data sovereignty with regard to other OSN users (no impact).

In addition to the legal dimension of data sovereignty, several technical approaches have been proposed to support a context-sensitive disclosure of personal data in an attempt to strengthen data sovereignty. For example, access control models that enable the user to map their real world trust relationships to OSNs have been introduced [28]. Such technical approaches, in general, attempt to recreate real world social norms. Thus, they can be considered a useful means to strengthen data sovereignty, but their overall impact is minor due to their limited supportive character.

From a social point of view, data sovereignty is threatened if personal information is taken out of its intended context. Tagging people on pictures – a common feature of OSNs – is a typical example of losing control of personal data flow. Gross and Acquisti argue that social norms can strengthen data sovereignty if the fine-grained social relations of the real world can be transferred to OSNs, as these foster reliability and predictability in the behavior of other users [20]. However, adherence to social norms highly depends on the trust relationship between two users, which are commonly divided into weak ties and strong ties [29]. Strong ties typically reflect relations with well-known acquaintances, and an abuse of confidence is likely to have a negative impact on the associated real-world relationship [29]. In contrast, studies indicate that users tend to have increasingly weak ties in OSNs, lacking fine-grained social relations [30], [20]. Individuals are commonly viewed as "contacts" or are even called "friends." Examining the impact on privacy issues related to other OSN users, unauthorized disclosure could primarily be regarded a social problem that relies on strong ties to be effective. As a consequence, the overall impact of the social aspect is medium, due to the aforementioned prevalent weak ties of current OSNs. Figure 2a illustrates our findings regarding data sovereignty.

4.2 Data Transience

Digitally mediated communication differs from real world communication; it adds persistence, searchability, replicability, and scalability by default [17]. However, other OSN users typically cannot be legally forced to delete voluntarily shared

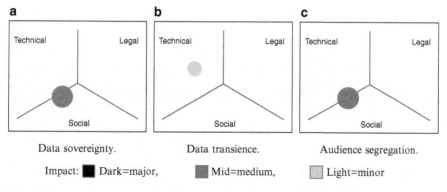

Fig. 2 OSN user privacy analysis (Part 1)

personal information after a given period of time. As a consequence, there is no legal impact on data transience regarding other users.

From a technical perspective, putting an expiry date on personal data is difficult because digital information that is eventually available can easily be copied. While approaches to technical data transience exist, successful attacks, as demonstrated in [31], substantiate their minor impact.

From a social point of view, the permanency of personal information in OSNs poses major challenges. According to Gross and Acquisti, OSN users are typically unaware of existing data storage periods [20]. Consequently, we deduce a lack of social norms regarding data persistence, and conclude that there is no impact stemming from social aspects. A summary of our results is shown in Fig. 2b.

4.3 Audience Segregation

Managing the presentation of the self to different audiences is a social challenge that is not governed by legal regulations (no impact). From a technical perspective, audience segregation is partially implemented in common OSNs (e.g., Facebook Groups[4] and Google Circles[5]). In addition, audience segregation is starting to gain attention in the research community. The prototypical OSN Clique,[6] developed within the PrimeLife project, for example, implements a fine-grained access control mechanism to present each audience with a different view on a user's identity [24]. Another approach presented in [32] automatically determines distinct audiences based on the user's relationships. In the current state, a medium impact of audience

---

[4] http://www.facebook.com

[5] https://plus.google.com

[6] http://clique.primelife.eu/

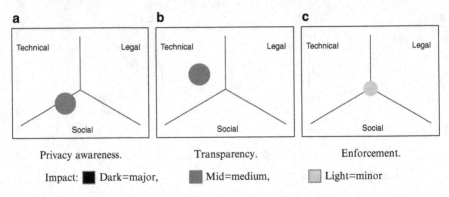

Privacy awareness.   Transparency.   Enforcement.

Impact: ■ Dark=major,   ■ Mid=medium,   ◻ Light=minor

Fig. 3 OSN user privacy analysis (Part 2)

segregation on OSN user privacy can be deduced. However, increasing research activity indicates future growth of the importance of technical means.

From the social point of view, audience segregation is a useful concept that can be used to apply the theory of contextual integrity, as outlined in Sect. 3. Currently, however, audience segregation is not well supported in existing OSNs. Consequently, users resort to behavioral strategies such as choosing appropriate communication channels (e.g., private messages) and to mental strategies (e.g., self-censorship) [33]. Studies show that managing different audiences is a burden to many users, and is rarely applied [34]. Based on the results of the aforementioned studies, only a medium level of social impact of audience segregation on privacy can be inferred, as shown in Fig. 2c.

4.4   Privacy Awareness

Awareness is an important requirement of social web privacy that affects many of the characteristics presented in Sect. 3. However, from a regulatory point of view, OSN user awareness cannot be legally enforced (no impact).

Technical aspects such as usable user interfaces influence perceived privacy protection and the awareness of privacy risks [35]. However, similar to previous characteristics, technical aspects only have a supportive character with which to facilitate privacy awareness and draw attention to potential privacy violations (minor impact).

Privacy awareness is primarily a social concept with a gap existing between theoretical and practical privacy awareness [26]. Privacy awareness is backed by further studies indicating that OSN users frequently underestimate privacy risks and rarely use the available privacy settings [20, 36]. According to Acquisti, immediate gratification outweighs long-term privacy risk and leads to a myopic evaluation of privacy risks [37]. As illustrated in Fig. 3a, there is a medium level of social impact on privacy protection from other users due to the discrepancy between the theoretical and practical effects of privacy awareness.

4.5 Transparency

Although similar to privacy awareness, transparency aims to enhance a user's understanding of the propagation of personal data within an OSN to better protect the data from unauthorized access. From a legal perspective, an individual has few means with which to force other users to make their spreading of others' personal data transparent because, typically, no applicable regulations exist.

Taking a technical point of view, transparency-enhancing approaches focusing on logging and retrospective analysis of personal data disclosures have been proposed [38]. Additionally, it has been shown that weak ties and loose sharing preferences (e.g., friend-of-a-friend) may lead to a large personal network and non-transparent personal data spreading [20]. Technical approaches to visually improving personal network transparency have been proposed, underlining that transparency strongly depends on the OSN service provider and related application programming interfaces (APIs) [39]. Following this reasoning, we assigned a medium level of technical impact because many transparency mechanisms rely on APIs that are provided by OSN service providers.

Similar to the legal dimension, the spreading of personal information by other OSN users is typically not governed by social norms, leading to no social impact on transparency. The results of our analysis of data transparency are shown in Fig. 3b.

4.6 Enforcement

The enforcement of law is an inherent property of any legal system. In the context of social web privacy, an individual can seek an injunction if reputation-damaging information is published. However, legal remedies are not universally applicable to the social web. Following the European Court of Justice, legal protection requires personal information to be restricted to close friends and family members in order to be applicable [40]. In addition, legal remedies only allow the suing others after a privacy breach, thereby resulting in a minor overall impact of legal enforcement on privacy protection against other users.

A technical means of redress may have a positive impact on the enforcement of legal remedies. However, current OSNs differ widely in providing the technical means to address problems (e.g., cyber-bullying) [41]. Thus, technical means are considered to have only a supportive function with minor impact.

In investigating privacy enforcement from a social perspective, tie strength plays an important role. In some cases, a specific group of an individual's OSN (e.g., family members) may have established social norms that allow each member to employ peer-group pressure to enforce privacy interests [42]. Following the reasoning in [20] that relationships in OSNs often consist of weak ties, the effect of social norms on the enforcement of peer pressure can be considered minor. Figure 3c summarizes these findings.

Table 2 Summary of OSN user-related privacy impact analysis

	Data sovereignty	Data transience	Audience segregation	Privacy awareness	Transparency	Enforcement
Legal						○
Technical	○	◍	●	○	●	○
Social	●		●	◍		○

Impact: ■ Dark = major, ▦ Mid = medium, ▢ Light = minor

4.7 Summary

Table 2 summarizes the results of our impact analysis using the proposed framework. This section has described how privacy protection from other social web users is predominately covered by social norms. This corresponds to the real world, where users mainly rely on selective sharing of personal data and highly differentiated relationships to ensure privacy. The mediated nature of OSNs (e.g., permanent storage and searchability of personal data) adds a new layer of complexity that influences privacy because the informational environment of OSNs is counterintuitive to the norms of personal data distribution in the real world. This often leads to a violation of contextual integrity [43]. Table 2 shows that technical approaches to privacy can be seen as a supportive means to translate social norms to the OSNs with potentially increasing importance in the future. On the contrary, legal measures play a minor role and are a last resort to retroactively punish privacy violations. These observations correspond to those of Strahilevitz, who suggested that the law does little to shape people's actual expectations of privacy [44].

5 Privacy Issues Related to Service Providers

Following the analysis of privacy issues related to social web users, we considered the impact of service provider-related privacy issues in this section. These results were then summarized and integrated into our framework.

5.1 Data Sovereignty

To ensure data sovereignty, legal norms have been enacted to control the exploitation of personal data by OSN service providers [40]. For instance, according to the German Teleservices Act and the Federal Data Protection Act, service providers require a user's explicit consent to use personal data for advertising purposes [40]. Furthermore, legal requirements for OSN service providers comprise the secure

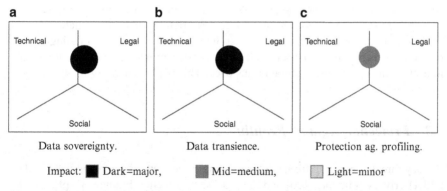

Data sovereignty.   Data transience.   Protection ag. profiling.

Impact: ■ Dark=major,   ■ Mid=medium,   □ Light=minor

Fig. 4 OSN service provider privacy analysis (Part 1)

storage of personal data and exclusion of search indexes by default. Consequently, legal aspects have a high impact on strengthening an individual's data sovereignty.

From a technical point of view, several approaches to facilitate data sovereignty have been proposed (e.g. [14, 45]). These approaches rely on cryptographic and steganographic means to effectively protect an individual's personal data from service provider access. Although they can easily be integrated into current OSN, they commonly infringe the service provider's general terms and conditions because their business model typically relies on free access to personal data for advertising purposes [4]. Hence, despite the theoretical effectiveness of the afore-mentioned approaches, the practical difficulties lead to only a medium level of technical impact on data sovereignty.

Commonly, OSN users do not have any social relationship with OSN service providers. As a consequence, an individual cannot rely on social means to ensure service provider adherence to data sovereignty. Therefore, there is no impact from this dimension. Figure 4a shows that data sovereignty with regard to OSN service providers is mainly legally driven with a medium level of technical influence.

5.2   Data Transience

Similar to data sovereignty, data transience is fully covered by legal norms and regulations to be fulfilled by OSN service providers. Providers are required to entitle a user to delete all personal data stored in a OSN profile and to cancel his membership [40]. Similarly, the European Data Protection Framework requires personal data to be removed if the purpose for which the data was collected ceases to exist [9]. This places the user in a strong position and leads to a high legal impact on data transience.

Approaches described in [31] can be applied to technically enforce data transience with respect to OSN service providers. However, their general impact can be considered minor; in their general terms and conditions, most OSN service providers prohibit any tools that place access restrictions on personal data.

Similar to the description of data sovereignty (see Sect. 5.1), the missing social relationship between OSN users and OSN service providers leads to no social impact on the enforcement of data transience. This is illustrated in Fig. 4b.

5.3 Protection Against Profiling

Privacy threats stemming from OSN service providers have been recognized in the OECD privacy principles [46] and the EU Data Protection Framework [9], which stipulates that data minimization is one of the key principles preventing service providers from linking personal information and building digital dossiers. However, several of the underlying principles of the social web counteract data minimization. For example, the business models of OSN service providers mostly rely on personal data being used for advertising purposes. As a consequence, several personal attributes are mandatory for registration. Studies indicate that only 3 out of 29 OSNs allow for a fully pseudonymous registration [41]. This leads to the conclusion that despite existing legal regulations to protect the user against profiling, the legal impact in practice can be considered minor.

Technically, the approaches presented in Sect. 5.1 can be applied to prevent profiling. Other research directions include the application of user-centric identity management systems on OSNs to strengthen user control, and to prevent service provider and third party access without prior approval. Maliki and Seigneur focused on the concept of Identity 2.0 and respective implementations [47]. They concluded that technical approaches in practice only have a minor impact on protection against profiling because the general terms and conditions of OSNs commonly prevent their application.

Again, due to the typically missing strong ties between OSN users, social norms are not applicable for protecting against profiling (no impact). Figure 4c highlights the lack of social impact.

5.4 Privacy Awareness

Similar to user-related privacy threats (see Sect. 4.4), awareness is primarily influenced through a social perspective, while legal and technical means do not contribute at all.

For example, studies reveal that users of Facebook place more trust in the service provider than in average Facebook users [36]. They also show that 56 % believe that Facebook does not share personal information with third parties, and 70 % believe that Facebook does not combine information about them collected from other sources. Less than one out of four users claim to have read Facebook's privacy

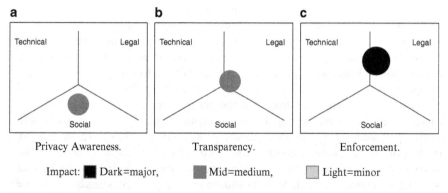

Fig. 5 OSN service provider privacy analysis (Part 2)

policy. While privacy risks tend to remain invisible to the average user [48], awareness increases if privacy-invading features are introduced such as Facebook's News Feed [49]. A high awareness is generally seen as a major obstacle in generating revenue by OSN service providers [12]. This leads to the conclusion that while awareness increases in exceptional situations, OSN users become accustomed to privacy threats stemming from service providers, thus leading to a medium social impact on privacy awareness (see Fig. 5a).

5.5 Transparency

The primary source of information used to assess the legal impact on transparency is the service provider's privacy policy. Bonneau and Preibusch extensively analyzed the privacy policies of 45 OSN providers [41]. As a result, flaws in almost all privacy policies, ranging from bad technical accessibility (e.g., by requiring JavaScript) to extensive use of legal jargon that is far too difficult for ordinary users to understand, have been identified. Other issues include a missing specification of applicable national data protection laws and the nation in which the data is stored and processed. These results show that there is no significant correlation between a network's privacy score and actually privacy practices.

A similar study on service provider transparency revealed that users are often unable to determine the amount of personal data required prior to registration [26]. The study additionally shows that even upon request by e-mail, service providers often do not provide adequate support to increase the transparency of their data handling practices. Consequently, despite the existence of privacy policies as a valuable legal means of fostering transparency, there is only a medium legal impact due to the aforementioned restrictions in terms of practical implementation.

In addition to legal means, several technical approaches to service provider transparency have been developed. P3P is a prominent example [10]. P3P requires service providers to publish a machine-readable privacy policy that subsequently can be matched with the user's predefined privacy preferences. However, most OSN service providers do not provide a machine-readable version of their privacy policy, thereby making P3P inapplicable [41]. Also, the task of defining privacy preferences can hardly be executed by non-technical users [50]. Taking these shortcomings into account, technical means have only a low impact on facilitating transparency.

Considering transparency from a social perspective, media coverage plays an important role in communicating the personal data handling practices of social web service providers [41]. However, they typically do not provide a substantive analysis of privacy problems; rather, they focus on partial aspects of privacy. The minor impact of mass media on transparency is also supported by the lack of privacy awareness (see Sect. 5.4). As illustrated in Fig. 5a, this leads to a minor overall impact of social means with respect to fostering transparency.

5.6 Enforcement

The inherent enforceability of legal measures (see Sect. 4.6) also applies to OSN service providers, and is reflected in the dominance of the aforementioned legal impact. OSN service providers typically employ a privacy-by-policy approach (e.g., as defined in [3]), notifying and obtaining the user's consent to its privacy policy prior to registration and thereby strengthening the legal impact of enforcing privacy interests (high impact).

Regarding the technical perspective, several means of enforcing OSN user privacy preferences are available (see Sects. 5.1 and 5.2). However, their overall practical impact is minor, taking into consideration that these tools are often prohibited by the service provider's general terms and conditions.

While social norms have a significant impact on enforcing privacy interests toward other users (see Sect. 4.6), there is typically no social relationship between a social web service provider and its users. As a consequence, the power structures of social groups do not apply. In addition, the effect of mass media coverage is limited in its ability to put pressure on service providers, as outlined in Sect. 5.5. Thus, privacy interests toward service providers cannot be socially enforced (no impact). Figure 5a shows the dominance of legal remedies on the enforcement of privacy preferences.

5.7 Summary

Table 3 summarizes the results of our analysis of privacy issues related to OSN service providers. Two major conclusions can be derived. First, a shift of impact from the social dimension to the legal dimension, as compared to the results of Sect. 4, can be seen. Second, our results show a general increase in the impact of all

Table 3 Summary of OSN service provider-related privacy impact analysis

	Data sovereignty	Data transience	Protection ag. Profiling	Privacy awareness	Transparency	Enforcement
Legal	● (major)	● (major)	○ (minor)		◐ (medium)	● (major)
Technical	◐ (medium)	○ (minor)	○ (minor)		○ (minor)	○ (minor)
Social				◐ (medium)	○ (minor)	

Impact: ■ Dark = major, ▨ Mid = medium, □ Light = minor

dimensions compared to the impact of Sect. 4.7. In particular, the major legal impact is noteworthy and shows that legislators realize the existence of an unequal distribution of power. Consequently, they try to strengthen the position of OSN users. In contrast, the minor impact of social norms can be explained by a diffusion of responsibility. Service providers are typically not embedded in an individual's social structure; thus, social norms do not apply. Similar to the results described in Sect. 4.7, technical tools can be seen as a supportive in nature, although their impact is often limited. Finally, the limited means of all three dimensions to protect an individual against profiling is noteworthy, emphasizing the service providers' efforts to protect their business model.

6 Conclusion and Future Work

The rising popularity of online social networks poses many challenges in the field of privacy. Unlike the real world in which personal information is ephemeral, in the online-world, such information is almost infinitely available. This poses great challenges in managing identities online, and in context-sensitive sharing of personal information with other users. In addition, the prevalent oligopolistic social web landscape threatens privacy as it fosters the growth of identity silos.

We proposed an interdisciplinary approach to address the aforementioned privacy risks. Consequently, as the main contribution of this chapter, we developed a framework to systematically analyze social web privacy issues from a legal, technical, and social perspective. Furthermore, the impact of these three different perspectives on privacy among OSN users themselves, and between OSN users and service providers, has been highlighted based on a thorough literature review. Our results support our initial assumption that the challenges of social web privacy cannot be addressed from a single direction; rather, they must be addressed by a comprehensive interdisciplinary approach.

Our results lead to a variety of research directions for future work. For example, the role of technology in pursuing social privacy violations should be investigated in detail. Additionally, we wish to overcome the limitations of subjective and qualitative characterizations of privacy effects by conducting a quantitative study to investigate social web privacy based on the framework presented in this chapter. This could lead to a further convergence of research activities.

Acknowledgement The authors would like to thank Ludwig Fuchs (Department of Information Systems, University of Regensburg) for his helpful remarks and valuable suggestions to improve this work. This research was partly funded by the European Union under the FP7 PADGETS project (grant agreement no. 248920). The authors gratefully acknowledge this support. Any opinions, findings, and conclusions or recommendations expressed in this material are those of the authors and do not necessarily reflect the views of the European Union.

References

1. Tufekci Z (2008) Can you see me now? Audience and disclosure regulation in online social network sites. Bull Sci Technol Soc 11:544–564
2. Post RC (2001) Three concepts of privacy. Georget Law J 1:2087–2098
3. Spiekermann S, Cranor LF (2009) Engineering privacy. IEEE Trans Softw Eng 35(1):67–82
4. PrimeLife: D1.2.1 – Privacy Enabled Communities (2010)
5. Gutwirth S, Gellert R, Bellanova R, Friedewald M, Schiitz P, Wright D, Mordini E, Venier S (2011) Deliverable D1: legal, social, economic and ethical conceptualisations of privacy and data protection, Karlsruhe
6. Warren SD, Brandeis LD (1890) The right to privacy. Harv Law Rev 4:193–220
7. Solove DJ (2006) A taxonomy of privacy. Univ Pa Law Rev 154(3):477560
8. Patil S, Kobsa A (2009) Privacy considerations in awareness systems: designing with privacy in mind. In: Markopoulos P, Mackay W, Ruyter B (eds) Awareness systems, human-computer interaction series. Springer, Heidelberg
9. European Parliament (1995) EU-Directive 95/46/EC. Official Journal of the European Communities
10. Cranor L, Dobbs B, Egelman S, Hogben G, Humphrey J, Langheinrich M, Marchiori M, Presler-Marshall M, Reagle JM, Schunter M, Stampley DA, Wenning R (2006) The platform for privacy preferences 1.1 (P3P1.1) specification. NOTE-P3P11-20061113
11. Nissenbaum H (2010) Privacy in context: technology, policy, and the integrity of social life. Stanford Law Books, Palo Alto
12. Ziegele M, Quiring O (2011) Privacy in social network sites. In: Trepte S, Reinecke L (eds) Privacy online. Perspectives on privacy and self-disclosure in the social web. Springer, Heidelberg/New York
13. Beye M, Jeckmans AJP, Erkin Z, Hartel PH, Lagendijk RI, Tang Q (2010) Literature overview – privacy in online social networks. Technical report TR-CTIT-10-36, centre for telematics and information technology, University of Twente, Enschede
14. Guha S, Tang K, Francis P (2008) NOYB: privacy in online social networks. In: Proceedings of the 1st workshop on online social networks, Seattle
15. van den Berg B, Leenes R (2011) Keeping up appearances: audience segregation in social network sites, Chap. 10. Springer, Dordrecht/Heidelberg, pp 211–231
16. Aimeur E, Gambs S, Ho A (2010) Towards a privacy-enhanced social networking site. In: Proceedings of the 5th international conference on availability, reliability and security, Corvallis
17. Boyd D (2008) Taken out of context: American teen sociality in networked publics. Ph.D. thesis, University of California, Berkeley

18. Mayer-Schonberger V (2009) Delete: the virtue of forgetting in the digital age. Princeton University Press, Princeton
19. Solove DJ (2008) The future of reputation: gossip, rumor, and privacy on the internet. Yale University Press, New Haven
20. Gross R, Acquisti A (2005) Information revelation and privacy in online social networks. In: Proceedings of the ACM workshop on privacy in the electronic society, New York
21. Hogben G (2007) Security issues and recommendations for online social networks. Technical report, ENISA
22. Altshuler Y, Aharony N, Pentland A, Elovici Y, Cebrian M (2011) Stealing reality: when criminals become data scientists (or vice versa). IEEE Intell Syst 26:22–30
23. Goffman E (1959) The presentation of self in everyday life. Anchor, New York
24. van den Berg B, Leenes R (2010) Audience segregation in social network sites. In: Proceedings of the 2nd international conference on social computing, Delft
25. Pötzsch S (2009) Privacy awareness: a means to solve the privacy paradox? In: Maty V, Fischer-Hübner S, Cvrcek D, Lvenda P (eds) The future of identity in the information society, IFIP advances in information and communication technology, vol 298. Springer, Heidelberg
26. Burghardt T, Buchmann E, Bohm K (2008) Why do privacy-enhancement mechanisms fail, after all? A survey of both the user and the provider perspective. In: Proceedings of the international workshop on web 2.0 trust, Trondheim
27. Carminati B, Ferrari E (2008) Access control and privacy in web-based social networks. Int J Web Inf Syst 4(4):395–415
28. Carminati B, Ferrari E, Perego A (2009) Enforcing access control in web-based social networks. ACM Trans Inf Syst Secur 13(1):1–38
29. Donath J, Boyd D (2004) Public displays of connection. BT Technol J 22(4):71–82
30. Boyd D (2004) Friendster and publicly articulated social networking. In: Proceedings of the SIGCHI conference on human factors and computing systems, Vienna
31. Federrath H, Fuchs KP, Herrmann D, Maier D, Scheuer F, Wagner K (2011) Grenzen des digitalen Radiergummis. Datenschutz und Datensicherheit – DuD 35(6):403–407
32. Netter M, Riesner M, Pernul G (2011) Assisted social identity management – enhancing privacy in the social web. In: Proceedings of the 10th international conference on Wirtschaftsinformatik, Zürich
33. Lampinen A, Tamminen S, Oulasvirta A (2009) All my people right here, right now: management of group co-presence on a social networking site. In: Proceedings of the ACM international conference on supporting group work, Sanibel
34. DiMicco JM, Millen DR (2007) Identity management: multiple presentations of self in Facebook. In: Proceedings of the international ACM conference on supporting group work, Sanibel Island
35. Grimmelmann J (2009) Saving Facebook. Iowa Law Rev 94(4):1137–1206
36. Acquisti A, Gross R (2006) Imagined communities: awareness, information sharing, and privacy on the Facebook. In: Proceedings of the 6th workshop on privacy enhancing technologies, Cambridge
37. Acquisti A (2004) Privacy in electronic commerce and the economics of immediate gratification. In: Proceedings of the 5th ACM conference on electronic commerce, New York
38. Kolter J, Netter M, Pernul G (2010) Visualizing past personal data disclosures. In: Proceedings of the fifth international conference on availability, reliability and security, Krakow
39. Tscherteu G, Langreiter C (2009) Explorative Netzwerkanalyse im living web. In: Social semantic web. Springer, Berlin/Heidelberg
40. Dix A (2010) Daten- und Personlichkeitsschutz im Web 2.0. In: Klumpp D, Kubicek H, Rob Nagel A, Schulz W (eds) Netzwelt-Wege, Werte, Wandel. Springer, Berlin/Heidelberg, pp 195–210
41. Bonneau J, Preibusch S (2009) The privacy jungle: on the market for data protection in social networks. In: Proceedings of the 8th workshop on the economics of information security, London

42. Feldman DC (1984) The development and enforcement of group norms. Acad Manag Rev 9 (1):47–53
43. Peterson C (2010) Losing face: an environmental analysis of privacy on Facebook. SSRN eLibrary
44. Strahilevitz L (2005) A social networks theory of privacy. Univ Chic Law Rev 72(3):919–988
45. Baden R, Bender A, Spring N, Bhattacharjee B, Starin D (2009) Persona: an online social network with user-defined privacy. In: Proceedings of the ACM SIGCOMM conference on data communication, Barcelona
46. Organisation for Economic Co-operation and Development (1981) Guidelines on the protection of privacy and transborder flows of personal data, vol 11. Organisation for Economic Cooperation and Development, Paris
47. Maliki TE, Seigneur JM (2009) Identity management. In: Vacca JR (ed) Computer and information security handbook, Chap. 17. Burlington, Morgan Kaufmann
48. Debatin B, Lovejoy JP, Horn AK, Hughes BN (2009) Facebook and online privacy: attitudes, behaviors, and unintended consequences. J Comput-Mediat Commun 15(1):83–108
49. Hoadley CM, Xu H, Lee JJ, Rosson MB (2010) Privacy as information access and illusory control: the case of the Facebook news feed privacy outcry. Electron Commer Res Appl 9 (1):50–60
50. Agrawal R (2002) Why is P3P not a PET? In: Proceedings of the W3C future of P3P workshop, Dulles

Recognizing Your Digital Friends

Patrik Bichsel, Jan Camenisch, and Mario Verdicchio

Abstract Interpersonal relationships are increasingly being managed over digital communication media in general, and by electronic social networks in particular. Thus, digital identity, conceived as a way in which to characterize and recognize people on the Internet, has taken center stage. However, this concept remains vague in many of its aspects, which complicates the definitions of the requirements or goals of digital, remote communication. This work aims to shed light on this topic by sketching a basic conceptual framework, including the terminology that captures the essence of digital identity, to analyze those issues of concern to Internet users regarding recognizing their communication partners, and to propose possible solutions.

1 Introduction

In recent years, the Internet has radically changed the way in which people interact. The Web 2.0 wave, in particular, has enabled people to take center stage on Web sites, such as electronic social networks (ESNs). Consequently, the focus has shifted from published content to those people who created it. A major benefit of this development for users is the dramatically increased ease of keeping in touch with each other, with the result that people spend more time online. This trend for an increased online presence also provides for new business opportunities. For example, it allows companies to create targeted advertising campaigns or to simplify and streamline corporate communications by using social media platforms.

P. Bichsel (✉) • J. Camenisch
IBM Research, Zurich, Switzerland
e-mail: pbi@zurich.ibm.com; jca@zurich.ibm.com

M. Verdicchio
Università degli Studi di Bergamo, Bergamo, Italy
e-mail: mario.verdicchio@unibg.it

Y. Altshuler et al. (eds.), *Security and Privacy in Social Networks*,
DOI 10.1007/978-1-4614-4139-7_3, © Springer Science+Business Media New York 2013

However, the differences between the offline world, where people physically interact with each other or with organizations, and the electronic realm of the Internet also pose challenging issues that cannot be neglected. Two important challenges are: (1) electronic data can be easily copied, and (2) it is hard to determine the "origin" of electronically transmitted data. Not only do these factors complicate the representation of a person or an organization online, as well as the communications with these entities, they also pose serious threats for users in terms of the theft and resale of personal data [1–3] or online predators [4, 5].

Our work focuses on the gap between what traditionally characterizes a person or an organization and what is made available in digital form. In particular, we focus on how we can recognize a person or an organization when we interact with them over a network that has no intrinsic security guarantees, such as the Internet.

In the offline world, a person has certain characteristics or attributes (e.g., name, hair color and length, facial features) that enable others to identify her; these constitute her *identity*. The same is true for less tangible entities like organizations; some characteristics can define them (e.g., name, date of establishment, address) and allow others to refer to them. The recognition of people or organizations is tightly bound to these identifying attributes. The question then arises regarding the role of these attributes in the definition of identity, and it is legitimate to ask whether the same concepts and mechanisms work on the Internet.

We will not get into the protracted philosophical debates on the essential characteristics that make up entities [6], or attempt to classify them based on whether or not they change over time [7]. We think that such distinctions are not very significant in the usual practice of identity management. In our view, a characteristic or attribute, c, can enable us to identify an entity, E, so as long as it has not changed since the encounter when we registered c as belonging to E and it uniquely characterizes E in the multitude of other entities from which we single out E.

Our inspiration derives from how the identities of people and organizations are managed in the offline world. Our goal is to build a model of *identity* on the Internet and explore to what extent the criteria we use offline to recognize and authenticate people are supported in the online world. In particular, we tackle those issues that arise from the lack of physical interactions in the context of the Internet.

2 Basic Concepts

In this section we present the fundamental concepts we use in this paper. In our view, communication between *entities* plays a fundamental role in defining identity. These entities − *individual persons* and *organizations* − are characterized by certain attributes, which include their name, date of birth (or establishment), as well as their communication exchanges with other entities. In Sect. 2.1 we introduce some characteristics of communication that are relevant to our work. We do not aim to provide a comprehensive definition of the concept of identity; rather, we want to provide a conceptual framework that will assist us in identifying similarities and differences between the recognition of persons and organizations in the offline and online worlds. We define those concepts related to recognition in Sect. 2.2, and continue in Sect. 2.3 by comparing and contrasting recognition in the offline and online worlds.

2.1 Characteristics of Communication

In general, communication serves the purpose of exchanging information and can occur in several different forms. Examples of the ways in which people can communicate include talking in person, sending an e-mail, making a phone call, leaving a voicemail, having a video chat, or writing a letter. All of these possibilities can be exploited for the same objective; however, they have different characteristics that affect the ways in which communicating entities perceive each other's attributes. In our view, the *attributes* of some person E are comprised of not only personally identifiable information, such as her first name, last name, or date of birth, but also all the impressions and attitudes that are transferred during the communication processes with which she is involved.

Proposition 1 (Attribute) *An attribute is information that is linked to an entity E that helps other entities to distinguish E within a set of entities.*

Communication can be characterized as either *synchronous* or *asynchronous,* depending on whether or not it takes place simultaneously in the presence or absence of all communicating entities. Synchronous communication is probably the most common way in which people get to know each other better (e.g., during a conversation in a bar, at a work meeting, or talking on the phone). In contrast, asynchronous communication does not require the presence of the communicating parties at the same time. This is implemented when one entity leaves persistent information (i.e., a set of attributes) that will be observed by another entity at a later time. Examples of this type of communication are letters, memos, and photos.

Synchronous communication allows for faster exchange of information among participants and usually provides for a broader variety of attributes, such that identities are presented and perceived in a more effective way. For instance, we can think of how much faster we get to know a person through several phone conversations and dates rather than by exchanging letters as pen pals. By comparison, asynchronous communication has the benefit of preserving messages because it relies on objects that can store information typically for a much longer period of time than can the error-prone memory of a human. For example, think of how we can better recall the details of an event through photos as compared to our remembrances.

Another important distinction between these types of communication depends on whether it takes place *offline* or *online*. The increase in computational power, the availability of computing devices, and the introduction of the Internet have provided a number of new communication possibilities. For synchronous communication, this started with scant text-based chats and evolved to fully-fledged vis-a-vis conversations due to developments like Skype. However, in the Internet era, asynchronous communication plays an even more important role, as shown by the unprecedented success of electronic social networks (ESNs) and blogs like Facebook, Twitter, and Tumblr. The services provided by these Web sites allows for the creation of persistent descriptions of an entity (i.e., its attributes), including physical features, personal tastes, and opinions.

The immense impacts of these kinds of services show that a new way to communicate with people and organizations has been established. We intend to investigate how such communications can be enhanced and improved; therefore, we first need to analyze its foundations by providing an adequate conceptual framework.

2.2 Identity Concepts

We begin with the basic concepts that characterize identity, which we illustrate using examples from the offline world. As we said before, in our view, identity is strictly dependent on communication, and the simplest, most common form in which offline communication can take place is a physical meeting between two people or a telephone conversation. Whether intentionally or not, a person E exhibits some of her attributes during communication. These enable the other person to associate them with E, and this association is the fundamental component of what it means to know, remember, or recognize E. Thus, we intuitively define the *identity* of a person E as that set of all the attributes E communicates in any way to any other entity.

The same basic principle of the association of attributes for recognition holds in more complex examples of communication. For example, these include communication scenarios where more than two parties are involved or when one of them is an organization rather than a person. In fact, although a person cannot communicate with an organization in the same way she would communicate with another person, an organization can also be characterized by attributes that people can use to identify and distinguish it from others. For organizations, the presentation of such attributes to other entities is often delegated to a specific person, usually in the organization's public relations office.

In general, during a communication between two entities, E and U, some of the attributes that contribute to the definition of the identity of E are revealed to U.

Proposition 2 (Facet) *A facet of the identity of an entity E is that set of attributes that describe E and are presented by E in a well-defined communication context. A facet of E is denoted by f^E.*

This is a very general view in that whatever a person looks like, says, or does in front of other people can be seen as defining part of her identity; indeed, our appearance, our opinions, and our actions define our identity. We indicate by F^E the set of all facets ($\{f_i{}^E\}$) that entity E is presenting. F^E is a dynamic set, in that the attributes that E shows vary continuously. Examples of a facet are a person E's Facebook page or her appearance at a dinner party. Note that online facets are closely related to how van den Berg and Leenes [8] imagined realizing audience segregation in ESNs. Temporal issues are not within the scope of this work, although we again point out the role played by communication in the definition of identity. Thus, it is not fundamentally important whether F^E changes quickly or remains constant; rather, its effects on the other entities that perceive, record, and remember a subset of F^E are important.

In fact, not all of the attributes made available by E are gathered and retained by her communication partner U. Rather, people can be distracted and may miss some particulars, or they may forget some information due to their imperfect memory and the passage of time. Hence, the result of the communication between E and U is not equivalent to a simple transmission of information of the facet that E is revealing. Thus, we need to introduce the concept of a *perceived identity* of E by U.

Proposition 3 (Perceived Identity) *Entity U's perceived identity of entity E, indicated by $I^U(E)$, is that set of all the information on E's identity that is kept in U's memory or stored in her device's memory.*

While E's facets define her identity, a perceived identity is the impression that those facets made on U, which consist of all those attributes that U retains and associates with E. Similar to F^E, $I^U(E)$ is a dynamic set, although it changes more slowly than F^e. One reason for this is that $I^U(E)$ represents a coherent image that U associates with E. Thus, it can only be updated when U learns new information about E and, accordingly, fundamental changes require verification before $I^U(E)$ is changed. Note that while a synchronous communication that affects $I^U(E)$ also affects $I^E(U)$, an asynchronous communication typically leads to an update of only one of the two.

We illustrate our concepts using the example depicted in Fig. 1, which shows the different facets a person called John Doe reveals to his employer, the state in which he lives, the jurisdiction, or his biking friends. For example, the employer and the state both get to learn John Doe's first name, last name, and his salary. Apart from these entities, John does not want anybody else to know his salary; thus, this is not part of any facet John reveals to other entities. An important difference between offline and online facets is that the former are not persistent and typically only become manifest during synchronous communication. The latter are persistent, easily accessible, and through the implementation of features such as the Facebook timeline, they provide access to a fine-grained facet.

The perceived identities are not shown in Fig. 1, but we point out that even though John communicates a single facet directed towards a group of people, the resulting perceived identities will all be different. For example, this is notable with his friends that remember different parts of a conversation and come to different conclusions. Moreover, in the offline world, John naturally has different

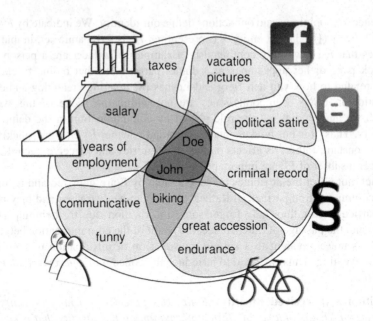

Fig. 1 Facets of a person called "John Doe" depicted as the attributes that John shares with entities, such as (from *top left*, counterclockwise) the state, his employer, his friends, his cycling mates, and law authorities. The picture includes digital facets created of John; namely, a political blog and his Facebook profile

conversations with his friends, corresponding to revealing different facets, which contribute to the diversity of the perceived identities.

Another example where we see differences between a facet and the resulting perceived identities involves the company where John works. Although John consistently presents his "professional facet," we can be certain that his boss, his closest colleague, and the human resources manager who interviewed him all have different perceptions of John. In fact, each individual within each group of people has a different perceived identity of John.

Using the concepts of perceived identity and facets, we can specify what we mean by *recognizing a friend*: a person U seeing a facet $f^{E'}$ attempts to map this facet to some already existing perceived identity.

Proposition 4 (Recognition) *In the case when U can match a facet $f^{E'}$ to an established perceived identity $I^U(E)$, we say that U recognizes $f^{E'}$ as a facet of E; that is, for U, E' corresponds to E.*

If a person U cannot map $f^{E'}$ to any existing perceived identity, then either (1) the information disclosed in $f^{E'}$ may not be sufficient to attain a mapping or (2) U did not have a previous encounter with E'. We now discuss differences between the online and offline scenarios before outlining the challenges that we face in recognizing digital friends.

2.3   Comparing the Offline and Online Worlds

We analyze our identity concepts by focusing on new elements that arise in the online context in order to make comparisons with the offline world. Just as a person communicates with others and reveals some of her characteristics in the offline world, so can a person describe a side of herself on a blog or a social network page. A digital facet of an entity E, f^E, is any set of attributes in a digital format that refers to E, is created and managed by E or an authorized entity, and is presented in a unitary way on a computer system. E's Google+ page and an email from E are examples of digital facets.

The information provided by a digital facet, possibly in the form of text, pictures, or multimedia files, can be considered as the digital counterpart of a person's offline facet; that is, what she presents when people physically meet her. Analogously, just as entity U builds up a perceived identity of entity E by communicating with E in the offline world, she can form a perceived digital identity of E (i.e., $I^U(E)$) by checking some of E's digital facets from F^E (the set of all data that has been published by E or by an authorized entity).

Thus far, we have focused on the similarities between the offline and online worlds with regard to dealing with identity; but, there are indeed important differences! Digital facets are scalable, that is, they are persistent, easily accessible, and potentially address a broad audience. This is opposite to offline facets, which are typically volatile and limited to a very restricted audience. Moreover, their digital nature makes them easily copyable, which marks an important difference with the offline world, where biometric, hard-to-copy features typically pertain to a facet. Also, ever-improving search algorithms make the retrieval of digital information more and more efficient.

This, in combination with cheaper storage, causes information on the Internet to become virtually un-erasable, that is, the *Internet does not forget*. This can be a desirable feature for a blogger who seeks to convince people, spread ideas, or simply entertain. However, it may not be true for ESNs, where users possibly publish personal information intended only for a small group of very close friends (e.g., vacation pictures that are not meant to be shared with work colleagues and superiors).

Persistency and retrieval of digital facets play significant roles when entities change their attributes. While the interests and opinions of people, and even their physical features typically change over time, they evolve so slowly that they can be considered as constant over significant intervals of time. In fact, we usually recognize the people with whom we communicate and interact on the basis of their biometric properties, such as facial features, voice, or handwriting. This occurs automatically, and we only become aware of this process when a mismatch occurs, as for example when a person calls and pretends to be someone we know, although their different voice quality gives the scam away.

In effect, in the offline world we only notice changes in attributes when we do not communicate with someone for an extended period of time. Because people's memories fade with time, such changes to a person's attributes hardly ever undermine the coherence of the person's perceived identity. In addition, negative but non-repeating attributes, such as a bad temper, may be forgotten and quickly forgiven in the offline world. In contrast, statements that were made online in the distant past have a potential impact on the present and the accessibility of ESN attributes has reportedly caused people to get fired [9, 10].

In summary, in the offline world, people's physical features provide fundamental support in the recognition process. A major difference in the online world is the lack of such direct contact. In the following sections we will illustrate the issues that arise from this lack of direct contact. But, for now, we want to shed some light on the increase in freedom that it allows. On the Internet, nobody is tightly bound to their physical features; thus, the immediate recognition processes that take place in the offline world are not inevitable. *Anonymity* has become possible, but there is more.

We have said that entities build up perceived identities of the people and organizations with which they communicate thanks to the digital facets presented to them. Thus far, we have taken for granted that these digital facets are based on some real-world entity; that is, they correspond to a person or an organization. However, we can imagine completely new identities that can be designed from scratch, where their digital facets present a coherence that induces a perceived identity in the audience, but are not based on any physical person or existing organization. We call this new type of identity − with a purely digital existence − a *purely digital identity* (DiD).

Thus, while each person or organization has one identity, they may create and control any number of DiD's. Note that a person U coming across a digital facet representing a previously unknown entity X cannot decide whether this facet represents a real-world entity or merely a DiD. In the following we will deal with the challenges that stand in the way of recognizing that a digital facet belongs to a real-world entity, as well as the mechanisms that foster such recognition processes.

3 Challenges for Recognizing Digital Facets

Several issues arise in a context where entities present themselves through digital facets; that is, communication takes place without any physical contact. We will discuss the main challenges in this section and propose possible solutions in Sect. 4. We begin our discussion in Sect. 3.1 where we focus on the authenticity of facets and the attributes of which they are comprised. In Sect. 3.2 we elaborate on the case in which authentication leads to identification because the attributes are personally identifiable. In specific scenarios, identification is undesirable and a person may prefer to keep facets separated. We cover such privacy aspects of facets in Sect. 3.3.

3.1 Authenticity

Like every other type of information that is transmitted over the Internet, digital facets are affected by security issues, such as integrity, confidentiality, and authenticity. In our context, the predominant concern is the authenticity of facets, because, as said before, the lack of physical contact and the ease with which digital data can be copied and transported pose serious threats. In this context, we use the term *authenticity* in the following way.

Proposition 5 (Authenticity of a Facet) *A facet f^E is said to be authentic when it has been published either by the entity E to which it refers or by an authorized person.*

We distinguish two types of possible attacks from malicious users that are based on *alteration* and *duplication* of facets. Alteration attacks target an already existing facet and change it or add new content. Duplication attacks aim to create a new facet designed to look like it is part of an existing F^E, where the set of facets may relate to a pure DiD or the identity of an entity E. The goal of both attacks on the facet of E is to convince an entity U who views the attacked facet to add these maliciously placed attributes to $I^U(E)$.

To support the correct use of facets and identities on the Internet, users need instruments that guarantee the authenticity of the facets they are viewing. A first good starting point for attaining authentic facets is to support the authenticity of relevant (i.e., personally identifying) attributes of which these facets are comprised. However, some considerations must be made first.

Not all attributes in a facet play the same roles in supporting its authentication; their importance depends on whether or not they constitute identifiable information. Consider the following example: a picture-less Facebook page of one John Smith from New York City in which the name and surname are shown to be authenticated. How certain can we be that this page actually belongs to our friend John who lives in New York City? The problem is that a very common name within a very large city does not sufficiently identify any particular person. Thus, although we can be sure that these are indeed the name and surname of the person managing the page, we are far from recognizing our friend.

Clearly, the situation would be different if the authenticated name and surname were 'Michiko' and 'Kakutani'; these attributes are so uncommon in New York City that our trust in this digital facet is much greater. It should be noted that such trust implicitly relies on the confidence we have in the authentication mechanisms used by the server that hosts the facet. The advantage of relying on the authentication of some identifying attributes is efficiency; we can authenticate an entire facet by checking only a small (but significant) fraction of it.

A second mechanism is the creation of a link between all facets in F^E. If there were universally accepted specifications on how to represent the fact that different facets are all part of the same identity or DiD, then recognition of different facets belonging to one F^E would be straightforward. However, there are no such specifications and the Web sites that host facets do not share a uniform data structure for their users. An external service could provide a similar link for facets, which comes with implications for trust.

3.2 Identifiability

In some situations, the authentication of a facet is sufficient, and may even be the best that we can hope for. This certainly holds for facets that are part of a pure DiD, which is not based on any real-world identity, such as a Facebook page for a fictional character, or a political blogger who keeps her real identity hidden. In such situations, we use the authentication of facets to be able to recognize that two facets belong together (e.g., the Facebook page and the Twitter page of our fictional character).

However, it is much more common for a facet to present some attributes that can be linked to the identity of a real person, E for example, through a picture or E's work address. A person U who already knows E has a perceived identity $I^U(E)$. When U is viewing such a facet, she will naturally update $I^U(E)$ with the new information provided by the facet. Consequently, identification goes one step further than authentication. That is, if U knows the link to the person E that has published a facet f^E, as well as another facet f'^E, she can conclude that both facets belong to F^E and use the published information to enhance $I^U(E)$.

We will illustrate alteration and duplication attacks by a malicious user with some examples. It still often happens that, especially with small family-run hotels, we are required to fax our credit card data to make a reservation. If the hotel's Web page (or its business ESN page) has been altered to show a different fax number, it is easy to imagine the consequences.

The most common examples of duplication attacks on the Internet are phishing websites, but this problem affects social networks as well. For example, fake profiles on Facebook are often used to spread malware by enticing the average user into befriending them and obtaining access to more and more profiles [11]. In front of a page that shows attributes, such as the first and last names and the date of birth of E, users are naturally led to think that E has published the displayed data and also manages this page. Such a supposition is true in most cases, but it cannot be taken for granted, especially considering that digital content can be easily copied and reused.

The immediate advantage of duplicating a facet of an ordinary person may not be apparent; but, let us consider a Facebook page presenting itself as an official facet of a pop star. With the pretense of a competition, this page could easily trick a considerable number of people into giving out personal information, such as their email addresses.

The facets in these attacks, whether the result of an alteration or a duplication, are not part of F^E and, by extension, of the identity of E, because they have not been published by E or an authorized person.

3.3 Privacy

It has been said that the best way to keep a secret is to never have it. In this context, we may say that the best way to avoid *privacy* issues is to never sign up for anything on the Internet. Because an increasing number of services are moving to the digital domain, such advice has become very hard to follow. The issue here is the opposite of identification; some, or possibly all of the facets published by an entity E may not be supposed to be ascribed to E. In other words, sometimes there is the need for avoiding *linkability* between a facet and a perceived identity $I^U(E)$.

These needs can arise in many different contexts. We are not only thinking about a controversial political blog in countries with controlled media, but also much more mundane cases like a teacher who manages a comic book discussion forum and does not wish to be recognized by his students. The possibility of separating facets only arises due to the lack of physical contact and it may look like a call for *anonymity*, although users often have more complex needs. In fact, complete anonymity would not serve the purposes of the aforementioned political blogger; the blog's existence relies on the connection between all the entries, which is normally given by the URL that publishes them and provides the authentication required to post new messages. Should the blog be transferred to another address because of technical or safety reasons, how could the readers recognize it when it is back online at a different site?

We are looking for solutions to support *pseudonymity*; a means to tackle the trade-off between having easy recognizability that a facet belongs to F^P, the set of facets of a pure DiD, and keeping the details on the entity behind it private.

4 Security and Privacy for Digital Facets

In this section we propose solutions to the problems raised in Sect. 3. We begin by analyzing ways to authenticate attributes in Sect. 4.1, which may be used to authenticate facets. This is followed by a discussion of identification possibilities in Sect. 4.2. Finally, we propose solutions to the issues of separating facets and achieving online privacy in Sect. 4.3.

4.1 Authentic Facets

In the offline world, we primarily use biometric attributes during synchronous and asynchronous communication processes to authenticate others. For example, we recognize the faces, voices, speaking patterns, or handwriting of the people with whom we regularly interact. However, we may not use such approaches online, as we are confronted with digital information transmitted over an insecure channel.

We will first see how we can attain authenticated attributes before thinking about how we can authenticate entire facets.

4.1.1 Authentic Attributes

The authenticity of attributes can be achieved in several ways: (1) attributes may have intrinsic authenticity; (2) attribute authenticity can be verified directly; or (3) an entity vouches for the attribute's authenticity. We will discuss these three approaches.

Intrinsically authentic attributes. We can identify attributes that assert authenticity in the digital domain. Even if they are exchanged in an asynchronous manner over a digital channel, they still bear authenticity information. This is the case for attributes that are tightly bound to how an entity expresses herself, which makes them hard to copy. Examples are writing style, humor, style of postings, or the style of taking pictures. As soon as a person U recognizes an intrinsically authentic attribute, she then recognizes to which $I^U(E)$ the attribute belongs.

Note that intrinsically authentic attributes do not necessarily lead to identification, even though they are tied to a person. Imagine a situation in which E creates a pure DiD, G, consisting of a set of facets F^G. E uses an original writing style that fits the DiD and its purpose. Assuming that a person U knows one facet, f_i^G, which constitutes U's image of G ($I^U(G)$), then U can match the writing style of a second facet, $f_j^{\ G}$, that she observes and, thus, recognize the correspondence of f_j^G to $I^U(G)$. This allows U to update her perceived identity $I^U(G)$ using the information from f_j^G.

Verified attributes. We distinguish two ways for attaining verified attributes. A first approach relies on certificates, such as X.509 [12], U-Prove [13], and idemix [14], with which E can add certified attributes to her facets. Let us assume that E has a certificate from her government that comprises, among other attributes, her first name, last name, and date of birth. When registering on a host (e.g., Facebook), E can provide the certified attributes instead of simply inserting them into a Web form. The host would provide a mechanism to distinguish certified from non-certified attributes and show which entity provided the certification.

Consequently, a user visiting the facet can verify the set of certified attributes and decide how confident she is that it authentically represents E (i.e., corresponds to $I(E)$ of some person). As an example, Facebook could check the eID of its users during the authentication process and show the verified information in the form of attributes authenticated by the country that issued the eID. In this situation, each new post would implicitly be bound to the authenticated attributes of the eID card.

A second, alternative way is to directly verify attributes. This is only possible when they come with an external authentication mechanism. An example is an email address where access to emails is only granted after successful authentication to the email provider. Thus, by sending an email to an address provided as an attribute in a facet, the host of that facet can verify if the user can authenticate to the email provider. In fact, most services, including ESNs, use such an approach to verify that a user signing up for the service has indicated a working email address. Other examples of attributes with external verification mechanisms are mobile phone numbers (using an SMS to communicate a verification code) and a physical address (using a letter bearing verification information).

However, using verified attributes imposes several requirements. First, the hosts need to adapt and expand the registration process to incorporate a verification step in which information like a certificate could be checked. Note that the frequent use of email address verification has lead to services that provide short time addresses; that is, a user obtains a temporary email account to receive the verification code without the host (e.g., the ESN) learning a permanent contact for the user. A further adjustment would be incorporating mechanisms to show whether an attribute is verified and, if so, by whom.

Second, the requirement of possessing a certificate is currently only practical for entities such as companies or larger organizations. These organizations typically use the certificates to allow their customers to authenticate communication. For example, bank customers can authenticate the correct bank using certificate information. However, as governments (e.g., Belgium, Germany) start issuing electronic identity (eID) cards, certified attributes may become available for a broader audience.

Third, users need to trust the certificate issuers used by their digital friends, as well as the host of the facet for verifying the certification correctly. Note that while the increase in trustworthiness of attributes appears to be coupled with a loss of users' privacy with respect to the host of a facet, the use of privacy-friendly authentication techniques can mitigate this issue [15, 16].

Externally-verified attributes. If we use a weaker trust model, we may consider additional entities for providing a verification of attributes. The fact that people interact with each other through their digital as well as their offline facets on a daily basis comes to mind. Therefore, after a user has assessed the authenticity of an attribute, she could share her findings, as for example by assigning a confidence rating or a recommendation. For such a process to work, the person recommending an attribute as authentic needs to authenticate it to the host of a facet. That is, depending on the trust model used, whether the viewer of a facet trusts the recommendations to be processed correctly by the host, the latter may need to provide information on the people that provided the recommendations. This is required because, otherwise, there would be no means of establishing trust in such a rating or recommendation.

We may view ratings or recommendations as a certification provided by a community of users. A mechanism like this can already be seen in several websites, where users authenticate themselves to the host by using one of their ESN accounts and, depending on the number of times they have visited the site and written comments, they acquire a status (e.g. "top commenter") from the host that is meant to increase the trust of the other users. A mechanism for bootstrapping trust in the authenticity of attributes using community-based certification has been proposed by Bichsel et al. [17]. Their intention was to build a public key infrastructure (PKI) using certification information.

Verified attributes may be communicated between hosts using protocols like the Security Assertion Markup Language (SAML). For example, assuming that Google verified the phone number of a person E, it can forward this information to another host. The latter concludes, based on knowledge of the process and a trust in Google, that the attribute bears the correct value. Thus, it shows in E's facet that the phone number is verified by Google. The drawbacks of externally-verified attributes are similar to those of verified attributes; namely, the required changes during these processes on the parts of the hosts of the facets. Additionally, the original verifier of an attribute – Google in our example – learns information about a user's activities.

4.1.2 Authentic Sets of Facets

As we know, facets can reflect several aspects of the entity to which they refer. For example, a profile on LinkedIn shows professional aspects, while a blog on Blogger reflects snippets of ideas or tips, and movie reviews on Rotten Tomatoes reveal interests in a particular movie. We will now focus on mechanisms that support linking these facets and recognizing that they belong to the same set, F^E.

Attribute equality. The same information published under different facets (e.g., the same first and last names in several facets) seems to imply a link between them. However, we must not forget that the simplicity of copying digital information makes it easy to create a facet that is seemingly equal to another one. It is important to note that relying on the equality of general attributes or on similar information (e.g., different facets stating that they are leaving for vacation) is not *per se* a guarantee. However, we can consider authentic attributes (see Sect. 4.1.1) when judging whether or not a facet belongs to a set F^E.

Depending on the mechanisms used, authentic attributes can serve the purpose of recognizing a link among facets in several ways. First, authentic attributes, such as certified and community-certified attributes we described in Sect. 4.1.1, can be a means to verify if several facets have been created by the same entity. The reason for this limited use lies in the fact that users only have to prove authenticity during the creation of a facet.

Second, intrinsically authentic attributes help to establish a link, as for example between posts released on behalf of several facets. More concretely, a blog entry using a specific writing style and a status update on Google+ using the same pattern allows an observer of these two facets to recognize the link between them. The same functionality may also be achieved by mechanisms like the release of certified attributes with each update of a given facet. Note that some mechanisms used to recognize the correspondence of facets lead to the identification of the entity publishing the information of the facet. We will treat cases related to identification in extensive detail in Sect. 4.2.

A requirement for all cases in which we derive authenticity of a facet based on authentic attributes are that the host of a facet must use a dependable authentication mechanism and the viewers of the facet must trust in the verification process carried out by the host. In addition, compared to current implementation, this approach requires adaptations to many processes, such as the display of authenticity information for attributes in ESN profiles.

Unique reference. A more direct solution to link several facets is to publish them by endowing them with a unique reference. This reference supposedly works as an identifier by showing viewers from among a unique set of facets F^E they are observing one facet f^E. This assumes that the reference works across multiple domains of the Internet. Such a reference needs to be coupled with an authentication mechanism. A cryptographic public key is one possible way to achieve these results by using a secret key as an authentication mechanism. Another possibility is a uniform resource locator (URL) coupled with a mechanism like OpenID [18].

Consider the following example. If user U visits some blog on Blogger and sees a comment by John Smith, she should be able to recognize if he is the same John Smith that U knows from Facebook. A unique reference can be established in accordance with the trust model we rely upon. If there are trusted hosts, then identity providers can possibly endow a facet with a unique reference, as for example a public key or an OpenID URL [19].

When we rely on such hosts, we assume that the username of the facet on the trusted host is unique. For a reference to be fully recognizable, it should explicitly include the trusted host's name. But, this is not part of current practice by many Web sites. Thus, when Web users see that a John.Smith entered a comment in a blog, there is no way to automatically establish that it is John.Smith@facebook. com, (i.e., the John Smith U already knows).

Publishing unique references will require adapting the current practices of how facets are handled. If the hosts of different facets could agree on a mechanism that supports such a solution, this would allow for the automated detection of several facets. Such an agreement, although very desirable, appears to be unlikely. Instead, alternative solutions have emerged. For example, a dedicated service that provides a unique reference to all social network activities of an entity, called about.me,[1] has been introduced. Another, simpler practice is to publish in the form of an information item within one facet a link to another facet (e.g., Facebook users often post a link to their Flickr accounts). This user-initiated linkability of facets, however, does not allow for any automation and comes with a poor user experience.

4.2 Identifiable Facets

Several of the authentication mechanisms presented above are related to the entity represented by a facet. They are very natural choices to support authentication, because facets depicting real-world entities are very frequent, as opposed to pure DiD's that are relatively rare (e.g., a political blog that should not be linked to the

---

[1] https://about.me/

actual person issuing the posts). What follows are some forms of interactions that ensure that a facet does indeed refer to a real-world entity.

Synchronous attribute exchange. More and more facets offer the possibility of having synchronous interactions that closely resemble communications in the offline world. Examples of these are Skype, which offers voice and video conversations, and "hangouts" in Google+, where a group of users can video-chat. Such interactions allow for authentication mechanisms that transport biometric features that are hard to copy. In addition, people are familiar with these authentication mechanisms, which allows for a very smooth user experience. Consequently, this mechanism closely resembles the offline experience; thus, it provides a seamless authentication experience.

Out-of-band information. Finally, if a person U has already interacted with a person E, by having met her in person or called her on the phone as examples, then all attributes that are coherent with the information exchanged during the offline interaction and published in a facet of E's digital facets increase U's confidence in the authenticity of these facets. For example, if E mentions her vacation in Rome while on the phone with U, then U gains confidence that the Flickr account with the Colosseum pictures belongs to the DiD of E. Note that we have assumed two things: (1) the phone conversation was private (i.e., it would be relatively difficult for an imposter to learn that the information exchange had occurred), and (2) the Flickr account was protected by an appropriate authentication mechanism.

While such out-of-band information can prove to be useful, the observer must consider the effort required to fabricate the information published digitally. For example, the correspondence between a new Skype status message "Vacation in Rome. Yeah!" and new Colosseum pictures on a Flickr page can increase a viewer's confidence in the fact that those facets belong to the same set of facets. However, the Skype message can be easily fabricated by an imposter who plans to impersonate the owner of the indicated Flickr account.

4.3   Private Facets

The lack of physical association might seem to be a disadvantage with regard to identity management, as it elicits a need for verification of the authenticity that determines whether a facet actually represents an implied entity. However, this lack of physical association can introduce new and interesting types of communication. Unless we are in specific law-defined contexts that require a user to release her attributes according to some real-world definition, there is no limit to the choices for her published characteristics.

In these situations, entities are free to create facets of pure DiD's that present a meaningful coherence and, possibly, make them look like they represent an existing entity without actually corresponding to any real person or organization. This would be the case, for instance, for the aforementioned blogger who wants to protect her real identity, but still wants to be represented on the Internet with a facet. One can also surrender any pretense of realism and create facets with such unrealistic features that it becomes obvious they are fictional.

Pure DiD's, however, are also affected by the authenticity issues outlined above. For example, the DiD of some blogger B may also have a social network page. While these two facets should be recognized as belonging to one set of facets, F^B, it should remain difficult for an imposter to create additional facets that are mistakenly interpreted as being part of F^B. In addition, the link to facets of the person publishing content in F^B must not be recognizable; that is, the person's privacy should remain guaranteed.

Most of the mechanisms we described in Sect. 4.1 for recognizing that several facets belong to some entity also work for pure DiD's. More precisely, all mechanisms that do not rely on the recognition of a real-world entity that controls a set of facets can be used directly, as they keep the entity's privacy intact. However, there are implications on the trust relationships that users entertain with the entity that hosts their facets.

Let E be an entity whose DiD has a facet on host H. When E trusts H not to leak any personal information, her real identity can be considered protected. Then, all E needs to do to manage her DiD is to authenticate it to H. Currently, this is usually done by using a username/password pair. The host H requests the release of personal information at registration time, which makes the actions of E identifiable to H. When this trust is missing, E needs to rely on an authentication mechanism, which also protects her identity from H. Indeed, suitable authentication technologies, such as pseudonym or anonymous credential systems [15, 20, 21], are already available. These allow E to authenticate pseudonymously by prescribing the use of certified attributes combined with strong cryptographic mechanisms. Thus, these systems maintain the level of assurance that H needs, while at the same time allowing E to remain pseudonymous.

Another cryptographic primitive that can be used to maintain facets in a privacy-friendly way is *verifiable encryption* [22]. This prescribes that, when entity S communicates an attribute type and its value to entity R, R receives the information encrypted in such a way that it can be decrypted only by a designated mediator, although the attribute type can nevertheless be verified by R. S and R agree on the terms under which the mediator is supposed to decrypt the encrypted attribute value. Note that while S trusts the mediator only to decrypt the attributes in case S "misbehaves" according to the agreed upon terms and not before, R trusts the mediator to decrypt in the former case.

Verifiable encryption enables management of the facet of a pure DiD to be passed from one person to another. For example, the aforementioned blogger, who we call A, can be substituted for by a new author B without anyone else knowing about this change. We assume that A verifiably encrypts her public key and publishes it with each post. Then, the blog's host, checks that the public key verifiably encrypted with the previous post matches the public key used to sign the current post in order to be assured that the post was submitted by the legitimate author. All that A needs to do to pass the authorship to B is to verifiably encrypt B's public key in her last post.

5 Related Work

Researchers from several fields have intensively investigated the analogies and the differences in the concepts of identity in the physical and digital worlds.

Allison et al. provide an overview of this concept from several different perspectives: legal (authorship and ownership issues), philosophical (logical relations among digital objects), and historical (chronological models and records of the evolution of digital identities) [23]. Cameron attempts to provide a more unified definition of this concept with a synthesis of all its aspects in a list of "laws of identity" [24]. Pfitzmann and Hansen [25] provide an extensive terminology on privacy-related concepts, such as anonymity, pseudonymity, or linkability.

Other efforts focus on singling out the available technologies in order to implement online the principles that are traditionally attached to identity. For example, Windley considers the support of digital identity to be fundamental for businesses on the Internet to succeed, and provides several pointers to existing proposals and standards [7]. Van den Berg and Leenes claim that people exploit the compartmentalization of social spheres in order to have different audiences in accordance with the context, and prescribe that social networks should provide instruments that enable users to do so also online. They show that this is possible with current technology by proposing a social network of their own [8]. Korolova et al. also deal with the trade-off between social connectivity and privacy. In particular, using experiments with a crawler in a social network, they show that user pages with too large a look-ahead enable attacks on privacy in the form of knowledge extraction that involves a significant fraction of the links in their networks [26].

Regarding proposals on standards, two main research guidelines can be found in the literature. Low-level computational instruments continue to be elaborated in the context of cryptographic research in order to expand the boundaries of what can be provided to users in terms of security and privacy. For example, Lysyanskaya et al. aim to find means to handle pseudonyms or anonymous access [16]. On a higher level, in the context of distributed system research, standards are proposed to support the expression of identity attributes for authentication and access control purposes, such as in OpenID [19]. More and more of these studies, as for example Ardagna et al. [27], consider privacy issues as fundamental.

6 Conclusions and Future Work

Internet users deal with digital identities in a manner similar to how people deal with each other's identity in the real world. Nevertheless, the lack of a physical dimension leads to greater freedom and anonymity, which allows for new types of identity to arise in the digital context of the Internet. People seek out and find each other based on the attributes that they exchange through their digital counterparts. The aim of this work was to shed some light on the basic concepts related to digital identities and to propose solutions based on existing technologies to support recognition of people over the Internet, with an eye on both security against attacks and privacy for users who intend to remain anonymous.

We think that the next steps on this research path should deal with the digital identities of organizations. These have the peculiarity of either being managed by more than one person at the same time or by different people throughout their life cycles. This topic is particularly interesting, because it calls for a compromise in the tradeoff between anonymity of the users on the Internet and the accountability of their actions within their organization.

Acknowledgements This work was partially supported by the EC within the 7th Framework Programme, under grant agreement 257129 (PoSecCo), and by the MIUR in the framework of the PRIN project Gatecom. In addition, we thank the reviewers of previous versions of this work for their valuable input.

References

1. Altshuler Y, Aharony N, Pentland A, Elovici Y, Cebrian M (2011) Stealing reality: when criminals become data scientists (or vice versa). IEEE Intell Syst 26(6):22–30
2. Svensson P (2011) Possible e-mail theft from epsilon slams banks, retailers. USA Today, April, 2011
3. Wingfield N, Sherr I, Worthen B (2011) Hackers raid Sony videogame network. The wall street Journal, (April, 2011)
4. Hitchcock JA (2007) Cyberbullies, online predators, and what to do about them. MultiMedia Internet@Schools 14(3):13–15
5. Wolak J, Finkelhor D, Mitchell KJ, Ybarra ML (2008) Online predators and their victims: Myths, realities, and implications for prevention and treatment. Am Psychol 63(2):111–128
6. Matthews G (1990) Aristotelian essentialism. Philos Phenomenol Res 50:251262
7. Windley P (2005) Digital identity. O'Reilly Media, Sebastopol, CA
8. van den Berg B, Leenes R (2011) Computers, privacy and data protection: an element of choice, Chapter keeping up appearances: audience segregation in social network sites, 1st edn. Springer, Dordrecht, pp 211–231
9. Farrell R (2010) 8 ways to get fired because of social media. http://www.careerrookie.com/Article/CB-221-8-Ways/. Accessed 8 Feb 2012
10. Madden K (2011) 12 ways to get fired for Facebook. http://msn.careerbuilder.com/Article/MSN-2349-Workplace-1ssues-12-Ways/. Accessed 8 Feb 2012
11. Barracuda Labs (2012) Attackers use fake friends to blend into Facebook. http://www.barracudalabs.com/wordpress/index.php/2012/02/02/attackers-use-fake-friends-to-blend-into-facebook/. Accessed 19 Jun 2012
12. Cooper D, Santesson S, Farrell S, Boeyen S, Housley R, Polk W (2008) Internet X.509 public key infrastructure certificate and certificate revocation list (CRL) Profile. RFC 5280 (Proposed Standard). http://www.ietf.org/rfc/rfc5280.txt. Accessed 19 Jun 2012
13. Paquin C (2011) U-Prove cryptographic specification V1.1. Technical report, Microsoft Corporation, Feb 2011
14. Security Team (2010) IBM Research – Zurich. Specification of the identity mixer cryptographic library (a.k.a. cryptographic protocols of the Identity Mixer library). IBM Technical Report RZ3730 (# 99740), IBM Research, Zurich, April 2010

15. Brands S (2000) Rethinking public key infrastructures and digital certificates: building in privacy. MIT Press, Cambridge, MA
16. Lysyanskaya et al. (1999) Pseudonym systems. In: Proceedings of SAC 1999, LNCS, vol 1758. Springer, Berlin, pp 184–199
17. Bichsel P, Mtiller S, Preiss FS, Sommer D, Verdicchio M (2009) Security and trust through electronic social network-based interactions. In: Workshop on security and privacy in online social networking (SPOSN09), vol 4. IEEE Computer Society Press, Vancouver, Aug 2009, pp 1002–1007
18. OpenID Consortium (2007) OpenID authentication 2.0. http://openid.net/specs/openid-authentication-2_0.html. Specification
19. Recordon D, Reed D (2006) OpenID 2.0: a platform for user-centric identity management. In: DIM'06: Proceedings of the second ACM workshop on digital identity management. ACM, New York, pp 11–16
20. Camenisch J, Lysyanskaya A (2001) Efficient non-transferable anonymous multi-show credential system with optional anonymity revocation. In: Pfitzmann B (ed) EUROCRYPT'01. LNCS, vol 2045, Springer, Innsbruck, March 2001, pp 93–118
21. Lysyanskaya A (1999) Pseudonym systems. Master's thesis. MIT, Cambridge, MA
22. Camenisch J, Shoup V (2002) Practical verifiable encryption and decryption of discrete logarithms. http://eprint.iacr.org/2002/161. Accessed 19 Jun 2012
23. Allison A, Currall J, Moss M, Stuart S (2004) Digital identity matters. J Am Soc Inf Sci Technol 56(4):364–372
24. Cameron K (2005) The laws of identity. http://www.identityblog.com/?page_id=354. Accessed 15 Dec 2011
25. Pfitzmann A, Hansen M (2010) A terminology for talking about privacy by data minimization: anonymity, unlinkability, undetectability, unobservability, pseudonymity, and identity management (v0.34). http://dud.inf.tu-dresden.de/literatur/Anon_Terminology_v0.34.pdf. Accessed 13 Feb 2012
26. Korolova A, Motwani R, Nabar SU, Xu Y (2008) Link privacy in social networks. In: Proceedings of the 17th ACM conference on information and knowledge management, CIKM'08, ACM, New York, pp 289–298
27. Ardagna CA, De Capitani di Vimercati S, Paraboschi S, Pedrini E, Samarati P (2009) An XACML-based privacy-centered access control system. In: WISG'09: proceedings of the first ACM workshop on information security governance, ACM, New York, pp 49–58

Encryption for Peer-to-Peer Social Networks

Oleksandr Bodriagov and Sonja Buchegger

Abstract To address privacy concerns over online social networking services, several decentralized alternatives have been proposed. These peer-to-peer (P2P) online social networks do not rely on centralized storage of user data. Rather, data can be stored not only on a profile owner's computer but almost anywhere (friends' computers, random peers from the social network, third-party external storage, etc.). Because external storage is often untrusted or only semi-trusted, encryption plays a fundamental role in the security of P2P social networks.

Such a system needs to be efficient for use on a large scale, provide functionality for changing access rights suitable for social networks, and, most importantly, it should preserve the network's privacy properties. That is, other than user data confidentiality, it has to protect against information leakage regarding users' access rights and behaviors. In this paper we explore the encryption requirements for P2P social networks and propose a list of evaluation criteria that we use to compare existing approaches. We have found that none of the current P2P architectures for social networks achieve secure, efficient, 24/7 access control enforcement and data storage. They rely on trust, require constantly running servers for each user, use expensive encryption, or fail to protect the privacy of access information. In a search for solutions that better fulfill our criteria, we found that some broadcast encryption (BE) and predicate encryption (PE) schemes exhibit several desirable properties.

Keywords P2P social network • Encryption-based access control • Broadcast encryption • Predicate encryption

---

O. Bodriagov (✉) • S. Buchegger
KTH – The Royal Institute of Technology, Valhallavägen 79, 100 44 Stockholm, Sweden
e-mail: obo@kth.se; buc@csc.kth.se

Y. Altshuler et al. (eds.), *Security and Privacy in Social Networks*,
DOI 10.1007/978-1-4614-4139-7_4, © Springer Science+Business Media New York 2013

1 Introduction

In current online social networks (OSN), users do not have complete control over who can access their data. While most OSN services provide some privacy settings to limit the audience to which a user's content is published, some default settings will make this content public. Because most users reveal an astonishing amount of information in their profiles and tend not to change the default privacy settings [19], the privacy situation is quite alarming. In addition, other privacy settings can be overridden by a user's friends' decisions; for example when granting access to a third-party application. In other systems that do allow third-party applications (e.g. Android and iOS) users can install information flow monitoring applications and detect private information leakages [10, 11]. However, OSN users do not have this capability and can only react *post factum* when it becomes evident from other sources that information was leaked.

More importantly, there is no real protection against access by the service provider itself both for user-generated content and inadvertently generated information, such as, among others, behavioral patterns in linking, messaging, interacting, commenting, logging on and off, locations, browser types, and operating systems used. This content can then be mined and used for targeted advertising or be released to third parties. Whether this is done and to what extent the users' privacy preferences can be enforced, depends primarily on the privacy agreements of the service provider and other legal issues such as the location of the service provider, the servers, the content, and the user. The business model of current OSN providers is based on advertisements and, thus, the collection and mining of user data. The OSN providers or anyone who can access and collect user information can sell it either legally or illegally [2].

To prevent such undesired disclosure of user data, efforts have been made to circumvent the OSN service providers and give data control back to the users. While some proposals use the existing infrastructure of the OSN provider, others decentralize control and take a peer-to-peer approach. In this paper, we focus on these latter types of solutions and, more narrowly, on those that enforce privacy policies by cryptographic means. We use the term *encryption* throughout this paper as a shorthand for this concept, including key management and other required mechanisms.

Access control based on encryption is fundamentally different from that in existing centralized, provider-dependent social networks, because the centralized provider has control over how their servers behave, given their configurations and security measures, and can enforce policies using the operating system. If all users had their own constantly running servers, then a P2P social network could be achieved via direct end-to-end communication and access control would be similar to the centralized case (though performed locally on each server). However, this is currently an unrealistic assumption and enforcement needs to occur on a different level. Encryption is a means to accomplish this for a P2P environment with data storage that is either untrusted or semi-trusted. Several P2P OSN proposals use this.

In this paper, we discuss and compare several prominent approaches: PeerSoN, Safebook, Persona, Diaspora, and our new proposal using public-key predicate encryption and private-key identity-based broadcast encryption (IBBE).

To arrive at a good solution for the effective and efficient use of encryption for access control and privacy-policy enforcement in P2P social networks, we first need to define the requirements for such systems. In this paper we group these into the following categories: efficiency, functionality, and privacy. Efficiency refers to how much the encryption scheme requires in terms of storage, computational cost, and communications overhead. Functionality refers to categorizing possibilities when using the encryption scheme to manage permissions. Privacy refers to the side-effects of the distributed system of leaking information *about* the user data and not just the user's data (confidentiality).

The remainder of the paper is organized as follows. First, in Sect. 2, we state the criteria that are crucial for the encryption schemes in P2P social networks. In Sect. 3, we describe existing P2P social network architectures and what encryption methods they use. We continue by evaluating existing encryption schemes according to the stated criteria in Sect. 4. In Sect. 5, we explain broadcast encryption and how it works in a P2P social network and evaluate it according to our criteria. We describe and analyze predicate encryption in Sect. 6. We summarize the results of our evaluation in Sect. 7 and table (Table 1). Finally, we draw some conclusions in Sect. 8.

2 Essential Criteria for the P2P Encryption Systems

The P2P environment and the absence of a trusted party place many security constraints on encryption-based access control systems. In addition, for acceptable usability, it is imperative that all actions can be executed fast enough to achieve a positive user experience. In this section we first analyze these constraints and subsequently state requirements for encryption systems.

The National Institute of Standards and Technology (NIST) established criteria for the evaluation of the Advanced Encryption Standard (AES) candidates. We derived similar criteria although we adapted these to suit the P2P social network environment. The NIST uses the following criteria groups [25]:

1. Security: "*resistance of the algorithm to cryptanalysis, soundness of its mathematical basis, randomness of the algorithm output*", etc.;
2. Cost: speed and memory requirements
3. Algorithm and Implementation Characteristics: flexibility, algorithm simplicity, etc.

We omit security evaluation because we will compare different families of encryption systems and not specific algorithms and their implementations. While a security evaluation according to the NIST criteria would be meaningless in the context of this paper due to differences between algorithms that are within

Table 1 Comparison of encryption systems for P2P social networks

	Safebook (unknown encryption system)	Diaspora (trivial BE with Push model)	Persona (CP-ABE)	Early PeerSoN (trivial BE with Pull)	Dynamic IBBE	Predicate encryption with KEM
Storage cost (data)	Size(d_{own})	Size(d_{own} + $d_{friends}$)	Size(d)	Size(d)	Size(d)	Size(d)
Storage cost (header)	Unknown	$O(1)$	$O(a)$	$O(n)$	$O(1)$	$O(v)$
Encryption time	Unknown	$O(1)_{symm} + O(n)_{asymm}$	$O(1)_{symm} + O(a)_{ABE}$	$O(1)_{symm} + O(n)_{asymm}$	$O(1)_{symm} + O(n)_{BE}$	$O(1)_{symm} + O(v + log(q))_{PE}$
Decryption time	Unknown	$O(1)$	$O(a)^a$	$O(1)$	$O(1)$	$O(v)$
Transmission cost	$2(s-1) \cdot enc_{asymm} + 2(s-1) \cdot dec_{asymm}$	0	0	0	0	0
Permissions mod cost (add/remove)	Unknown	$O(1)$ / —	$O(a)_{ABE}$ / $O(1)_{symm} + O(a)_{ABE}$	$O(1)$ / $O(1)_{symm} + O(n)_{asymm}$	$O(n)_{BE}$ / $O(1)_{symm} + O(n)_{BE}$	$O(v + log(q))_{PE}$ / $O(1)_{symm} + O(v + log(q))_{PE}$
Cost of user addition/removal to a group	Unknown	$1 \cdot enc_{asymm}$ / $k \cdot enc_{symm} + n \cdot enc_{asymm}$	$1 \cdot keyCreate$ / $k \cdot en\,c_{symm} + k \cdot enc_{ABE} + (n \cdot keyCreate^b)$	$1 \cdot enc_{asymm}$ / $k \cdot enc_{symm} + n \cdot enc_{asymm}$	$k \cdot enc_{BE}$ / $k \cdot enc_{symm} + k \cdot enc_{BE}$	$1 \cdot keyCreate$ / $k \cdot enc_{symm} + k \cdot enc_{cPE} + n \cdot keyCreate$
Can encrypt for the conjunction/disjunction of groups	Unknown	✗ / ✓	✓ / ✓	✗ / ✓	✓ / ✓	✓ / ✓
Can encrypt for a group that one is not a member of	Unknown	✗	✓	✗	✗	✓
Can encrypt for "friends of friends"	Unknown	✗	✓	✗	✗	✓
Will not reveal access structures in the encryption header	Unknown	✓	✗	✗	✓	✓

[a] Some CP-ABE schemes are linear in the set of attributes from the user's key that satisfy the access structure

[b] For schemas with monotonic access structures

one family, it should be revisited for concrete examples as they become available. We divide our criteria into three categories: efficiency, functionality, and privacy. The efficiency category roughly corresponds to the cost category of NIST, and the functionality and privacy categories correspond to the NIST's algorithm characteristics category.

2.1   Efficiency

In ordinary centralized access control the security subsystem authenticates the user and enforces policies provided by access control lists (ACLs) or capabilities. In contrast, in a P2P system we cannot rely on untrusted storage for authentication and authorization. We do not have access to the operating system of a replica holder and, thus, we use encryption and key management to replace this functionality. Encryption-based access control relies on authentication during a key setup phase, when a decryption key is given to the user after authentication. This key has a role similar to an access token in systems like Kerberos, while the encryption scheme in a P2P social network plays the role of the security subsystem in a centralized system in the sense that it takes a user's key and authorizes access to the data.

An access token has a short lifetime and can be easily renewed, whereas a users' key is given out for a much longer period; thus, there is a higher probability that it might be stolen or lost. Cryptographic keys are also prone to aging. And, although user key renovation is not too frequent, it can have significant consequences because of its fined-grained access control requirement.

To achieve fine-grained access control, each object should be encrypted separately for different sets of recipients, such that encrypted objects are completely unrelated and a change in one of them does not influence the others. That is why, all objects to which this key provides access should be re-encrypted during a key renovation procedure, which is clearly a performance issue. It might be better that such a procedure for all the user's keys for the system is done at one time, so that a single object becomes re-encrypted only once. With a large number of objects, however, re-encryption of all data might be quite time consuming. Thus, it is important to have rapid encryption. Also from the perspective of usability, the speed of encryption/decryption is very important. Operations like posting a single message, a photo, and so on will not take much time even with inefficient encryption, although retrieval of recent wall posts, messages, and entire photo albums can be more time consuming. The speed of encryption/decryption depends not only on the speed of the underlying cipher, but also on the scheme's scalability. Therefore, the first requirement is a constant cost encryption/decryption that does not depend on the number of recipients. To the best of our knowledge, however, there are no encryption schemes that have both encryption and decryption that do not depend on the number of recipients.

In a centralized system the addition/removal of a group member influences all objects to which this group has access, although this is not generally true for encryption-based access control systems. Some encryption schemes require that all objects are re-encrypted if the group changes. This is not scalable and might have a strong impact, especially in P2P networks, because the number of objects (posts, photos, etc.) can be quite large and groups can change quite frequently (e.g. adding new friends). Thus, the second requirement is that the addition/removal of users from a group should not depend on the number of subjects/objects and it should have constant cost, as in centralized systems. If the encryption system does not have a constant cost for the addition/removal of users from a group, then re-encryption should be as fast as possible.

Another issue is encryption overhead in terms of storage. For P2P storage with replication it is crucial to save as much space as possible, as otherwise the system will not be scalable. Encryption overhead (headers) can be quite considerable for short messages and may even require more space than the actual encrypted data. If the size of the header depends on the number of receivers, then such an encryption scheme is not suitable for a P2P social network with considerable numbers of possible recipients. Therefore, the next criterion is the header scalability with respect to the number of recipients. Another concern is the storage cost of the encrypted data.

2.2 Functionality

Different types of encryption schemes (symmetric, asymmetric, and others) have different properties and thus can be used to realize different P2P social network features. Yet, an encryption system that combines different encryption schemes should be able to provide all functions of the social network. The encryption system defines the P2P social network's functionality, the security provided, and the privacy levels.

A P2P social network's encryption system should be able to encrypt objects for a single subject as well as for any possible set of subjects in a cost-effective way. However, efficient encryption for the conjunction/disjunction of groups is not supported by all encryption systems, although this is quite a useful operation for users of social networks because users' connections can have different origins (colleagues, family, etc.) and different levels of trust. Such operations as encryption for a group of which one is not a member and encryption for "friends of friends" are even less frequently supported, although these operations have analogies in every-day life.

2.3 Privacy

The security subsystem within a centralized environment controls all of the flows of information from a single point of control. However, it is much harder to implement such control with the encryption system of a P2P network with untrusted storage, as the encrypted objects' contents are not the only things requiring protection. It is also important to protect that information regarding which subjects have access to what objects, the quantity of objects, and their types. It should also not be possible to verify if a particular user has access to some particular object. The user should be able to see only those objects that are encrypted for her or for the group of which she is a member. The requirement for fine-grained access control results in a set of separately encrypted objects. The users should be able to determine which files they are able to open without checking all of the files; otherwise the system looses scalability. At the same time, an object's encryption header should not reveal those subjects who have access to this object. If the access list accompanies the encrypted data, malicious users can completely reconstruct a network of contacts from these lists. Additionally, they will know who can access which encrypted objects, and thus be able to infer some information from that knowledge.

2.4 List of Criteria

In summary, we have derived the following evaluation criteria: efficiency of addition/removal of users from a group; efficiency of user key revocation; encryption/decryption efficiency; encryption header overhead, capability to encrypt for the conjunction/disjunction of groups; capability to encrypt for a group of which one is not a member; capability to encrypt for "friends of friends"; and not reveal access structures in the header.

3 Existing P2P OSN Architectures

In this section we describe and analyze existing P2P architectures for social networks.

An early version of a P2P social network, developed under the PeerSoN project [1, 5], relied on the conjunction of symmetric and asymmetric cryptography. Data were first encrypted using a symmetric key, after which this key was encrypted with recipients' public keys. Users' IDs and encrypted symmetric keys were stored alongside the encrypted data.

Safebook [6] is based on two design principles: decentralization and exploitation of a real-life trust. It relies on matryoshkas that provide data storage, profile data retrieval, and communication obfuscation. A matryoshka is comprised of a set of nodes that are grouped in several concentric rings according to the level of trust that each node associated with the matryoshka has towards them. The innermost layer/ring is the most trusted and consists of 'friends.' This ring is actually responsible for storing replicated data for the node associated with the matryoshka. The innermost layer stores published data in both encrypted and unencrypted forms, although private data are stored by the owner himself and are not replicated to the innermost layer. According to Cuttilo et al. [7], a "*simple group-based encryption scheme*" is used for encryption, and users receive opportune keys [6] to decrypt the published data. The owner should explicitly authorize and republish to the inner ring every message written by other users.

Anonymity in Safebook is achieved by multi-hop routing. A distributed hash table holds pointers to nodes on the outermost ring of the matryoshka. The incoming request is routed from the outermost ring to the matryoshka's core. Using asymmetric cryptography, the routed messages are encrypted on a hop-by-hop basis.

The Diaspora project [14] uses a client-server architecture, but does so in a decentralized way. It requires a constantly running server for each user to achieve end-to-end communications. Users without servers can choose from one of the existing servers to store their data. Encryption is used to insure confidentiality of stored data. Not many people may be willing to run a server and provide storage for other users for free. Even if a user finds such a server there is no guarantee that the server will not be shut-down at a later time, which could potentially result in a complete loss of all the user's data. This risk is mitigated in systems that use multiple replicas held by peers, rather than having one instance as is done in Diaspora.

According to Diaspora's security architecture proposal there are three levels of data security [15]: unencrypted information that is available to everyone; and information encrypted by the server for some intended receivers, information encrypted by the owner herself for some intended receivers.

Encryption is executed in two stages [16]. First, a random encryption key is generated (symmetric cryptography) and the message is encrypted using this key. Second, the sender encrypts this secret key for each of the receivers with a corresponding public key and sends it to them. Currently, an AES-256-CBC cipher is used for symmetric encryption and RSA is used for public key encryption [18].

Diaspora works according to the Push model [17, 18]. Data posted by a user are encrypted for the recipients and pushed to the recipients' servers in an encrypted form. To delete posted data, a *retraction* request is sent to the recipients' servers.

Another P2P architecture is Persona [3]. This stores data in an encrypted form; thus access control is encryption-based. As with PeerSoN, storage is not trusted, and confidentiality is ensured by encryption. To provide specific rights to stored objects the profile owner defines access control lists (ACLs) and instructs the storage medium to set them. ACLs contain users' public keys and their access rights. The storage medium authenticates the users and authorizes their actions based on the entries in the ACL. This scheme provides limited data integrity protection. However, the credibility of access control enforced by untrusted storage is not that strong, so the main protection mechanism is encryption, which only ensures confidentiality.

Persona relies on a ciphertext-policy attribute-based encryption (CP-ABE) scheme [13]. With CP-ABE, a user's private key is associated with a number of attributes (e.g. 'friend', 'family'). During encryption, an access structure over attributes is attached to a ciphertext. The user can decrypt the ciphertext if that user's attributes pass through the ciphertext's access structure.

Because ABE is computationally expensive, encryption in Persona is a two-stage process. Data are first encrypted with a symmetric key, after which they are ABE-encrypted.

4   Evaluations of Existing Encryption Schemes Based on Our Criteria

In this section we evaluate the suitability of encryption systems in existing architectures for the P2P social network environment. Our evaluation is based on the criteria described in Sect. 2.

As described in the previous section, existing P2P architectures for social networks use the following two types of encryption systems: a conjunction of symmetric and asymmetric cryptography (i.e., trivial broadcast encryption scheme [9]) used in Diaspora and the early version of PeerSoN; and CP-ABE used in Persona. There is not enough information on the encryption system used by Safebook, except that it is a *"simple group-based encryption scheme"* and users receive opportune keys [6] to decrypt published data. In addition, expensive asymmetric cryptography that is used for communicating between hops inside the matryoshka defines the time cost of information retrieval and posting by other users. The time required for encryption/decryption of data is negligible compared to the time required for information retrieval and posting. Other relevant drawbacks of Safebook are its reliance on trust relationships, and authorization and republishing of every message written by others.

4.1   Efficiency

It is well known that asymmetric cryptography is much more computationally intensive than symmetric cryptography. Even Elliptic Curve Cryptography (ECC), which is the most efficient type of public-key cryptography [20], is much slower than symmetric cryptography. Moreover, storage efficiency is inadequate because for each of the receivers the object must be encrypted separately. This is why encryption systems based solely on asymmetric cryptography are not used.

Compared to a purely asymmetric cryptography scheme, an encryption system based on the conjunction of symmetric and asymmetric cryptography is much more efficient because the object itself is encrypted using a symmetric cipher, after which this symmetric key is encrypted multiple times for each of the receivers with their public keys. However, even this approach is not quite suitable because the number of objects in the typical profile is very large. Thus, the overhead associated with encrypting the same keys multiple times is quite significant both in terms of time and space. Encryption for a group means that data are first encrypted with a symmetric key and then this symmetric key is encrypted with the public key of each member. The addition of a user to a group is very simple; it only requires encryption of the symmetric key(s) of that group with the public key of that user. Conversely, the removal of a user or a set of users from a group requires the re-encryption of all data encrypted for that group, which is considerably harder.

Both the early version of PeerSoN and Diaspora use this encryption system. PeerSoN uses it in a Pull model, while in Diaspora it is used in a Push model that has the disadvantage that the same encrypted object has to be transferred multiple times (i.e., separately to each of the recipients).

The CP-ABE scheme used in Persona [4] was the first CP-ABE scheme introduced and had many drawbacks. The size of the ciphertext and the speed of encryption/decryption are crucial parameters for the P2P social network environment. In the original scheme, they were linear in the number of attributes in the access structure, which is not adequate for a P2P social network. In addition, so far as we know, there are no CP-ABE schemes with constant size ciphertexts or decryption that does not depend on the number of attributes and have constant cost. The encryption time with existing schemes also scales linearly with the size of the access formula [21, 29]. To our knowledge, the most efficient CP-ABE schemes in terms of decryption, such as the scheme described by Waters [21], are linear in the set of attributes from the user's key that satisfy the access structure. Encryption for one contact can be accomplished using the public key of that person (or as with conjunction of symmetric and asymmetric cryptography), while encryption to groups uses CP-ABE because of its advantages in efficiency and functionality. An attribute defines a group; to encrypt for that group, one encrypts for that attribute. If all receivers have some common attribute, then CP-ABE is quite efficient from the point of view of ciphertext size; although, if the receivers are members of different groups then the overhead can be suboptimal (depending on the number of attributes), even though the encryption time is very favorable.

The CP-ABE scheme used in Persona is limited to monotonic access structures (no negations) which leads to inefficient encryption; for example, in cases when access is allowed for the entire group except for a few members. This scheme has troublesome user revocation, as several different users might match the decryption policy [4] and there are no negations to prohibit access for some specific users. In the worst case scenario, revocation of a user's access rights basically means creating a new group of users that corresponds to some new attribute that the members of this new group have in common and re-encrypting all of the old group's data with new symmetric keys. To the best of our knowledge, the only CP-ABE scheme that allows negations is the one described by Ostrovsky et al. [27]. This scheme, in conjunction with using identities as attributes, yields simple revocation, although the decryption time and the storage cost are still linear in this scheme.

4.2 Functionality

The combination of symmetric and asymmetric cryptography allows for encrypting for the disjunction of several groups by encrypting data with symmetric keys that correspond to those groups. However, it is impossible to encrypt for the conjunction of groups. Encryption for some arbitrary set of users that do not belong to the same group is equivalent to creating a new group, as, after encryption, these users will share the symmetric key used for encryption. We have described the encryption procedure from the perspective of group creator/group member, but it is impossible to encrypt for a group for which one is not a member unless that group has a public-private key pair shared among its members. Encryption for "friends of friends" is also not supported.

CP-ABE schemes seamlessly support encryption for the conjunction/disjunction of two groups using the conjunction/disjunction of their attributes. They also allow "friends of friends" encryption. Additionally, a user can encrypt for a group even if he is not a member of that group.

4.3 Privacy

In the early version of PeerSoN it was possible to determine which subjects could access what objects from the encryption headers that contained the subjects' IDs. A cryptosystem based on conjunction of symmetric and asymmetric cryptography does not, however, need to reveal for whom the data is encrypted (the problem of identifying what one can decrypt can be solved by different means). In contrast, so far as we know, all CP-ABE schemes have clear access structures; thus, anyone who can download encrypted data can learn which groups have access to them. On the other hand, there are BE schemes with hidden access structures. One of these schemes is described by Jiang et al. [22].

4.4 Summary

To summarize our evaluation, an encryption system that combines symmetric and asymmetric cryptography is quite efficient, although it is quite limited from the functionality point of view. Encryption systems based on CP-ABE schemes are moderately adequate in terms of efficiency, and have quite rich functionality. However, because none of the CP-ABE schemes achieves non-monotonic, hidden access structures and low (constant) storage and computational cost at the same time, we propose using an encryption system based on broadcast encryption or predicate encryption schemes. We describe these in the following sections.

5   Broadcast Encryption

Broadcast encryption (BE) schemes [12] are used to distribute encrypted data to a dynamic set of users in a cost-effective way. In general, a BE scheme consists of a sender and a group of recipients. Each recipient has her own private decryption key to decrypt the encrypted data sent by the sender.

BE schemes can be either symmetric or public-key based. In the first case, only a trusted source/broadcaster of the system that generated all the private keys can broadcast data to receivers. If the system is public-key based, then anyone who knows a system's public key can broadcast.

The efficiency of BE schemes is measured in terms of transmission, storage, and computational cost. In addition to efficiency, one of the main requirements for a BE scheme is that it should be easy to revoke a key or a set of keys. Other important security concepts are collusion resistance and statelessness. A fully collusion-resistant scheme is robust against collusion of any number of revoked users. A BE scheme is said to be stateless if, after revocation of some subset of users, the remaining users do not have to update their private keys.

A BE scheme is called dynamic [9] if it allows the following: new users can join without the need to modify existing users' decryption keys; the ciphertext size and the system's initial key setup do not depend on the number of users; for a symmetric key based scheme, the encryption key should not be changed and for a public key scheme, the group public key should be incrementally updated with complexity of at most $O(1)$. Because dynamic BE schemes provide so many advantages from the perspective of key management and efficiency, we will narrow our discussion to only this type of BE scheme.

It is obvious that the properties of BE schemes we have described are very desirable. Thus suitable candidates for application to a social network environment are BE schemes that have the following properties: stateless; fully collision resistant; and dynamic with constant size ciphertexts and keys, and with computationally efficient encryption/decryption.

We will use a dynamic identity-based broadcast encryption (IBBE) scheme that meets all these requirements [22]. IBBE schemes involve a third-party authority: a Private Key Generator (PKG). However, this role is given to the profile owner when adjusting this scheme for our scenario. Thus, the profile owner is responsible for creating a group of receivers and assigning private BE keys.

The IBBE scheme is formaly defined as a tuple of algorithms *IBBE = (Setup, Extract, Encrypt, Decrypt)* [8]. Although the DIBBE scheme defined in Jiang et al. [22] has the same structure, there are some differences in the algorithms' input parameters that reflect the dynamic nature of the scheme. The algorithms for the DIBBE scheme have the following form.

The *Setup* algorithm generates some system parameters, a secret master key, and a group public key, *GPK*. The *Extract* algorithm uses as input a secret master key, *MK*, known only to the broadcaster and produces a private key for each user. The encryption algorithm *Encrypt* uses as input a set of receivers, *S*, and a *GPK* (additionally used for the DIBBE scheme) and outputs a pair *(Header,K)*, where K is a symmetric secret key to encrypt data and *Header* is an encryption of this symmetric key for the set of receivers. Data are stored in the form *(Header, encrypted data)*; only a user whose ID/label is in the set can decrypt the *Header* using his/her private key. Some schemes work with plain Headers that show who can decrypt the data, while other schemes are more privacy preserving and reveal no information about the set of receivers or any other parameters (e.g. scheme described in [22, 30]). The *Decrypt* algorithm for the privacy preserving scheme mentioned above uses *GPK*, *Header*, the user's private key, and the user ID as input and outputs a symmetric key, K; for the ordinary IBBE schemes, the *Decrypt* algorithm also requires the set of receivers, S.

Because each time during encryption the user can create a set of receivers "on the fly" in the IBBE scheme, it is possible to encrypt to any conjunction/disjunction of groups, because a group is merely an arbitrary set of users. In addition, in IBBE schemes, users that are not members of the group can still encrypt to the group if they know the *GPK*. However, the DIBBE scheme defined by Jiang et al. [22] requires the secret master key, *MK*, as input for the encryption algorithm. Thus, encryption to a group of which one is not a member and encryption for "friends of friends" are not supported.

User revocation for stateless BE schemes does not require re-keying for other users. Thus, for stateless IBBE schemes, this means re-encryption of data with a new symmetric key and consequently regenerating *Headers* for the new set of receivers. User addition in any IBBE scheme requires re-encryption of *Headers* for the new set of receivers in addition to creating a private key for that user.

Some broadcast encryption schemes (e.g. [8, 21]) achieve constant size ciphertext. In addition, the scheme described by Jiang et al. [21] has decryption complexity of $O(1)$, while the encryption cost is linear in the number of receivers.

6 Predicate Encryption

In Predicate Encryption (PE) [23], a cipher text is associated with some attribute from a set of attributes, Σ. This attribute defines who can decrypt the text. User secret keys for decryption are associated with predicates (characteristic Boolean functions) in some class F. A user can decrypt a cipher text if and only if $f(I) = 0$, where $f \in F$ is a predicate associated with a user's secret key and $I \in \Sigma$ is an attribute associated with the cipher text. As with BE schemes, PE schemes can be divided into private-key and public-key schemes. In a public key scheme, any user who knows the public key for encryption can define attributes and encrypt data for some set of receivers. However, only an owner of the master secret key can create user decryption keys. In a private-key scheme only, the owner can encrypt and generate decryption keys for users.

The primary distinguishing feature of predicate encryption is "attribute-hiding." According to the definition of "attribute-hiding" [23], an attacker that possesses l

secret user keys can learn only values $f_1(I), \ldots, f_l(I)$ and nothing more about the attribute I. In other words, a cipher text does not reveal attributes, although the user secret key may leak some information. There is also an additional notion of "predicate privacy" [28], which means that it should not be possible to learn a description of the encoded predicate from the corresponding user secret key. However, this property can only be achieved by symmetric PE schemes because, with asymmetric schemes, an attacker can attempt to guess the predicate associated with a key by crafting arbitrary plain text and encrypting it under any chosen attribute using an available master public key. The "predicate privacy" property is not very valuable in a social network environment, because users can infer information about their access rights from the decrypted information. In addition, a private-key scheme does not support encryption for a group of which one is not a member and for friends of friends.

Many PE schemes [23, 24, 26] use inner-product predicates when a secret key corresponds to a vector $\bar{x}$ and the attribute corresponds to a vector $\bar{v}$. Then the following condition holds: $f_{\bar{v}}(\bar{x}) = 1$ if $\bar{x} \times \bar{v} = 0$. PE schemes based on inner-products support a wide class of predicates [23]: conjunctions/disjunctions; polynomials; CNF/DNF formulas. Katz et al. [23] show how polynomial-based constructions can be used to evaluate conjunctions/disjunctions of attributes against predicates. Yet, despite all this variety, the expressiveness of inner-product predicates is lower than the expressiveness of ABE access structures [24]. Current PE schemes work only with monotonous structures and do not allow negations. We would like to point out that anonymous identity based encryption and hidden vector encryption are just special cases of PE schemes based on inner-product predicates [24].

The PE scheme for inner-product predicates is formally defined as a tuple of probabilistic polynomial-time algorithms: *PE = (Setup, KeyGen, Enc, Dec)* [24]. The algorithms have the following form.

The *Setup* algorithm uses as input some security parameter(s) and generates a secret master key, *SK*, and a public master key, *PK*. The *KeyGen* algorithm uses as input a predicate vector $\bar{v}$ and both master keys and produces a user private key (decryption key) $sk_{\bar{v}}$ that corresponds to the predicate. The encryption algorithm *Enc* uses as input an attribute vector $\bar{x}$, the public master key, and plain text and then produces a cipher text, *C*. The decryption algorithm *Dec* uses the master public key, *PK*, the user private key $sk_{\bar{v}}$. It produces either cipher text or the distinguished symbol $\perp$ which means that decryption failed.

Although neither the original PE definition [23] nor the PE definition for inner-product predicates [24] mentions anything about bilinear pairing operations, all of the mentioned PE schemes use them. Therefore, because of performance implications, we will consider PE usage in a key-encapsulation construction; that is, symmetric encryption is used to encrypt the data, and the corresponding secret key will be PE-encrypted.

PE schemes were not constructed with underlying symmetric encryption, as for BE schemes, but taking into account that some algorithms for PE encryption require expensive bilinear paring operations, we will consider them in combination with underlying symmetric encryption (as in Persona with CP-ABE). Using multivariate polynomials for predicates inner product PE schemes can handle arbitrary CNF or

DNF formulas [23]. Therefore, all arguments, except for attribute-hiding, in favor of or against combination of symmetric cryptography and CP-ABE can also be applied to the case of public-key predicate encryption based on inner-product predicates.

7 Comparisons and Discussion

In Table 1 we summarize our evaluation of different encryption schemes (with best performance schemes taken as representatives) according to the stated criteria and transmission costs. Transmission cost is defined as the number of decryption/ encryption operations that have to be performed in order to transfer an encrypted object from the source to the destination. Of course, there is also a cost of sending messages. So, for example in the case of Diaspora when all the keys and data are sent to recipients and in early PeerSoN where they are stored locally, it is evident that the difference is very significant. However, the transmission costs shown in Table 1 do not take into account the costs of sending messages, and focuses solely on encryption/decryption.

The following notation is used in Table 1: d_{own} – own data of the profile owner; $d_{friends}$ – data that was received from friends as posts; a – the size of access structure in a CP-ABE scheme; n – the number of recipients; $O(1)_{symm} + O(n)_{asymm}$ – a symmetric operation with a constant cost followed by an asymmetric operation with a linear in the number of recipients n cost; $O(a)_{ABE}$ – ABE operation with a linear in the size of access formula a cost; s – number of shells in the Matryoshka; v – the inner-product vector length in PE (this number can be quite small, e.g. anonymous IBE can be obtained from PE using $v = 2$ [23]); q – the order of a multiplicative group in the PE scheme; enc_{asymm} – one asymmetric encryption operation; dec_{asymm} – one asymmetric decryption operation; enc_{symm} – one symmetric encryption operation, k – number of affected objects.

As we mentioned in Sect. 4, there is not enough available information on the encryption system of Safebook. Any assumptions about the encryption system that may be used in Safebook would lead to the same evaluation results as for other P2P systems that use the same encryption systems and follow the Pull model.

We should note that, in Table 1 the encryption operations are performed for groups of receivers, and the decryption operations are performed by one receiver each. Thus, although the encryption operation in Diaspora for one receiver requires only one symmetric and one asymmetric encryption, for the group of receivers we would need one symmetric and n asymmetric encryption operations; thus, the cost is linear.

In Table 1 we see that Diaspora (because of the Push model) has the highest storage cost storing not only own data, but also data received from others. The early version of PeerSoN with a trivial BE scheme has the worst storage cost for headers; although, CP-ABE schemes are also not optimal in this regard. The encryption cost of Persona with its underlying CP-ABE scheme and the encryption cost of the PE scheme are generally lower than for other systems, because the number of attributes is usually smaller than the number of receivers. Additionally, CP-ABE with PE schemes have the worst decryption costs that depend on the number of attributes (attribute vector length for PE), while all the other systems have constant decryption costs. Moreover, CP-ABE and PE decryption algorithms contain bilinear pairing operations; because they are computationally expensive and their number linearly depends on the number of attributes, we can conclude that these algorithms are quite expensive.

The permissions modification cost is defined as the cost of changing permissions (set of receivers) in one object. Because all objects are pushed in Diaspora, it is impossible to modify a set of receivers of an already shared object; thus, there is a dash in Table 1.

The cost of user addition to a group (a set of identities for identity-based schemes) is the highest for dynamic IBBE, and the cost of user removal from a group is the highest for CP-ABE and PE (unless the schemes allow negations). Nevertheless, both of these schemes can encrypt for the conjunction/disjunction of groups. And, while CP-ABE also provides the capability to encrypt for the group of which one is not a member and for friends of friends, the IBBE scheme is more secure and does not reveal access structures in encryption headers. PE is the best from the functionality point of view, as it supports the capability to encrypt for the group of which one is not a member and for friends of friends. It also supports attribute-hiding.

We should note that, although there are public-key BE schemes that would provide the same functionality as CP-ABE or PE, they have worse performances than the private key DIBBE scheme described in Table 1. However, we do not know of any theoretical limitations that would not allow creating a public-key BE scheme with a hidden set of receivers and comparable or better performance. By comparison, CP-ABE schemes are limited only to visible access structures [24]. PE schemes have no such limitations and might achieve better performances.

8   Conclusions

We analyzed the scenario of P2P social networks without trusted parties and the impact this environment has on encryption-based access control systems. Based on this analysis, we stated the following evaluation criteria that encompass efficiency, functionality, and privacy areas: efficiency of addition/removal of users from a group; efficiency of user key revocation; encryption/decryption efficiency; encryption header overhead; capability to encrypt for the conjunction/disjunction of groups; capability to encrypt for a group of which one is not a member, capability to encrypt for "friends of friends"; and capability not to reveal access structures in the header.

We analyzed existing P2P architectures for social networks that focus on encryption as a means to ensure data confidentiality. We evaluated the types of encryption systems that these architectures use (combination of asymmetric and symmetric cryptographies, CP-ABE) based on the stated criteria.

We also evaluated existing broadcast encryption (BE) and predicate encryption (PE) schemes in terms of how they were in accord with the stated criteria and defined properties that are crucial for the BE schemes to be used in the P2P social network environment. We found one BE scheme that met all of the requirements and adapted it to the social network environment. The PE scheme was considered in combination with underlying symmetric encryption. Within the scope of the current evaluation, the public-key predicate encryption schemes behave almost like CP-ABE schemes, so all arguments (except for attribute hiding) that apply to CP-ABE also apply to PE schemes.

The combination of asymmetric and symmetric cryptography does not have sufficient efficiency and functionality for the P2P social network environment. CP-ABE schemes are inferior to PE and BE schemes because none of the current CP-ABE schemes achieve non-monotonic, hidden access structures, while at the same time achieving low storage and computational costs. Hidden access structures cannot be achieved for any future CP-ABE schemes, because this class of schemes is limited to open access structures only. Current broadcast encryption schemes with hidden access structures do not have the aforementioned drawbacks, although they do not support the capability to encrypt for a group of which one is not a member and the ability to encrypt for "friends of friends" because they are private-key schemes. On the other hand, current PE schemes offer the same functionality as CP-ABE schemes and have attribute-hiding properties, although they are not as efficient as BE schemes. In addition, there are no theoretical limitations that might prevent the creation of public-key BE schemes with hidden access structures and more efficient PE schemes. Thus, we propose the use of either public-key inner-product predicate encryption schemes or BE schemes with high performance encryption/decryption, regardless of the number of identities/groups, for an efficient encryption-based access control for the P2P social network environment.

Acknowledgements This research was funded by grant SSF FFL09-0086 from the Swedish Foundation for Strategic Research and by grant VR 2009-3793 from the Swedish Research Council.

References

1. Afify Y (2008) Access control in a peer-to-peer social network. Master's thesis, EPFL, Lausanne, Switzerland
2. Altshuler Y, Aharony N, Pentland A, Elovici Y, Cebrian M (2011) Stealing reality: when criminals become data scientists (or vice versa). Intell Syst IEEE 26(6):22–30
3. Baden R, Bender A, Spring N, Bhattacharjee B, Starin D (2009) Persona: an online social network with user-defined privacy. SIGCOMM Comput Commun Rev 39:135–146. http://doi.acm.org/10.1145/1594977.1592585
4. Bethencourt J, Sahai A, Waters B (2007) Ciphertext-policy attribute-based encryption. In: Proceedings of the 2007 I.E. symposium on security and privacy, SP '07, Berkeley. IEEE Computer Society, Los Alamitos, pp 321–334. http://dx.doi.org/10.1109/SP.2007.11

5. Buchegger S, Schiöberg D, Vu LH, Datta A (2009) Peerson: P2p social networking: early experiences and insights. In: Proceedings of the second ACM EuroSys workshop on social network systems, SNS '09, Nuremberg, pp 46–52. http://doi.acm.org/10.1145/1578002.1578010

6. Cutillo L, Molva R, Strufe T (2009) Safebook: a privacy-preserving online social network leveraging on real-life trust. Commun Mag IEEE 47(12):94–101

7. Cutillo L, Molva R, Strufe T (2010) On the security and feasibility of safebook: a distributed privacy-preserving online social network. In: Privacy and identity management for life. IFIP advances in information and communication technology, vol 320. Springer, Boston, pp 86–101

8. Delerablee C (2007) Identity-based broadcast encryption with constant size ciphertexts and private keys. In: Advances in cryptology ASIACRYPT 2007. Lecture notes in computer science, vol 4833. Springer, Berlin/Heidelberg, pp 200–215

9. Delerablee C, Paillier P, Pointcheval D (2007) Fully collusion secure dynamic broadcast encryption with constant-size ciphertexts or decryption keys. In: Pairing-based cryptography pairing 2007. Lecture notes in computer science, vol 4575. Springer, Berlin/Heidelberg, pp 39–59

10. Egele M, Kruegel C, Kirda E, Vigna G (2011) Pios: detecting privacy leaks in ios applications. In: Proceedings of the ISOC network and distributed systems security (NDSS) symposium, San Diego

11. Enck W, Gilbert P, Chun BG, Cox LP, Jung J, McDaniel P, Sheth AN (2010) Taintdroid: an information-flow tracking system for realtime privacy monitoring on smartphones. In: Proceedings of the 9th USENIX symposium on operating systems design and implementation (OSDI), Vancouver

12. Fiat A, Naor M (1994) Broadcast encryption. In: Advances in cryptology CRYPTO 93. Lecture notes in computer science, vol 773. Springer, Berlin/Heidelberg, pp 480–491

13. Goyal V, Pandey O, Sahai A, Waters B (2006) Attribute-based encryption for fine-grained access control of encrypted data. In: Proceedings of the 13th ACM conference on computer and communications security, CCS '06. ACM, New York, pp 89–98

14. Grippi D, Sofaer R, Salzberg M, Zhitomirsky I (2010) Diaspora. A little more about the project. http://blog.joindiaspora.com/2010/04/21/a-little-more-about-the-project.html. Accessed Nov 2011

15. Grippi D, Sofaer R, Salzberg M, Zhitomirsky I (2010) Diaspora security architecture proposal. https://github.com/diaspora/diaspora/wiki/Security-Architecture-Proposal. Accessed Nov 2011

16. Grippi D, Sofaer R, Salzberg M, Zhitomirsky I (2010) Encryption. https://github.com/diaspora/diaspora/wiki/Encryption. Accessed Nov 2011

17. Grippi D, Sofaer R, Salzberg M, Zhitomirsky I (2011) Diaspora roadmap. https://github.com/diaspora/diaspora/wiki/Roadmap. Accessed Nov 2011

18. Grippi D, Sofaer R, Salzberg M, Zhitomirsky I (2011) Diaspora's federation protocol. https://github.com/diaspora/diaspora/wiki/Diaspora\%27s-federation-protocol

19. Gross R, Acquisti A (2005) Information revelation and privacy in online social networks. In: Proceedings of the 2005 ACM workshop on privacy in the electronic society, WPES '05. ACM, New York, pp 71–80

20. Gupta V, Gupta S, Chang S, Stebila D (2002) Performance analysis of elliptic curve cryptography for ssl. In: Proceedings of the 1st ACM workshop on wireless security, WiSE '02. ACM, New York, pp 87–94

21. Ibraimi L, Tang Q, Hartel P, Jonker W (2009) Efficient and provable secure ciphertext-policy attribute-based encryption schemes. In: Proceedings of the 5th international conference on information security practice and experience, ISPEC '09. Springer, Berlin, pp 1–12

22. Jiang H, Xu Q, Shang J (2010) An efficient dynamic identity-based broadcast encryption scheme. In: Data, privacy and E-commerce (ISDPE), 2010 second international symposium on, Buffalo, pp 27–32

23. Katz J, Sahai A, Waters B (2008) Predicate encryption supporting disjunctions, polynomial equations, and inner products. In: Proceedings of the theory and applications of cryptographic

techniques 27th annual international conference on advances in cryptology, EUROCRYPT'08, Istanbul. Springer, Berlin/Heidelberg, pp 146–162

24. Lewko A, Okamoto T, Sahai A, Takashima K, Waters B (2010) Fully secure functional encryption: attribute-based encryption and (hierarchical) inner product encryption. In: Advances in cryptology EUROCRYPT 2010. Lecture notes in computer science, vol 6110. Springer, Berlin/Heidelberg, pp 62–91

25. Nechvatal J, Barker E, Bassham L, Burr W, Dworkin M, Foti J, Roback E (2000) Report on the development of the advanced encryption standard (aes). Technical report MSU-CSE-99-39, Computer Security Division, Information Technology Laboratory, National Institute of Standards and Technology. http://csrc.nist.gov/archive/aes/round2/r2report.pdf

26. Okamoto T, Takashima K (2009) Hierarchical predicate encryption for inner-products. In: Advances in cryptology ASIACRYPT 2009. Lecture notes in computer science, vol 5912. Springer, Berlin/Heidelberg, pp 214–231

27. Ostrovsky R, Sahai A, Waters B (2007) Attribute-based encryption with non-monotonic access structures. In: Proceedings of the 14th ACM conference on computer and communications security, CCS '07. ACM, New York, pp 195–203. http://doi.acm.org/10.1145/1315245.1315270

28. Shen E, Shi E, Waters B (2009) Predicate privacy in encryption systems. In: Proceedings of the 6th theory of cryptography conference on theory of cryptography, TCC '09. Springer, Berlin/Heidelberg, pp 457–473

29. Waters B (2011) Ciphertext-policy attribute-based encryption: an expressive, efficient, and provably secure realization. In: Public key cryptography PKC 2011. Lecture notes in computer science, vol 6571. Springer, Berlin/Heidelberg, pp 53–70

30. Zhang W, Xu Q, He P (2010) Identity-based broadcast encryption with recipient privacy. In: 3rd IEEE international conference on Computer science and information technology (ICCSIT 2010), vol 8, Chengdu, pp 483–487

Crowdsourcing and Ethics

The Employment of Crowdsourcing Workers for Tasks that Violate Privacy and Ethics

Christopher G. Harris and Padmini Srinivasan

Abstract Crowdsourcing has received considerable attention for its ability to provide researchers and task requesters with an inexpensive, quick, and easy method to complete repetitive tasks and utilize human intellect. Most studies have expressed the merits of crowdsourcing; however, little discussion has been reported on the potential to use the crowd to accomplish unethical tasks. In this chapter, we start with a survey on crowdsourcing ethics that illustrates the crowd's reluctance to perform unethical tasks. We then conduct an experiment with crowdsourcing workers to explore selected influential factors that might encourage them to knowingly violate ethical norms of privacy.

Keywords Crowdsourcing • Privacy • Human computation • Anonymity • Computer ethics • Collective intelligence • Wisdom of crowds

1 Introduction

Crowdsourcing – the act of sourcing tasks traditionally performed by specific individuals to a group of people or community (the crowd) through an open call – has established itself as a mechanism for accomplishing routine tasks and conducting experiments that demand a large number of participants to be available on short notice. Crowdsourcing often involves single-purpose tasks designed around

C.G. Harris (✉)
Informatics Program, The University of Iowa, Iowa City, IA 52242, USA
e-mail: christopher-harris@uiowa.edu

P. Srinivasan
Informatics Program, The University of Iowa, Iowa City, IA 52242, USA

Computer Science Department, The University of Iowa, Iowa City, IA 52242, USA
e-mail: padmini-srinivasan@uiowa.edu

Y. Altshuler et al. (eds.), *Security and Privacy in Social Networks*,
DOI 10.1007/978-1-4614-4139-7_5, © Springer Science+Business Media New York 2013

a simple objective such as image classification, video annotation, form-based data entry, optical character recognition, translation, and document proofreading. Using crowdsourcing, task requesters are able to make use of workers who would otherwise be inaccessible due to global reach or labor restrictions. Often it is claimed that the large worker supply, scant regulation, and low labor costs provide crowdsourcing's strongest advantages [1]. We recognize four primary advantages of crowdsourcing: speed, cost, quality, and diversity [2]:

1. Tasks can be set up quickly and easily, and results can often be obtained in less than 24 hours.
2. Conducting tasks is usually inexpensive. A payment of only a few cents per task, even with task redundancy established to enhance quality, is a fraction of the compensation required if temporary in-house workers were used instead.
3. As long as tasks are designed with appropriate control mechanisms, results are usually of good quality [3, 4].
4. The diversity of available workers in the labor pool is good. This can be beneficial for creative tasks, or when a task requires a talent you cannot easily find through standard channels (such as a translator from a rare language to English).

Since Jeff Howe first coined the term "crowdsourcing" in a June 2006 *Wired* magazine article [5], the overwhelmingly popular view has been that crowdsourcing has benefitted both requesters and workers by more effectively allocating labor and resources [6]. In comparison, there are relatively few criticisms of crowdsourcing, and most are limited to discussions about the low pay workers receive [7]. However, these criticisms rarely go beyond lamenting the economic realities of a flexible global labor market. Furthermore, some critics have reported on poor worker quality, including worker "spam" – the act of workers submitting arbitrary answers to receive payment without effort. Consequently, most task requesters now use well-established techniques to address spam.

Interestingly, little discussion has been reported on the potential of using crowdsourcing platforms to accomplish unethical tasks. Thus, our goal is to explore several hypotheses related to unethical behavior in crowdsourcing. We start with a survey on crowdsourcing ethics that illustrates the crowd's overall reluctance to perform unethical tasks. We then conduct an experiment with crowdsourcing workers to explore factors that might influence the decision of whether or not to violate ethical norms with respect to particular expectations of privacy.

The remainder of this chapter is structured as follows. In the next section, we give an overview of ethics in crowdsourcing and describe related works. Next, the results of a worker survey we conducted are discussed. We then describe the tasks of our experiment, test the influencing factors and hypotheses for the overall procedure of our experiment, and a discussion of our results. We conclude with an analysis of our findings.

2 Background and Related Work

Consider an examination of positive and negative tasks that has been conducted online. At the far positive end of the spectrum, there would be tasks that benefit mankind (e.g., protein folding analysis, SETI-based tasks, or tasks enabling a cure for dreadful diseases). At the far negative end, we would find cybercriminal clearinghouses wherein bulk sales of stolen personal information are readily available for purchase. Although it is true that many online marketplaces offer passwords and cracks for popular software applications that violate the software piracy laws of most countries, these activities are generally not related to crowdsourcing.

More interesting is the middle region of this continuum: human computational tasks that are not considered illegal, but may be regarded by most people as unethical. The objective here is not to define ethical behavior – a definition that has been debated at least since the time of Socrates. The examples used here illustrate clear ethical violations understandable to most readers. For example, a jilted lover asking others to pose as potential (but phony) suitors to a former lover on a dating website to seek revenge may not be illegal, but many will find this action unethical. Or, consider advances in technology and the ease of sending micro-payments to parts of the globe. However, this ease of transferring work to economically-depressed geographical areas forces some workers to choose between maintaining their own ethical standards or accepting unethical work to feed their family.

Effective policing of computer ethics on the Internet is difficult, particularly because nobody owns the Internet. In crowdsourcing, one challenge in avoiding ethical quagmires is tied to one of crowdsourcing's strengths – the diversity of crowd demographics. Several studies on ethics have shown that there is a substantial variety of what is regarded as unethical behavior in different demographic groups; for instance, a reprehensible deed conducted within one group may be considered perfectly ethical in another.

Other studies have concluded that the anonymity of the Internet emboldens behavior that would not likely occur face-to-face, as described by Freestone [8] and Johnson [9]. Finding workers willing to perform unethical tasks increases when the pool of potential workers, regardless of distance or demographics, is anonymous and only an internet connection away.

In addition, there are various motivating factors for crowd participants. Several studies have examined the ways in which the crowd is motivated to work on low-paying tasks [10, 11]. For example, the compensation for *Wikipedia* article editing and fact-checking is limited to personal satisfaction [12, 13]. However, for potential participants in regions that offer few other employment opportunities, these tasks may represent a means to support an entire family [14]. With different motivations come different levels of acceptable behavior. Some may view every available task as an opportunity for additional compensation. Others may see their reputation as a paramount consideration in obtaining future tasks, and thus be far more reluctant to engage in potentially unethical tasks. Given these diverse crowdsourcing worker characteristics, it could be quite feasible to obtain the desired number of participants for most tasks of interest, including tasks that may seem unethical to a particular group.

Consider the task of using the crowd for surveillance. This could be desired by a person who wishes to monitor the actions of his ex-spouse and is physically restricted from doing so, or by family members who want to monitor their teenager's activities while away from home. She or he could hire an expensive private detective to engage in surveillance, or could solicit the crowd to observe the targeted person's activities and pay on the basis of validated pieces of information, making it harder for the person being monitored to notice. In a recent talk, Jonathan Zittrain illustrated how it is possible to identify a single Iranian demonstrator from a photograph by crowdsourcing a comparison of the photograph with the ID cards of 72 million Iranians, four photos at a time [15] He estimated that the total cost would be about US$14,000 using a crowdsourcing platform such as Amazon's Mechanical Turk[1] (MTurk) – but far less if this task was offered as a game to schoolchildren and played for no compensation. Even if the true motives were discovered by the crowd, it is still easy to find willing participants. Indeed, in societies where breaking social norms is lightly punished, a number of people may eagerly accept an opportunity to break social norms, especially when an incentive is introduced [16, 17], thereby providing a large number of potential participants from the crowd to engage in such tasks.

Consider a hypothetical "revenge"-oriented crowdsourcing platform that employs a crowd to conduct unethical information gathering tasks for various prices. Password cracking of a specific individual's e-mail accounts might be listed for a certain fee (along with information about that individual to make the task quicker and easier to perform). Creating a profile on an online dating website in order to attract an ex-spouse into a false sense of commitment would involve a different level of activity and list for a different fee. This platform, like most other crowdsourcing platforms, would seek to bring providers and requesters together at a market-clearing price; however, in this situation, this market-clearing price would be for potentially unethical tasks. One concern is that far more severe (and illegal) activities could be conducted based on these mild information-gathering techniques.

Malicious tasks requiring human computation can conceivably be accomplished using the crowd. Zhou et al. describes several such cases in [18]. The "Completely Automated Public Turing test to tell Computers and Humans Apart" (CAPTCHA) is a screening device used to distinguish virtual robots from humans on the web [19]. The premise is that computer programs such as bots cannot read distorted text as effectively as humans. CAPTCHA challenges remain a first line of defense against automated computer cracking techniques, although they are not undefeatable. Techniques such as CAPTCHA are designed to prevent automated systems from mimicking human intelligence; however, many consider the human worker to be the biggest risk to unethical behavior. Our objective is to examine factors that influence the crowd's ability to engage in unethical behavior.

---

[1] http://www.mturk.com

3 Survey of Unethical Behavior

We conducted a survey to obtain some understanding of the MTurk worker pool's views on unethical behavior. Our survey received 214 responses. To reduce survey spam and bot-based survey completion, we required participants to provide written comments to support their responses. The survey results provided insight into the crowd's view of unethical tasks, and are summarized in Table 1.

These results provided some interesting inferences. Seventy-seven percent of workers that responded to Question 1 believe that breaking into e-mail accounts is unethical. Ninety-two percent of workers responding to Question 2 believe that sending e-mails misrepresenting themselves as someone else for personal gain is unethical. Eighty percent of workers that responded to Question 3 believe that assisting others to send misrepresentative e-mails is unethical. This illustrates that our survey respondents understand the unethical nature of using e-mail accounts that do not belong to them, and of sending e-mails that misrepresent themselves. These results illustrate the relative ethical distinction between (a) breaking into another person's e-mail account, and (b) sending misrepresentative e-mails for personal gain.

From this survey, we observed another interesting behavioral issue: how the potential consequences of unethical acts influence a worker's inclination to participate. According to Question 4, if the possibility of being caught performing an unethical act exists, 85 % of survey respondents would not participate. However, as Question 5 indicates, if the possibility of being caught does not exist, the number of non-participants is reduced to 69 %. This represents a statistically significant decrease from the result obtained in Question 4.

Table 1 Results from survey on ethical behavior of MTurk workers (n = 214)

Statement	Strongly disagree	Disagree	Neutral	Agree	Strongly agree
1. Compromising (breaking into) e-mail accounts that do not belong to me is unethical	2	3	18	21	56
2. Sending e-mails pretending to be someone else for my own personal gain is unethical	1	2	5	15	77
3. Helping another person send e-mails pretending to be someone else is unethical	2	3	15	16	64
4. I would not violate my own personal ethics if there were a possibility of being caught, for any price	1	4	10	14	71
5. I would not violate my own personal ethics, even if there were no possibility of being caught, for any price	3	12	16	24	45

4   Experiment Description

We examined two subtasks: (1) the ability to recruit people from crowdsourcing platforms to compromise a "source" e-mail account, and (2) the ability to have them send an e-mail with specified content from the "source" e-mail account to a "target" e-mail account. Our survey of unethical behavior showed that a large percentage of survey participants regard both activities as unethical. Our goal was to determine if we could obtain consistent results by performing an actual crowdsourcing experiment involving these two unethical activities.

Our crowdsourcing tasks were set up as deception studies advertising the need for e-mail writing assistance. In an effort to attract the widest variety of potential workers, these tasks were written to imply that an urgent personal favor was needed in the form of writing an e-mail for a friend. Figures 1 and 2 show examples of the language used to recruit participants.

We created four different "source" e-mail accounts using pseudonyms, two of which represented male-owned accounts and two of which represented female-owned accounts. One account from each gender was used to complete a "positive" e-mail request, and one account from each gender was used to complete a "negative" e-mail request. The names and information we provided for each account were purely fictional and only used for the purposes of this study – at no time were any accounts from actual people used, and all e-mail accounts were solely under our

Please help me write an email to help a friend!

My best friend Alicia has an issue with her boyfriend, Brandon. Seems that she and Brandon are having some problems recently and honestly, Brandon is really a great guy. Alicia is kinda stubborn, so I am hoping that I somehow write an email to coax Brandon to come back to Alicia. Right now they aren't talking very much except through email. Alicia is a mess right now, but I have her e-mail and password: aisqueria@yahoo.com and her password is '0313ally' or 'ally0313' or 'snickers031388' - one of those should work. You can go there and see their last e-mail exchange. Anyways, can you help us out please? Brandon will know if I write something since he already knows my writing style, so I thought to have someone she doesn't know help out. It will help out if you can mimic Alicia's writing style. Brandon's email is skullkross@hotmail.com - just write him an e-mail pretending to be Alicia. If you can get them back together, oh, that will be super!!! If it works, I'll pay you a bonus of $0.50. Oh, please help... she really needs this to happen!

Thanks! Rosemarie Allen

Fig. 1 A request to break into a female's e-mail account to send a positive message

Please help me write an email for my friend!

My buddy, Gabe, has a problem with this psycho girl he dated a few times. Seems that this psycho, Lucy, is a stalker and won't leave him alone. She is way too aggressive towards Gabe. Gabe just doesn't have the guts to just tell Lucy to go away!! Right now he is avoiding her, but she still sends him emails wanting to meet up. My buddy is a bit soft and afraid of her, and I totally understand (you would too if you met her!). Anyways, please help by sending Lucy an email written from my buddy to tell her strongly to GET LOST!!! Gabe's email is gabe.bekker@gmail.com. And his password is 'GoCards11' or 'Stl4me2' - one of those should work. You can go there and see what a nuisance Lucy is. Lucy will know if I write something since she knows my writing style, so I thought to have someone she doesn't know help out. It will help out if you can copy Gabe's writing style. Just write this psycho-chick an email pretending to be Gabe and I will do the rest to convince my friend to tell this girl goodbye. Lucy's email is iconiclucy@hotmail.com. If it works, and she disappears, I will pay you a bonus of $4.50 on top of the $1.50 promised already! Please help!! My buddy's grades are starting to suffer and he is gonna lose his scholarship if things don't change!

Thank you so much! Arturo

Fig. 2 A request to break into a male's e-mail account to send a negative message

control. As shown in Figs. 1 and 2, we provided the e-mail account and a few possible passwords for each account and requested for the worker to enter the account we provided to complete the task. We provided the passwords since this experiment was not an examination of a worker's password-cracking abilities, but rather a characterization of willingness to engage in an unethical activity.

Workers were instructed to send an e-mail to one of the "target" accounts from a given "source" account. Workers were told that the e-mail had to contain a minimum of 50 words and be convincing, with the final decision on whether it would be sent to the other party left to us. We monitored the e-mails sent to these "target" accounts.

Once the accounts were created, we exchanged several e-mails between these four "source" accounts and one of the two "target" accounts to make the relationship seem more realistic. We assumed that these e-mail histories would be read by each worker once they entered the "source" account. Thus, we also corresponded with additional "third party" accounts that we had created to enhance their legitimacy. Each "source" e-mail account corresponded to a minimum of four other non-target e-mail accounts, thus resulting in the sending and receiving of an average of 22 messages with these additional e-mail accounts. Again, we assumed these e-mails would be read by each worker, and therefore these e-mails contained information that would support our requested demand.

In our experiment, a "run" involves a specific pair of source and target accounts and it consists of two subtasks: (1) entering the "source" e-mail account using the password provided, and (2) sending an e-mail with some required information to a "target" e-mail account. We created one of four types of run for each worker. These subtasks illustrate two potentially different levels of ethical violations. From the survey conducted previously, we observed that sending an e-mail from an account belonging to someone else is considered unethical by more respondents than simply compromising or entering an e-mail account. Although these subtasks are not independent events, we examined the number workers who entered the e-mail account but did not send the e-mail. We conducted a total of 120 runs. Each worker was allowed to participate in only one run. Each "source" e-mail account was involved in 30 runs, and each target e-mail account was involved in 60 runs.

Each worker was required go to a website for information for the assigned run (see Figs. 1 and 2). This allowed us to track the IP addresses and obtain timestamps of when workers started each subtask. Next, we tracked the login IP address and timestamp for each login to the "source" account. With this information, we could evaluate the success of the e-mail-entry subtask if the e-mail-sending subtask was not completed. In addition, we could read the e-mail sent to the "target" account, including the message header, IP, timestamp, and actual message, which indicated a completion of the overall task. After each run was completed, we refreshed the information for the "source" e-mail account and modified the "source" e-mail password information.

To allow us to compare ethical tasks and unethical tasks, we conducted a separate study of 60 workers, divided equally among pseudo-anonymous and identifiable platform workers and each with a similar request to help a friend

write an e-mail. However, we only asked the workers to provide the body of the
e-mail text to be sent for a given scenario; we did not require workers to enter
the e-mail account or actually send an e-mail. This study represented an ethical
"baseline" counterpart to the previously described study. The three influencing
factors described in the next section were also examined in this baseline task.

5 Influencing Factors

Despite the results obtained from our survey, when unethical tasks are posted on
crowdsourcing platforms, we believe we will still find enough workers agreeing to
offer their services. We believe that several factors could potentially influence a
worker's decision whether or not to participate in an unethical task. In this section,
we examine three potentially influencing factors and their effects on subtask
success: worker anonymity, anticipated consequence of the task, and payment.
In addition, we present specific hypotheses exploring these factors.

5.1 Level of Anonymity

Many crowdsourcing platforms such as MTurk rely on a large, pseudo-anonymous,
and transient workforce. Because these workers are known to requesters only by a
platform-established unique identifier, they are not completely anonymous
(requesters can determine if the same worker ID was used more than once, but
cannot identify the worker), we consider them to be "pseudo-anonymous." This
characterization, combined with their non-persistent nature, makes it nearly impossible for requesters to establish an ongoing relationship with reliable crowd workers.

Other crowdsourcing platforms (e.g., Elance[2] and oDesk[3]) address this anonymity
by allowing workers to establish an identity and list their relevant skills and
experiences. They also allow task requesters to establish transactions directly with
workers, with the platforms serving as a marketplace. These platforms are usually
reserved for larger and more specialized tasks, such as website design or business plan
development. These workers are often specialists who turn to crowdsourcing
platforms for supplemental income. Workers on such platforms frequently command
a premium rate for their work compared to those using pseudo-anonymous platforms
such as MTurk. We call these workers "identifiable" since a requester is able to
locate and contact a specific worker directly through the platform for subsequent
tasks at any time.

---

[2] http://www.elance.com

[3] http://www.odesk.com

5.2 Anticipated Task Consequence

Most unethical behavior is perceived to have a negative consequence, but it is possible for unethical behavior to have a positive consequence [20]. Behavior such as moving an item without permission from a location where it is likely to be damaged, temporarily holding on to a lost wallet, or taking a lost child home until his or her parents can be located, are examples of positive consequences that come from potentially unethical behavior. In our experiments, Figs. 1 and 2 illustrate examples of tasks with anticipated positive and negative consequences, respectively.

We believe that a worker will be more willing to engage in an unethical task with a stated positive consequence than to a task with a stated negative consequence, as it is easier to justify the behavior. This view is validated by several studies in consumer behavior [21, 22]. We examined how the perceived consequence of unethical behavior might influence a worker's decision to participate in the task.

5.3 Level of Payment Expected

Payment has been shown to be a factor in numerous crowdsourcing studies; the survey we conducted indicated that financial incentives could encourage some workers to engage in unethical work if the price was sufficiently high. However, other studies have shown that other factors are also important; these include task satisfaction, the level of challenge, or intrinsic motivation [23]. Moreover, some studies have indicated that financial incentives can actually hurt performance [10]. Although our task was designed to be challenging, our objective is to observe the effects of payment on the willingness to participate in unethical tasks.

We established task payments in the following way. We began with the identifiable anonymity platforms, since these workers usually offer prices for their services at an hourly rate. We negotiated a US$1.50 fixed price with the participants directly based on their quoted hourly rate with the strong potential of earning a bonus of $0.50 (low-paying), $2.50 (medium-paying), or $4.50 (high-paying). This provided a wage plus a bonus of $2.00, $4.00, or $6.00, respectively. Similarly, for the pseudo-anonymous platform, we offered tasks at rates close to the mean wage offered by the identifiable anonymity platforms. We offered task payments of $1.50, with the strong potential of earning a bonus of $0.50 (low-paying), $2.50 (medium-paying), or $4.50 (high-paying). The same base payment and three levels of incentives were provided for the ethical baseline study, for which only the body of the text needed to be supplied. Each group was equally represented, so the mean anticipated financial incentive to each participant was $4.00.

5.4 Specific Hypotheses Explored

We explored the following four hypotheses:

1. Crowdsourcing platforms include workers that can be enticed to engage in unethical behavior.
2. Workers from pseudo-anonymous crowdsourcing platforms are no more likely to be enticed to engage in unethical behavior than workers from crowdsourcing platforms in which identity can be determined.
3. Crowdsourcing workers who engage in unethical tasks are more likely to be enticed to perform unethical tasks with a perceived positive impact compared with those with a perceived negative impact.
4. Crowdsourcing platforms include workers that are more likely to be enticed to participate in unethical tasks, provided that the final expected compensation offered to them is sufficiently high.

5.5 Measures of Task Success

We took the following measurements when the worker initially visited the web page to obtain instructions, and at the completion of each of our subtasks. In parentheses, we indicate the measurements obtained from each subtask.

1. When the worker enters the e-mail account and supplies the correct password (visitor IP address, timestamp).
2. When the worker sends an e-mail from the "source" e-mail account of 50 words or greater, conveying the message we requested to the "target" e-mail account specified at the instructions web page (e-mail timestamp, e-mail message).

Workers decided to connect and perform their work through proxy servers for a number of reasons. Prior to geo-location of the IP address in each subtask, we checked the IP addresses recorded against known proxy server lists and excluded those found to be proxies.

In our study, we calculated the time spent on each subtask by subtracting the synchronized timestamps between the subtasks. We assumed that the subtasks were done in succession in one session. We discarded any time differences that exceeded 1.5 times the inter-quartile range as outliers.

6 Experimental Procedure

We used a $2 \times 2 \times 3$ factorial design to investigate the effects of various conditions (two types of worker anonymity, two types of anticipated consequence, and three financial incentive levels) on our measurements (speed and completion rate).

6.1 Identifiable Platforms

We provided 36 tasks on oDesk.com and 24 tasks on Elance.com using several different requester identities. We provided financial incentives to identifiable platform workers as previously described. As with the pseudo-anonymous platform, we provided each worker with a link and obtained basic information, including IP address and a task initiation timestamp.

6.2 Pseudo-anonymous Platforms

We posted 60 tasks on MTurk over a 30-day time period. We designed each task so that it could be attempted by a single worker only. To avoid reputation effects from the requesters' side, we used a different MTurk identity to list each task. Therefore, each task was posted by a unique requester ID with no previous MTurk history. A link in the task description instructed the worker to visit a web page that provided specific information about the task and obtained some basic information from their visit, including IP address and a task initiation timestamp. We provided financial incentives to pseudo-anonymous platform workers as previously described.

The success of the experiment depended on each task being perceived as a unique request. To ensure that this information was not passed along to other workers, we periodically monitored the popular worker forums Turkernation[4] and mTurk Forum[5] for any criticisms of our sponsored tasks.

7 Results

7.1 Worker Engagement

Table 2 illustrates the success rates for each of the subtasks (accessing the website, the ability to compromise the e-mail password, and sending an e-mail to the target e-mail account). Subtask 1 was to enter a "source" e-mail account, representing an account owned by a friend of the task requester. The success rate of subtask 1 is 71.7 % and 78.3 % for the pseudo-anonymous and identifiable groups, respectively. Subtask 2, sending an e-mail with specified content from the "source" e-mail account to a "target" e-mail account, had a success rate of 63.3 % and 70.0 % for the pseudo-anonymous and identifiable groups, respectively. Comparing the results of this unethical task to the results from our survey conducted prior to the

---

[4] http://www.turkernation.com
[5] http://www.mturkforum.com

Table 2 Success rates per subtask broken out by anonymity group

Number (percent) of workers	Pseudo-anonymous group	Identifiable group
Accept task	60	60
Access web page to obtain information	58 (96.7 %)	60 (100 %)
Subtask 1: Compromise the source e-mail account password based on the information provided	43 (71.7 %)	47 (78.3 %)
Subtask 2: Send an e-mail with specified content from the source e-mail account to a target e-mail account	38 (63.3 %)	42 (70.0 %)

experiment, we see that the percentage of those who participated in this unethical task was significantly higher than the percentage of surveyed crowdsourcing workers who had reported they would participate in unethical activities. This supports our first hypothesis that there are workers on crowd source platforms who can be enticed to participate in both of the unethical goals of our experiment.

We observed that in general it took longer to recruit workers in the identifiable group compared to the pseudo-anonymous group. This could be due to several reasons (beyond the level of anonymity). First, the identifiable group participants asked to be compensated at an hourly rate. To provide parity, we negotiated for a fixed price for the task, significantly slowing the worker recruitment process. In contrast, recruitment was far simpler with the pseudo-anonymous group. We put the task description at a wage level of $1.50 plus one of the incentives, and waited for workers to accept and complete the tasks. Second, we believe that there are far more pseudo-anonymous workers available for the tasks we advertised, permitting more workers to be hired within the window of time allocated for these experiments. A third reason could be due to self-selection: we attempted to negotiate with many workers from the identifiable group that did not respond. This could be a result of these workers making an ethical decision prior to the discussion of payment.

7.2 Level of Anonymity

We made comparisons between the two platform types for the likelihood of completing each subtask. We used a t-test (two sided, $\alpha = 0.05$) to compare the likelihood of a pseudo-anonymous group worker completing the first subtask to that of an identifiable group worker. We also used a t-test (two sided, $\alpha = 0.05$) to compare the likelihood of completing the second subtask between the two worker groups. We did not find a significant difference between the two anonymity groups completing either sub-task. Therefore, our second hypothesis is supported by these findings.

Next, we examined the time taken to complete the subtasks between these two groups. The difference in time was calculated by subtracting the timestamp for the web page visit from the time the password on the e-mail account was entered. We assumed that both subtasks were completed within a single session and discarded the outliers, as previously described. The mean difference in the time periods was 12 min for the pseudo-anonymous group and 14 min for the identifiable group.

We also examined the time taken to send the e-mail to the target e-mail account. We repeated the assumption that the subtasks were performed within a single session, and we discarded the outliers. The mean difference in time periods was 27 min for the pseudo-anonymous group and 28 min for the identifiable group.

Using a t-test (two sided, $\alpha = 0.05$), we did not find a significant difference in either of these tests – the time it took to complete the first subtask or the second subtask – based on worker anonymity level. This supports our second hypothesis. Similarly, we did not find a significant difference in our ethical baseline task based on anonymity.

7.3 Anticipated Task Consequence

We examined the differences between subtasks with requests for perceived positive and negative anticipated consequences for both worker groups. To accomplish this, we used a t-test (two sided, $\alpha = 0.05$) to compare the likelihood of a worker with a negatively-perceived task completing the first subtask to that of a worker assigned a positively-perceived task. We also used a t-test (two sided, $\alpha = 0.05$) to examine the likelihood of completing the second subtask between the perceived positive and negative task groups. From both t-tests, we did not find a significant difference between the two groups to complete either subtask as a result of the positive and negative task groups. Thus, our third hypothesis is not supported by these results.

7.4 Financial Incentive Effects

For the three financial incentive groups (low, medium, and high), we wanted to see the effects of the expected financial incentive levels on the success of accomplishing each of the subtasks (compromising the e-mail password, and the subtask of sending an e-mail as agreed). For each platform, there were 20 workers assigned to each of the three wage groups. Table 3 gives the breakdown of the number of workers in each wage group entering the e-mail account and sending the e-mail as agreed.

We conducted a one-way between-subjects analysis of variance (ANOVA) test to determine if there is a difference between success rates for each of the three wage levels in the combined group. There was a significant effect of wages paid on the

Table 3 Percentage of workers completing each subtask by expected compensation and platform type

		Low (%)	Medium (%)	High (%)
1. Pseudo-anonymous	Enter e-mail account	50.0	65.0	100.0
	Send e-mail as agreed	45.0	70.0	95.0
2. Identifiable	Enter e-mail account	40.0	90.0	100.0
	Send e-mail as agreed	35.0	90.0	100.0
3. Combined	Enter e-mail account	45.0	77.5	100.0
	Send e-mail as agreed	40.0	80.0	97.5

task success rate at the $p < 0.05$ level for the three conditions [$F_{(2,3)} = 9.55$, $p = 0.0078$]. Further examination using Tukey's Honestly Significant Difference (HSD) test and Scheffé's test as post-hoc methods determined that the lower-wage worker group had a lower likelihood of completing each of the two subtasks compared to the medium- and high-wage groups.

Examining the high-wage group, we see that nearly all participants completed both subtasks, resulting in a conversion rate of 88.5 %. This supports our fourth hypothesis that crowd workers are more willing to perform unethical tasks if the financial incentives are sufficient. With the ethical benchmark test, we had 100 % participation regardless of financial compensation offered. We did not notice a significant effect of the wage offered on completion rates. This allowed us to contrast the effects of financial compensation on the success rates of ethical and unethical tasks.

7.5   Additional Analysis

Our experiment was designed with equal numbers of male and female "source" e-mail accounts. Although not tied to any of our stated hypotheses, we wanted to determine if the perceived gender of the "source" account holders was a factor in successfully completing each subtask. Table 4 presents the breakdown of the participants who visited the information web page for each worker group.

We used a t-test (two sided, $\alpha = 0.05$) to compare the likelihood of success for a worker completing the first subtask using a female's "source" e-mail account to that of a worker using a male's "source" e-mail account. We also used a t-test (two sided, $\alpha = 0.05$) to examine the mean likelihood of success in completing the second subtask between female and male "source" e-mail accounts. With both tests, we found a significant difference in the two subtasks as a result of the gender of the account holder.

We also determined whether the demographics of our workers matched the underlying demographics of crowdsourcing workers. A February 2010 survey on MTurk workers by Ross et al. – the most recently published demographic survey – reported that 39 % of workers were US residents, 46 % were from India, and the

Table 4 Percentage of workers completing each subtask by gender and platform type

		Male "Source" (%)	Female "Source" (%)
1. Pseudo-anonymous	Enter e-mail account	80.0	63.3
	Send e-mail as agreed	76.7	63.3
2. Identifiable	Enter e-mail account	83.3	70.0
	Send e-mail as agreed	80.0	70.0
3. Combined	Enter e-mail account	81.7	66.7
	Send e-mail as agreed	78.3	66.7

Table 5 Locations of task participants based on IP address geo-location

Platform	India	USA	Asia excluding India	Europe	Other	Total
Pseudo-anonymous	32	11	10	5	2	60
Identifiable	23	11	16	7	3	60
Ethical (baseline)	29	16	8	7	0	60
Total	84	38	34	19	5	180

remaining 15 % were from all other countries combined [24]. Table 5 reports the IP address geo-locations for those workers who participated in our study.

We note that when compared to other surveys that show the distribution of MTurk workers, the population agreeing to perform our tasks had a much larger-than-expected representation from India and other Asian countries. One interesting result of the Ross et al. study was the number of people who rely on crowdsourcing income to provide for their basic needs (27 % India, 14 % USA), which may be a factor in our observed demographics.

We realize that there are limitations to the experiment performed in this study. First, because of Institutional Review Board (IRB) requirements on deception studies, we disclosed information that may have limited the potential downside risk of participants. This may have influenced the workers we recruited. In other words, had we advertised for "revenge seeking password hackers" openly, we would have likely obtained a different pool of workers that may have been influenced our measurements. Second, despite our best attempts, we had no way of knowing if the participants could see through our experiment and treat our work requests as innocuous lab work.

8   Conclusion

We performed an experiment to better understand unethical behavior using workers from several crowdsourcing platforms. We tested four hypotheses. Our results show that our first hypothesis – crowdsourcing workers are willing to engage in unethical behavior – clearly has merit. Our experiment found no significant difference in participation rates based on the anonymity of the worker; in other words, the pseudo-anonymous crowdsourcing workers in our study were no more or less willing to engage in unethical behavior than identifiable workers. Investigation of our fourth hypothesis shows that larger financial incentives do have an influence on the success of unethical tasks; in other words, the crowd workers in our study were more likely to participate in unethical tasks if the wage offered was sufficiently high. Our experiments also showed that the expected impact of the study (positive or negative), by itself, had little bearing on the choice made by crowdsourcing workers to participate in an unethical task. This refutes our third hypothesis.

Overall, we showed that there is a sufficiently large pool of workers in crowdsourcing platforms to accomplish unethical tasks. This conclusion holds despite our earlier survey results. Even if our survey turns out to be representative of the crowd in a general sense, the fact borne out is that there are enough workers in the crowd to accomplish the unethical tasks tested here; even if only one one-hundredth of one percent of the two million reported workers would eagerly agree to perform unethical tasks, the number of available workers would exceed the number of workers used in our experiment. From the perspective of task requester with an unethical task to offer, we suggest that they would have no trouble finding workers willing to participate.

We note that some workers struggled with the ethics of our study. Of the 120 workers agreeing to take part in our study on unethical tasks, we later discovered that three workers sent an additional e-mail to our target soon after they completed the task to either confess to, or apologize for, their unethical behavior. Furthermore, one worker later sent an e-mail from his own personal account to the "target" e-mail account to provide information on e-mail requests in an attempt to warn the "target." Thus, we see that a number of workers – despite anonymity and the ability to financially benefit from an unethical work request – took an ethical approach and warned strangers who faced potential harm.

Our experiment is only a preliminary step in an examination of crowdsourcing ethics. In future work, we plan to investigate other tasks involving unethical crowd behavior, including influencing recommender systems and unethical assistance with academic tasks.

References

1. Bederson BB, Quinn AJ (2011) Web workers unite! Addressing challenges of online laborers. ACM, New York
2. Alonso O (2011) Perspectives on infrastructure for crowdsourcing. In: Proceedings of the crowdsourcing for search and data mining (CSDM 2011), Hong Kong
3. Ipeirotis PG, Provost F, Wang J (2010) Quality management on amazon mechanical turk. ACM, New York
4. Zaidan OF, Callison-Burch C (2011) Crowdsourcing translation: professional quality from non-professionals. In: Proceedings of the 49th annual meeting of the ACL-HTL, Association for Computational Linguistics, Portland

5. Howe J (2006) The rise of crowdsourcing. Wired, June 2006
6. Kimbarovsky K (2010) Ten crowdsourcing trends for 2011. http://blog.crowdspring.com/2010/12/2011-crowdsourcing-trends/
7. Silberman M, Irani L, Ross J (2010) Ethics and tactics of professional crowdwork. XRDS: Crossroads 17(2):39–43
8. Freestone O, Mitchell V (2004) Generation Y attitudes towards e-ethics and internet-related misbehaviours. J Bus Ethics 54(2):121–128
9. Johnson DG (2009) Computer ethics. Prentice Hall, New York
10. Horton JJ, Chilton LB (2010) The labor economics of paid crowdsourcing. ACM, New York
11. Mason W, Watts DJ (2010) Financial incentives and the performance of crowds. ACM, New York
12. Forte, A. and Bruckman, A. Why do people write for wikipedia? Incentives to contribute to open content publishing. In Proceedings of GROUP' 05 (2005), 6–9.
13. Johnson BK (2007) Incentives to contribute in online collaboration: Wikipedia as collective action. Ph.D. thesis, Michigan State University, East Lansing
14. Paritosh P, Ipeirotis P, Cooper M, Suri S (2011) The computer is the new sewing machine: benefits and perils of crowdsourcing. In: Proceedings of the 20th international conference companion on world wide web (Hyderabad, India, 2011), ACM, New York
15. Zittrain J (2009) Minds for sale. MIT Press, Cambridge, MA
16. Kandori M (1992) Social norms and community enforcement. Rev Econ Stud 59(1):63–80
17. Funk P (2005) Governmental action, social norms, and criminal behavior. J Inst Theor Econ (JITE) 161(3):522–535
18. Zhou CV, Leckie C, Karunasekera S (2010) A survey of coordinated attacks and collaborative intrusion detection. Comput Secur 29(1):124–140
19. Von Ahn, L, Blum, M., Hopper, N. J., and Langford, J. 2003. CAPTCHA: using hard AI problems for security. In Proceedings of the 22nd international conference on Theory and applications of cryptographic techniques (EUROCRYPT'03), Eli Biham (Ed.). Springer-Verlag, Berlin, Heidelberg, 294–311.
20. Broad CD (1930) Five types of ethical theory. Routledge & Kegan Paul, London
21. Vitell SJ, Singhapakdi A, Thomas J (2001) Consumer ethics: an application and empirical testing of the Hunt-Vitell theory of ethics. J Consum Mark 18(2):153–178
22. Hunt SD, Vitell S (1986) A general theory of marketing ethics. J Macromark 6(1):5–16
23. Von Ahn L (2006) Games with a purpose. Computer 39(6):92–94
24. Ross J, Irani L, Silberman M, Zaldivar A, Tomlinson B (2010) Who are the crowdworkers? Shifting demographics in mechanical turk. ACM, New York

The Effect of Social Status on Decision-Making and Prices in Financial Networks

Yoel Krasny

Abstract In this chapter, we examine the impact of status-seeking considerations on investors' portfolio choices and asset prices in a general equilibrium setting. The economy we study consists of traditional ("Markowitz") investors as well as status-seekers who are concerned about relative wealth. The model highlights the strategic and interdependent nature of portfolio selection in such a setting: low-status investors look for portfolio choices that maximize their chances of moving up the ladder, while high-status investors look to maintain the status quo and hedge against these choices of the low-status investors. In equilibrium, asset returns obey a novel two-factor model in which one factor is the traditional market factor and the other is a particular "high-volatility factor" that does not appear to have been identified so far in the theoretical or empirical literature. We test this two-factor model using stock market data and find significant support for it. Of particular interest is the fact that the model and the empirical results attribute the low returns on idiosyncratic volatility stocks documented by Ang et al. (2006) to their covariance with the portfolio of highly volatile stocks held by investors with relatively low status.

1 Introduction

The empirical literature in finance has provided many challenges to traditional asset-pricing theories. Although diversification is a fundamental tenet of modern portfolio theory, in reality, investors tend to hold underdiversified portfolios. Many households that hold individual stocks directly hold only a single stock, and the median number of stocks held is only about three [1]. In addition, less wealthy

This chapter is based on work that was published in the Quarterly Journal of Finance – Vol. 1(3), 2011

Y. Krasny (✉)
Department of Finance, Stern School of Business, New York University, New York, USA
e-mail: jkrasny@stern.nyu.edu

Y. Altshuler et al. (eds.), *Security and Privacy in Social Networks*,
DOI 10.1007/978-1-4614-4139-7_6, © Springer Science+Business Media New York 2013

investors are even less diversified than wealthier investors. A recent study by Kumar (2009) [2] has found that investors who earn less than their neighbors (within a 25-mile radius) invest more in stocks with lottery-like payoffs and experience greater underperformance. The latter finding agrees with a recent empirical asset-pricing study by Bali et al. (2009) [3] showing that stocks with lottery-like payoffs have significantly lower returns than others. This conclusion agrees with the puzzling empirical finding documented by Ang et al. (2006) [4] that stocks with high idiosyncratic volatility have exceptionally low average returns. These findings stand in stark contrast to asset-pricing theories that imply that idiosyncratic risk should not be priced or that in a market in which investors cannot properly diversify, one would expect idiosyncratic risk to be positively related to expected returns [5].

In this chapter, we argue that taking social-status-based concerns into account sheds some light on these puzzles. We develop a model that introduces social-status-conscious investors, for whom status is defined as their wealth-based rank in their reference group, into an economy populated with traditional "Markowitz" investors (mean-variance optimizers). Because some of these investors have low status and others have high status, each group uses a different investment strategy. We obtain closed-form solutions for portfolio choice in equilibrium and show that low-status investors hold portfolios concentrated in high-volatility assets in an effort to leapfrog high-status investors. High-status investors strategically hedge against these attempts by investing in a portfolio with high exposure to high-volatility assets. This gives rise to a two-factor asset-pricing model in a general equilibrium. We obtain exact solutions for prices and show that expected returns are a sum of a positive return premium on the market beta and a negative return premium on the beta with a high-volatility factor derived from a portfolio of the assets with the highest volatility in the economy.

We test the asset-pricing implications of the model using stock market data and find significant economic and statistical support. The two-factor model proves to price assets with high exposure to high-volatility stocks significantly better than the CAPM, the Fama-French (1993) [6] three-factor model, and the Carhart (1997) [7] four-factor model. The model sheds light on the idiosyncratic volatility puzzle posed by Ang et al. (2006) [4] because assets with high idiosyncratic risk are positively correlated with assets with high exposure to the high-volatility factor. Nevertheless, the two-factor model has a cross-sectional pricing ability above and beyond that of idiosyncratic risk.

The idea that individuals are often motivated in their behavior by a quest for social status is not new. It has been acknowledged by economists such as Smith (1776) [8], Marx (1849) [9], Veblen (1899) [10], and Duesenberry (1949) [11]. The importance of social status has long been recognized in psychology, sociology, and more recently in economics. These studies highlight the effects that status concerns have on individuals' decisions. We ask how such concerns affect agents' financial decisions—portfolio choices—and how these decisions affect aggregate outcomes, namely asset prices. In the context of financial markets, status concerns affect not only individual investors, but also mutual fund managers. The mutual fund tournament literature, originated by Brown et al. (1996) [12], hypothesizes that the portfolio choices of fund managers reflect their concern about their position relative to other managers because their compensation is linked to their performance relative to their peers.

We devise a model that captures several salient characteristics of status preferences. Most importantly, status is inherently positional in the sense stated by Heffez and Frank (2008) [13]. We capture the positionality of status by modeling status as the ordinal wealth-based rank of investors in their reference group. Modeling status as indicated by ordinal rank in the distribution of wealth was pioneered by Frank (1985) [14] in a study of the demand for positional and nonpositional goods. Later, Robson (1992) [15] and Becker et al. (2005) [16] considered preferences over absolute wealth as well as ordinal rank in wealth.

One consequence of the positionality of status is that an increase in one agent's relative status automatically translates into a decrease in the relative status of others in the relevant reference group. This zero-sum feature of status gives rise to a strategic interaction among agents in portfolio choice. Anecdotal evidence of this sort was stated by Harrison Hong (2008) [64] during an interview given to the *Wall Street Journal* on the topic of the high-tech bubble: "My sister's getting rich. My friends are getting rich... I think this is all crazy, but I feel so horrible about missing out, about being left out of the party. I finally caved in, I put in some money just as a hedge against other people getting richer than me and feeling better than me." To capture the strategic interaction among investors, status-conscious investors in our model strategically choose portfolios in Nash equilibrium.

Our work is consistent with the assumption that status concerns are primarily local. Sociological studies consistently confirm that the comparisons that really matter are highly local in character (Frank 1985) [17]. As Bertrand Russell once remarked, "Beggars don't envy millionaires; they envy other beggars who earn more than they do" (Frank 2009) [18]. Recent empirical work indeed confirms the importance of local comparisons. Luttmer (2005) showed that higher earnings of neighbors are associated with lower levels of self-reported happiness, and Clark and Oswald (1996) regressed job satisfaction on personal income and on predicted income of a comparison group and found coefficients of equal magnitude but opposite sign. Similarly, in the mutual funds context, local competitions emerge among funds with the same investment style. Within each such competition, there could be a nested local competition among the best-performing funds that compete for the top positions in the tournament, and another local competition among funds that compete to avoid the bottom positions. There could also be a competition among funds of the same family, as suggested by Kempf and Ruenzi (2008) [19].

Just as in every competition there are winners and losers, in every local reference group there must be high-status investors that are ahead in the competition ("leaders") and low-status investors that fall behind ("laggards").[1]

---

[1] We use the terms "leader" and "laggard" following Cabral (2002, 2003) [20, 21] and Anderson and Cabral (2007) [22], who studied the strategic choices of players competing in a dynamic race for positional rewards.

If status incentives are strong enough, then the leaders are satisfied with their position and are interested in maintaining the status quo. The laggards, on the other hand, are dissatisfied with their low rank and are interested in moving up the status ladder. We model each competition within a certain reference group as a two-player game where the leader is the richer investor and the laggard is the poorer investor. The players compete over wealth-based rank. We obtain the portfolio choices of the leader and the laggard in Nash equilibrium and then examine asset prices in an economy with many pairs of status investors representing many reference groups, as well as many traditional Markowitz investors who care only about maximizing mean and minimizing variance.

The model highlights the difference between the investment behavior of status-conscious investors who are concerned with upward comparisons (the "laggards" in our model) and those investors who are concerned with downward comparisons (the "leaders" in our model). In doing so, the model is aligned with the literature in psychology on social comparison processes, which offers a key distinction between the motivations and consequences of upward and downward comparisons (Buunk and Gibbons 2007) [23]. People seek social downward comparisons when the concern for self-enhancement predominates, but they seek upward comparisons when the desire for self-improvement prevails. Blanton et al. (1999) [24] found that students who compared themselves to better performers improved their academic performance more than those who used downward comparisons.

Inspired by this literature, Schoenberg and Haruvy (2009) [25] studied the effects of status-seeking considerations on market bubbles in a laboratory setting. In their experiment, subjects traded a 15-period finitely lived risky asset with a known distribution of dividends. Subjects received information about the earnings of either the best performer ("upward" traders) or the worst performer ("downward" traders). Consistent with our model, Schoenberg and Haruvy found that "upward" traders reported lower levels of satisfaction and bought risky assets at higher prices than downward traders. Moreover, as the proportion of "upward" traders increased, market prices of the risky asset increased, and deviations from fundamental values became larger.

At the heart of our proposed model is a game between two players, a laggard and a leader, who compete against each other for the top (wealth-based) rank. The leader is defined as the wealthier player at the onset of the game. The attitudes of investors toward the moments of return on their portfolios are determined endogenously as a function of this initial status. The laggard pursues a volatile portfolio because he has "nothing to lose." In addition, he seeks minimal correlation with the portfolio of the leader because differentiating himself is necessary to overtake her. On the other hand, the leader faces "status risk," the risk of losing her leadership. This status risk has two components. The first is that she will earn a low return and fall behind the laggard, and the second is that the laggard will earn a high return and overtake her. To manage the first risk, the leader tries to minimize the variance of her portfolio. Practically, this risk is the same as that faced by a traditional "Markowitz" investor. To manage the second risk, the leader is interested in increasing the covariance of her portfolio compared to that of the laggard. In the following discussion, we show that this twofold concern of the leader gives rise to a two-factor asset-pricing model.

To study portfolio choices and the cross-section of expected returns in this status-conscious economy, we introduce an economy with many groups of similar assets. There are many pairs of laggard and leader investors (status-conscious investors) and many Markowitz investors who care only about maximizing expected return and minimizing volatility. We find a Nash equilibrium, in which each laggard uses a mixed strategy to invest in a single asset from a specific group ("group V"), which is characterized by the high volatility of its assets. We obtain a closed-form solution for the leader's response. The leader's portfolio reflects her twofold concern for reducing her variance and increasing her covariance with the laggard as she invests in a linear combination of the tangency portfolio and group V. The tradeoff of the leader between the tangency portfolio and group V depends on her "hedging demand," which captures the extent to which the leader can hedge against the laggard. As the correlation within group V increases, the covariance between the return of group V and the return of the laggard's portfolio increases. Therefore, the leader can better hedge against the laggard using group V, and she increases her invested portion in group V accordingly.

We obtain exact solutions for asset prices and show that they follow a two-factor beta pricing model in which one factor is the market excess return and the other is the excess return on group V over the market return (VMM). Assets with high exposure to VMM obtain lower expected returns because they provide a hedge against the status risk of the leader. The negative premium for assets with high exposure to VMM depends on the hedging demand, which is derived from the correlation within group V, and on the variance of VMM. When the variance of VMM is lower, the leader can use other assets in the economy to hedge against the laggard, the overall demand for group V assets decreases, and exposure to VMM is rewarded less in equilibrium.

The model has both portfolio-choice and asset-pricing implications. It explains why some investors (the laggards in the model) hold undiversified portfolios of stocks with lottery-like payoffs and experience underperformance relative to traditional asset-pricing models. The model generates a cross-sectional two-factor beta pricing equation. It suggests that assets with higher exposure to the most volatile group of stocks in the market should have a negative return premium because they provide a hedge against status risk. In addition, the model provides a closed-form expression for the premium on this portfolio in terms of the correlation within that portfolio and its variance.

We test the asset-pricing implications of the model using stock-market data. In accordance with the model predictions, we construct 25 portfolios designed to maximize the cross-sectional variation in expected returns. We sort stocks first by their exposure to the market and then by their exposure to the high-volatility factor (VMM).

The empirical counterpart of group V is the portfolio of stocks with the highest total volatility. We examine the monthly returns on these portfolios and show that portfolios with higher exposure to VMM earn significantly lower risk-adjusted returns. For example, the portfolio with the highest exposure to VMM has monthly alphas of -1.08%, -0.84%, and -0.75% using the CAPM, the Fama-French (1993) [6] three-factor model, and the Carhart (1997) [7] four-factor model respectively during the period from 1945 to 2008.

We test the cross-sectional implications of the two-factor model using time-series regressions, the Fama-MacBeth method, and GMM-SDF tests. All these tests agree that the unconditional version of our two-factor model prices the 25 test assets significantly better than the CAPM, the Fama-French three-factor model, and the Carhart four-factor model. Using time-series regressions, we show that a joint test that all pricing errors are zero rejects the CAPM, the Fama-French three-factor model, and the Carhart four-factor model at the 1% significance level. However, the same test cannot reject our two-factor model even at the 5% significance level. The GMM tests reinforce this finding because Hansen's (1982) [26] test of overidentifying restrictions rejects the CAPM, the Fama-French three-factor model, and the Carhart four-factor model at the 5% significance level, while it cannot reject the unconditional two-factor model at the 10% significance level. Using the Fama-MacBeth method and GMM-SDF tests, we also find that exposure to the VMM factor remains statistically and economically significant in explaining the cross-section of expected returns after controlling for the Fama-French three-factor model and the Carhart four-factor model. Using GMM tests, we also show that the conditional version of the two-factor asset-pricing model, which incorporates variations over time in the risk premium of the VMM factor, performs better than the unconditional version.

Finally, we test the performance of this two-factor model versus that of idiosyncratic volatility, as measured by Ang et al. (2006) [4], using Fama-MacBeth regressions and GMM-SDF tests. The results show that the two-factor model performs better in the cross-section. Nevertheless, we find high positive correlation in the cross-section between idiosyncratic volatility and exposure to high-volatility stocks. The model and this empirical finding provide an explanation for the idiosyncratic volatility puzzle: the low returns that have been assigned to idiosyncratic risk are actually a result of the negative premium for covariance with the portfolio of highly volatile stocks. In this spirit, we show that the two-factor pricing model reduces the monthly alpha of the high/low idiosyncratic risk portfolio of Ang et al. (2006) [4] from -1.23% (using the Fama-French three-factor model) to -0.32% for the period from 1963 to 2008.

The rest of this chapter is structured as follows. In the next section, we review the literature related to this work. In Sect. 3, we present the model, and in Sect. 4, we test its asset-pricing implications. Section 5 then presents conclusions. It should also be noted that this chapter is based on work published in Krasny (2011) [27].

2 Related Literature

Several papers in the economics literature have studied the effect of status concerns on risk preferences. Friedman and Savage (1948) [28] used status concerns to interpret the concave-convex-concave shape of their well-known utility function. They interpreted the convex segment in their utility function as a transition between two socioeconomic levels and suggested that people are willing to take great risks to obtain a chance to move to a higher social class. Robson (1992) [15] and Becker et al. (2005) [16] illustrated that including status, modeled as ordinal rank in the distribution of wealth, in the utility function leads some agents to take on fair lotteries.

The behavior of the laggards in our proposed model is consistent with that of the agents that are induced to take on fair lotteries in the studies mentioned above. However, important distinguishing features of our model are that the investment opportunity set is common to all investors and that assets are not independent of one another. Therefore, in our model, the preference of the laggards for high-volatility assets cascades to other investors, the leaders, because they can create a hedge against the laggards. Becker et al. (2005) [16] stress that fair lotteries may take the form of wagers made through occupational choices and entrepreneurial activities and may not necessarily involve actual lotteries. The appropriate interpretation of assets in our model is public equity. Unlike occupational choices and entrepreneurial activities, investments in public equity are highly accessible and do not require drastic changes in the daily life of an individual.

In the context of portfolio choice and asset prices, Cole et al. (2001) [29] studied the effects of relative wealth concerns in a general framework and showed that these concerns can have two opposite effects: investors can bias their portfolios either toward or away from the portfolios held by other investors. Abel (1990) [30] and other researchers studying interdependent preferences in finance have modeled relative wealth using utility functions that exhibit the first effect, which is commonly termed "keeping up with the Joneses." Because investors in these models tend to bias their portfolios toward the portfolio held by the reference group, such models yield herd behavior. For example, DeMarzo et al. (2004) [31] showed that preference for a local good can give rise to relative wealth concerns, leading to undiversified portfolios as households in each community tilt their portfolios toward community-specific assets. Others, such as Lauterbach and Reisman (2004) [32] and Cole et al. [29] (2001) have used such preferences to explain the home bias. Roussanov (2009) [33] is the first paper, to our knowledge, in the finance literature to specify a utility function that leads investors to "get ahead of the Joneses" and to seek portfolios that are biased away from the aggregate portfolio.

Our proposed model takes the view that merging these two effects into a single framework is essential to understanding the effects of status on portfolio choice and asset pricing. Investors who are satisfied with their position relative to others will pursue the "keeping up with the Joneses" approach and will bias their portfolios towards the portfolios of others, whereas other investors who are dissatisfied with their position relative to others will pursue the "getting ahead of the Joneses" approach described by Roussanov (2009) [33] and will bias their portfolios away from the portfolios of others. Juxtaposing these two approaches gives rise to a strategic game because the decisions of both types of investors are interdependent. This chapter is a first step in studying such models.

This chapter also adds to earlier work that has shown that relative wealth concerns may lead to a preference for lottery-like securities. Robson (1996) [34] used a biologically motivated model to show that agents who are fundamentally risk-neutral are induced to take fair bets involving small losses and large gains in an environment in which the rewards are a function of relative wealth. Barberis and Huang (2008) [35] studied the implications of prospect theory (Tversky and Kahneman 1979 [36]) on asset prices. They showed that errors in the probability weighting of investors cause agents to overvalue stocks that have a small probability of a large positive return. The optimal beliefs framework proposed by Brunnermeier et al. (2007) [37] also predicts a preference for lottery-like securities. In their economy, agents optimally choose to distort their beliefs about future probabilities to maximize their current utility. In both these references, assets with positively skewed payoffs are overpriced. The asset-pricing implications of our proposed model are different in two aspects from the studies mentioned above. First, in our economy, high-volatility securities obtain high prices even if they are not positively skewed. Second, in our economy, agents seek *covariance* with high-volatility assets, giving rise to a two-factor beta pricing model in which covariance with high-volatility assets commands a negative premium.

Other studies that have used relative wealth concerns to try to explain occurrences of underdiversification are those of Roussanov (2009) [33] and DeMarzo et al. (2004) [31]. Unlike these studies, this chapter identifies the holders of underdiversified portfolios as investors who have fallen behind in the competition over status and identifies the assets held in these portfolios as the most volatile assets. A model that associates assets held in underdiversified portfolios with high-risk assets has been provided by Van Nieuwerburgh and Veldkamp (2010) [38], who argued that information acquisition can rationalize investing in a concentrated set of assets. In particular, they formalized the conditions under which the informed investor would hold an underdiversified portfolio of the riskiest assets. Liu (2008) [1] argued that portfolio insurance leads the poorest investors to hold underdiversified portfolios with assets that have the highest expected return and the highest risk. Unlike these studies, our proposed model predicts that the underdiversified portfolios held by poorer investors contain assets with low expected returns. Therefore, the model proposed here is better aligned with the findings of Kumar (2009) [2], who showed that investors who invest disproportionately more in lottery-type stocks experience greater underperformance.

Another potential consequence of relative wealth concerns is the creation of financial bubbles. Demarzo et al. (2007, 2008) [39, 40] have already pointed out that herd behavior due to relative wealth concerns can play a role in explaining financial bubbles and in particular the recent high-tech bubble. Other studies of the evolution of trends in financial networks have shown how these trends can be predicted (and potentially also influenced) through monitoring local social interactions between traders [41]. This chapter adds to this literature by identifying that the source of asset-pricing bubbles is likely to be high-volatility stocks, especially in times when these covary more and have high variance relative to the market. During the high-tech bubble, sophisticated investors such as hedge fund managers were heavily invested in technology stocks (Brunnermeier and Nagel 2004 [42]). From the vantage point of this research, these managers were using technology stocks as a hedge against their status risk. Corresponding to the characteristics associated with high prices in our model, at that time high-tech stocks were the most volatile stocks in the market and had high covariance with one another, and the high-tech industry as a whole had high variance relative to the market.

Another related strand in the literature is the mutual fund tournament literature, which examines whether underperforming mutual funds (the laggards in our model) increase risk in the latter part of the year. This phenomenon has been studied using return data, with different studies reaching different conclusions (see a review by Elton et al. (2009) [43]). There are at least two issues with this empirical approach that might hinder reaching a decisive conclusion about mutual-fund tournament behavior. First, while most studies examine the risk taken by the leaders and the laggards as measured by volatility or beta, Chen and Pennacchi (2009) [44] showed that laggard funds should increase a fund's "tracking error" volatility, but not necessarily its return volatility. This chapter provides support for both these approaches because the laggards in our model seek higher variance and lower covariance with the leaders.

The second issue with this literature is the identity of the leaders and the laggards. Although the common and intuitive approach is to view the underperforming funds as the laggards and the top performers as the leaders, this might not necessarily be the case. Chevalier and Ellison (1997) [45] studied the relationship between new cash flows and returns and found that it was nonlinear, with an extreme payoff from winning the tournament. Moreover, Chevalier and Ellison (1998) [46] identified implicit incentives created by the relationship between job termination and performance. Therefore, the career concerns of mutual-fund managers may provide an incentive to avoid ending up among the worst performers. These studies suggest that the competition might be a more complex and localized structure in which the best performers compete among themselves, as do the worst performers. Furthermore, it could be true that funds compete within families, as suggested by Kempf and Ruenzi (2008) [19]. Other research on the ability to monitor and identify personal features in a crowd is described in [47–52]. Our model provides an additional test to this literature because it predicts that both the leaders and the laggards should increase their holdings of highly volatile assets as the tournament-based incentives intensify (i.e., towards the end of the calendar year).

Finally, this chapter relates to the race literature that studies the choices of efforts and strategies by agents in a setting where rewards are positional in nature.

In particular, Cabral (2003) [21] and Anderson and Cabral (2007) [22] provided conditions under which the laggard will choose a risky strategy while the leader will choose a safe strategy. Cabral (2002) showed that when the competitors choose covariance, the laggard is willing to trade off lower expected value for lower correlation with respect to the leader. Both effects are consistent with our model.

3   The Model

In this section, we first define and examine the status game between the leader and the laggard in a general setting where assets have a multivariate normal distribution. Next, we define an economy with an additional structure imposed on the distribution of assets and derive the Nash equilibrium in the two-player game. Finally, we add many pairs of leaders and laggards (status-conscious investors) and many traditional Markowitz investors and examine asset prices in this economy.

3.1   The Two-Player Status Game

The model has two players: the laggard ("he"), with an initial wealth normalized to one, and the leader ("she"), with an initial wealth normalized to $k > 1$. There are finitely many risky assets with returns from a multivariate normal distribution as well as a risk-free asset with a gross return of one available for investment. Short sales are not allowed.[2] Time is discrete and runs for one period.

The gross return of the leader's portfolio is given by r_d, and the gross return of the laggard's portfolio is given by r_g. Therefore, at the end of the period, the wealth of the leader is kr_d, and the wealth of the laggard is r_g. The utility of the players is given by their wealth-based rank: the initial utility of the leader is one, and the initial utility of the laggard is zero. At the beginning of the period, each player chooses a portfolio to maximize his or her expected utility, which is equivalent to his or her probability of being the leader at the end of the period. We denote the difference in end-of-period wealth between the leader and the laggard by $D\,(r_d,\,r_g)$:

$$D(r_d, r_g) = kr_d - r_g. \tag{1}$$

---

[2] The results of this section can be derived under the assumption of limited short sales as well.

This is a zero-sum game in which the leader (laggard) tries to maximize (minimize) the expression:

$$Pr(D(r_d, r_g) > 0). \qquad (2)$$

Because D is normal, the objective function of the leader can be written as:

$$Max \ \Phi\left(\frac{kE(r_d) - E(r_g)}{\sqrt{k^2 Var(r_d) - 2kCov(r_d, r_g) + Var(r_g)}}\right) \qquad (3)$$

where $\varphi(.)$ is the cumulative distribution function (CDF) of a standard normal distribution. If short sales are not allowed, the expected return on any portfolio must be finite. Therefore, the leader can guarantee an expected return on her portfolio at least as high as that of the laggard, and the following proposition holds:

Proposition 1. *In Nash equilibrium, the choices of the players must satisfy:*

$$kE(r_d) - E(r_g) > 0, \qquad (4)$$

where r_d is the gross return of the leader, r_g is the gross return of the laggard, and $k > 1$ is the wealth ratio between the players.

Proof. The short sales constraint guarantees that any strategy η of the laggard yields a finite expected return. For any such strategy, the leader can use an imitation strategy with one unit of her wealth invested with η and the rest $(k - 1)$ invested in the risk-free asset. This guarantees a probability of winning the game (i.e., remaining the leader) greater than 0.5. In Nash equilibrium, the leader uses a strategy that is at least as good as the imitation strategy and therefore yields a probability greater than 0.5 of winning the game. Because assets are multivariate normal, Eq. 3 implies that a probability greater than 0.5 of winning the game is achieved if and only if the numerator of the CDF's argument is positive. Therefore, it follows that $kE(r_d) - E(r_g) > 0$.

In other words, in equilibrium, the laggard cannot choose a portfolio such that his end-of-period wealth, on average, will exceed or be equal to that of the leader. Otherwise, the leader will imitate his strategy.

The leader (laggard) chooses her (his) portfolio to maximize (minimize) the probability of the leader's maintaining her first-place rank at the end of the game. Using Proposition 1 and Eq. 3, we can gain some insight into the endogenous translation of the players' initial status to their portfolio choice preferences. Both players prefer higher expected returns on their portfolios. In addition, because the numerator in Eq. 3 is positive, the leader (laggard) prefers a lower (higher) variance in her (his) portfolio. Finally, the leader (laggard) prefers higher (lower) covariance between the wealth of the players.

3.2 The Economy

To examine further portfolio choices and asset prices, we impose an additional structure on the distribution of assets by introducing G groups of assets. To clarify notation, we will use capital letters to denote variables that relate to groups and small letters to denote variables that relate to individual assets.

All assets are multivariate normal. Each group $I \in \{1,...,G\}$ has N_I assets with the same distribution. The return of asset $k \in \{1,...,N_I\}$ in group I is denoted by r_i^k. The return of the equally weighted portfolio over all assets in group I is denoted by r_I. We refer to the "equally weighted portfolio over all assets in group I" as "group I" for brevity.

The expected return of every individual asset in the same group I is identical and denoted by μ_i. Because the return of group I is the average of the returns of individual assets, the expected return of group I, μ_I, is equal to the expected return of the individual securities:

$$\forall k \in \{1, \ldots, N_I\}, I \in \{1, \ldots, G\}.$$

The variance of every individual security in group I is the same and is denoted by σ^2. The correlation of every pair of assets in group I is the same and denoted by ρ_I. Hence, the N_I by N_I covariance matrix of group I can be represented as:

$$Cov\left(r_i^k, r_i^l\right) = \begin{cases} \sigma_i^2 & \text{if } k = l \\ \rho_I \sigma_i^2 & \text{if } k \neq l. \end{cases}$$

We assume that the correlation of every pair of assets within any group is positive, but less than one:

$$0 < \rho_I < 1, \quad \forall I \in \{1, \ldots, G\}. \tag{5}$$

The correlation between two assets of different groups $I, J \in \{1,..., G\}$ is denoted by $\rho_{i,j}$. Hence, the G by G covariance matrix for individual assets across different groups can be written as follows:

$$Cov\left(r_i^k, r_j^k\right) = \sigma_{ij} = \begin{cases} \sigma_i^2 & \text{if } i = j \\ \rho_{i,j} \sigma_i \sigma_j & \text{if } i \neq j. \end{cases}$$

The G by G covariance matrix for groups is denoted by E and can be expressed as follows:

$$Cov(r_I, r_J) = \sigma_{I,J} = \begin{cases} \sigma_I^2 = \sigma_i^2\left(\rho_I + \frac{1-\rho_I}{N_I}\right) & \text{if } I = J \\ \rho_{i,j}\sigma_i\sigma_j & \text{if } I \neq J. \end{cases}$$

Note that the covariance of two individual assets in different groups is equal to the covariance of these two groups.

3.3   Portfolio Choice in Nash Equilibrium

First, we characterize the laggard's response to the leader's strategy. Proposition 1 suggests that the strategy of the leader in a Nash equilibrium guarantees that her expected wealth in the next period will be greater than that of the laggard, regardless of the response of the laggard. Therefore, we examine the response of the laggard to such strategies. The following proposition characterizes the best response of the laggard (all remaining proofs are relegated to the appendix):

Proposition 2. *Given a strategy of the leader that satisfies condition (4) for all possible strategies of the laggard, the best response of the laggard is to use a mixed strategy whose support consists exclusively of pure strategies that employ a single asset.*

In other words, the laggard either chooses a single asset or a mix of single assets. Each asset can be either the risk-free asset or a risky asset. Because the laggard cannot choose a strategy such that his expected end-of-period wealth will be at least that of the leader, he prefers higher volatility and lower covariance with the leader. Investing in a single risky asset serves both objectives. The laggard may choose to invest in the risk-free asset if the leader is invested in risky assets and either the expected returns on these risky assets are too low, or the correlation between the risky assets is too high. In either of these cases, the laggard is better off waiting on the sidelines, hoping that the leader obtains a low return from the risky assets.

The symmetry of assets within each group makes it natural to focus the Nash equilibrium analysis on strategies that are symmetric within each group. Such strategies invest, on average, the same amount in each of the assets in the same group. Therefore, Proposition 2 implies that in Nash equilibrium with symmetric strategies within groups, if the laggard invests in some group I, then he must choose a single risky asset using a uniform mixed strategy over all assets in group I. If he were to invest exclusively in the risk-free asset, then the leader would imitate his investment to guarantee her first rank.

We now turn to the leader's response to the laggard's strategy of choosing a single risky asset using a uniform mixed strategy over a specific group that we denote as group V. The following proposition suggests that if the number of assets in group V is large enough, the leader's problem is reduced to choosing a portfolio over groups.

Proposition 3. *For N_V large enough, and given that the laggard invests his wealth in a single asset chosen uniformly by a mixed strategy over group V, within each group the leader invests an equal amount in each of the assets.*

The reason that a large enough number of assets in group V is required can be illustrated by the following example. Suppose that there is only one group in the economy and that there are only two assets in this group. In addition, the wealth ratio, k, is very close to one. In this case, if the leader holds the equally weighted portfolio, the probability that she will remain the leader is slightly greater than 0.5 because the result of the game depends primarily on whether the laggard's chosen asset performs better than the other asset. However, in the event that she invests everything in one asset, she will achieve a probability slightly greater than 0.75 of winning the game, because if she "catches" the laggard and invests in the same asset, she will undoubtedly remain the leader. Having a large enough number of assets is important to discourage the leader from pursuing such strategies.

With N_V large enough, because the laggard invests in an asset v, and within each group the leader invests an equal amount in each of the assets, we can treat the leader's problem as choosing a vector θ of length G over all groups. Therefore, the problem of the leader can be represented as:

$$Max_\theta \frac{k(\theta'\tilde{\mu}+1)-(\tilde{\mu}_v+1)}{\sqrt{k^2\theta'\Sigma\theta-2k\theta'\Sigma E_v+\sigma_v^2}}, \tag{6}$$

where $\tilde{\mu}$ is the vector of expected excess returns over the G groups, $\tilde{\mu}_v$ is the expected excess return of a group V asset, Σ is the covariance matrix over all groups, and Ev is a vector of zeros except for entry v, which is one.

The leader prefers higher expected return, lower variance, and higher covariance with group V. Therefore, the leader's problem is a special case of the problem of an intertemporal CAPM (ICAPM) investor who cares about her covariance with state variables. In our proposed model, the only "state" variable is the return on group V, and naturally the mimicking portfolio for group V is simply the return on group V. In accordance with Fama (1996) [53], we conclude that the leader chooses a multifactor-minimum-variance portfolio in the sense of Fama (1996) [53]. This portfolio is a combination of the risk-free asset, the tangency portfolio, and group V. Hence, the leader's risky portfolio can be described as follows:

$$\theta = x\Sigma^{-1}\tilde{\mu}+yE_v, \tag{7}$$

where x and y are scalars. Using this insight, we can now solve for a unique Nash equilibrium:

Theorem 4. *Under the conditions described in Appendix A.3, there exists a unique Nash equilibrium in which the laggard chooses a single asset using a uniform mixed strategy over group V assets and the leader invests in a risky portfolio θ over groups:*

$$\theta = \frac{\sigma_v^2-\sigma_V^2}{k(k-1)}\Sigma^{-1}\tilde{\mu}+\frac{1}{k}E_v, \tag{8}$$

where $k > 1$ is the wealth ratio between the players, σ_v is the volatility of an individual asset of group V, σ_V is the volatility of group V, Σ is the covariance matrix for groups, $\tilde{\mu}$ is the expected excess return over the groups, and E_v is a vector of zeros except for entry v, which is one.

The investment of the leader in the risk-free asset, the tangency portfolio, and group V reflects her preferences for lower variance, higher expected return, and higher covariance with the laggard. As the wealth ratio between the players, k, increases, the leader becomes less threatened by the laggard. Her status risk, the risk of losing her first rank, becomes primarily the risk of obtaining too low a return, and in some sense she becomes her "own worst enemy." Hence, as k increases, the leader increases her portion invested in the risk-free asset.

The leader's twofold concern for low variance and high covariance with the laggard is reflected in her risky portfolio as represented in Eq. 8, which is a linear combination of the tangency portfolio and group V. To obtain high covariance with the laggard, she matches his investment in group V in the second term $\frac{1}{k}E_v$. To obtain an efficient mean-variance tradeoff, she invests in the tangency portfolio. The balance between the two terms is a function of the following term:

$$\Psi = \frac{k-1}{\sigma_v^2 - \sigma_V^2}, \tag{9}$$

where Ψ reflects the hedging demands of the leader. When the volatility of an individual asset in group V (asset v) increases relative to the volatility of its group, the correlation within group V decreases, and it is harder for the leader to obtain a high covariance with the laggard. Therefore her hedging demands, as reflected by Ψ, decrease.

When hedging demands are high, the leader concentrates her efforts on the covariance with the laggard and decreases her investment in the tangency portfolio. When hedging demands are low, she finds it difficult to obtain a high covariance with the laggard, and she channels her concerns to obtaining a more efficient mean-variance portfolio by investing more in the tangency portfolio.

The first condition for the equilibrium described in Theorem 4 is that the number of assets in group V is large enough in the sense of Proposition 3. The second set of conditions is sufficient to have the laggard not deviate from investing in asset v. Condition (2.a), $\sigma_v > \sqrt{2}\sigma_j \forall j \in \{1, ..., g\}$, says that the volatility of asset v should be high enough relative to assets of other groups to encourage the laggard to invest in it. This condition identifies the attribute that makes group V the laggard's choice. It is the high volatility of group V that distinguishes it from other groups in the economy. Condition (2.b), $\sigma_{vj} > 0 \ \forall j$, tells us that there is no group with negative covariance with group V. If there were one, the laggard might have been enticed to invest in it to obtain a negative correlation with the leader, who is tilting her portfolio towards group V. Condition (2.c), $\sigma_{vj} > 2\sigma_V$, says that the volatility of asset v should be high enough relative to the volatility of group V. In other words, the correlation within group V should be low enough, otherwise the leader can easily hedge against the laggard. To prevent the laggard from deviating to the risk-free asset, a sufficient condition is $\sigma_v > \sqrt{2}\,\sigma_V$, which is included in the above conditions. The third set of conditions is necessary to ensure that the leader refrains from taking a short position in the risk-free asset or in any of the risky assets.

3.4   Asset Prices in General Equilibrium

To examine asset prices in this economy, we add many leader-laggard pairs (status investors) and many Markowitz investors. Let us examine the risky portfolio held by each type of investor. The risky portfolio of every Markowitz investor is simply the tangency portfolio. There are many laggards in the economy, and each laggard chooses a single asset from group V using a uniform mixed strategy. Therefore, the law of large numbers suggests that the aggregation of the portfolios of the laggards is simply group V. As already shown, the portfolio of the leader is a linear combination of the tangency portfolio and group V. Hence, the market portfolio, which is a linear combination of the portfolios held by all investors, is also a linear combination of the tangency portfolio and group V. This guarantees the existence of a two-factor beta pricing model. To obtain a closed-form solution for prices, we rearrange Eq. 8 to yield:

$$\tilde{\mu} = \Psi(k\Sigma\theta - \Sigma E_v). \tag{10}$$

The expected return of an asset is positively related to its covariance with the portfolio of the leader and negatively related to its covariance with group V. Because the leader's portfolio is a combination of group V and the tangency portfolio, it is also a combination of the market and group V. Hence, there exists a two-factor beta pricing model in which one of the factors is the market and the other is group V. To derive the closed form of this two-factor beta pricing model, further assumptions about the ratio of the status-conscious investors to the Markowitz investors are required.

3.4.1   An Economy with Only Status Investors

Suppose that there are only status investors in the economy. In this case, the market portfolio can be expressed as a combination of the leader's portfolio and the laggard's portfolio:

$$\theta_M = \frac{k\theta + E_v}{k\theta'\imath + 1}. \tag{11}$$

Using the expression for the leader's portfolio obtained in (8) and the pricing Eq. 10, the expected excess return for an individual asset can be represented as:

$$\tilde{\mu}_i = [\iota'\Sigma^{-1}\tilde{\mu} + 2\Psi] \, Cov(r_i, r_M) - 2\Psi Cov(r_i, r_V). \tag{12}$$

The exposure of an asset to the market positively contributes to its expected return. The term $\iota'\Sigma^{-1}\tilde{\mu}$ is the expected excess return divided by the variance of the tangency portfolio. It reflects the implicit risk aversion of the leader. The term Ψ reflects the hedging demands of the leader, as defined in Eq. 9. If the hedging demands are high, the leader is inclined to invest more in group V at the expense of other groups, leading to a higher price for group V and a lower price for the market.

A compact way to express the asset-pricing relation as a two-factor beta pricing model is to have the first factor be the excess return of the market portfolio and the second factor the excess return on group V over the market return. We denote the second factor by VMM. This form is not only algebraically simpler, but also leads to powerful empirical predictions, as we will see shortly. From Eq. 12, the two-factor beta pricing model for this economy can be derived:

Theorem 5. *In an economy with many pairs of leaders and laggards, where the Nash equilibrium described in Theorem 4 holds, the expected excess return of asset i ($\tilde{\mu}_i$) is:*

$$\tilde{\mu}_i = \beta^I_{i,MKT}[\iota'\Sigma^{-1}\tilde{\mu}] \, Var(r_{MKT}) + \beta^I_{i,VMM}[-2\Psi] \, Var(r_{VMM}), \tag{13}$$

where $\beta^I_{i,MKT}$ is the slope of a univariate regression of the asset excess return on the excess market return ($r_{MKT} - r_f$) and $\beta^I_{i,VMM}$ is the slope of a univariate regression of the asset excess return on the return of VMM. The return of VMM equals the return of group V minus the return on the market ($r_V - r_{MKT}$), ι is a vector of ones, E is the covariance matrix of all groups, and μ_i is the expected excess returns of groups.

Equation 13 illustrates how exposure to the high-volatility factor, VMM, translates into prices. By fixing the univariate beta of an asset on the market $(\beta^I_{i,MKT})$, a higher univariate beta on VMM $(\beta^I_{i,VMM})$, leads to a lower expected return.

The negative premium on VMM beta has two determinants. First, the hedging demands Ψ—when there are higher hedging demands, the premium becomes more negative as the demand for exposure to group V increases. The second determinant is the variance of the VMM factor. When $Var(r_{VMM})$ increases, it is harder to hedge against group V using other groups in the market, group V becomes more specific in its effectiveness as a hedge, and its price increases.

To derive the stochastic discount factor (SDF) in this economy, Eq. 12 can be manipulated to obtain a two-factor SDF:

$$M = 1 + \tilde{\mu}'\Sigma^{-1}\tilde{\mu} - \iota'\Sigma^{-1}\tilde{\mu}(r_{MKT} - r_f) + 2\Psi(r_V - r_{MKT}). \tag{14}$$

The SDF expression is useful if we want to think about the model in conditional terms. So far, our analysis has focused on a one-period game. To extend the asset-pricing implications to a multi-period setting, we use a nonoverlapping generations approach. In this case, for every time period t, we can write the SDF as:

$$
\begin{aligned}
M_{t+1} = {} & 1 + (\tilde{\mu}'\Sigma^{-1}\tilde{\mu})_t - (\iota'\Sigma^{-1}\tilde{\mu})_t (r_{MKT,t+1} - r_{f,t+1}) \\
& + 2\Psi_t(r_{V,t+1} - r_{MKT,t+1}).
\end{aligned} \tag{15}
$$

This form of the SDF stresses the role of the hedging demand term in the conditional asset-pricing model. The return on VMM is scaled by the hedging demand term. This implies that the importance of the covariance of a return with the VMM factor at time $t + 1$ depends on the hedging demands at time t. At times when the correlation within the most volatile group of stocks increases, the hedging demand term increases, and covariance with VMM leads to higher prices.

3.4.2 Status Investors and Markowitz Investors

Let us suppose that along with the status investors, there are Markowitz investors who invest solely in the tangency portfolio. In particular, suppose that for every pair of leader/laggard investors with wealth $(k + 1)$, there is one Markowitz investor that invests φ in the tangency portfolio. φ is positively related to the wealth of the Markowitz investors in the economy and negatively related to their risk aversion. Now the market portfolio is:

$$
\theta_M = \frac{k\theta + E_v + \frac{\phi\Sigma^{-1}\tilde{\mu}}{\iota'\Sigma^{-1}\tilde{\mu}}}{k\theta'\iota + 1 + \phi}. \tag{16}
$$

We can use the same derivation used in the previous section to obtain the two-factor beta pricing model as a function of φ:

$$
\tilde{\mu}_i = \beta_{i,MKT}^I \left[\frac{\iota'\Sigma^{-1}\tilde{\mu} + \phi\Psi}{1 + \frac{\Psi\phi}{\iota'\Sigma^{-1}\tilde{\mu}}} \right] Var(r_{MKT}) + \beta_{i,VMM}^I \left[\frac{-2\Psi}{1 + \frac{\Psi\phi}{\iota'\Sigma^{-1}\tilde{\mu}}} \right] Var(r_{VMM}). \tag{17}
$$

As φ increases, the effect of the status investors on prices in this economy decreases. In particular, the negative premium on VMM becomes less negative as φ increases. Nevertheless, the Markowitz investors do not reverse the effect of the status investors. In fact, in the presence of status investors, the Markowitz investors require a lower expected return on assets with high VMM beta than the expected return they require in a CAPM world. The Markowitz investors care about the beta of an asset with the tangency portfolio. The tangency portfolio, however, has a short position in group V, and therefore a higher beta with group V leads to a lower beta with the tangency portfolio.

Not surprisingly, as φ goes to infinity, the model converges to the CAPM world:

$$\lim_{\phi \to \infty} \tilde{\mu}(\phi) = \iota'\Sigma^{-1}\tilde{\mu}\Sigma\theta_M. \tag{18}$$

Finally, the stochastic discount factor can be obtained as a function of φ:

$$M = 1 + \tilde{\mu}'\Sigma^{-1}\tilde{\mu} - \left[\frac{\iota'\Sigma^{-1}\tilde{\mu} + \phi\Psi}{1 + \frac{\Psi\theta}{\iota'\Sigma^{-1}\tilde{\mu}}}\right](r_{MKT} - r_f) - \left[\frac{-2\Psi}{1 + \frac{\Psi\phi}{\iota'\Sigma^{-1}\tilde{\mu}}}\right](r_{VMM}). \tag{19}$$

4 Empirical Tests

The model provides two sets of testable implications. The first set relates to the portfolio choices of investors as a function of their status in their reference group. According to the model, low-status investors hold underdiversified portfolios which are concentrated in highly volatile securities, while high-status investors weight these assets more than traditional Markowitz investors. Kumar (2009) [2] provides empirical support for the portfolio choice implication because he shows that investors who earn less than their neighbors hold underdiversified portfolios concentrated in lottery investments like stocks. The mutual fund tournament literature provides indecisive empirical findings regarding the tournament behavior of mutual funds. As discussed in the related literature section, it is perhaps difficult to identify the "laggards" and the "leaders" in such a tournament. The second set of implications relate to the asset-pricing results of the model. In this section, we concentrate on testing these implications.

The model provides a linear two-factor beta pricing model in which the factors are excess returns. The first factor is the return on the market minus the risk-free rate, and the second factor is the return of the most volatile group of stocks minus the market (henceforth referred to as VMM). Because the model is a member of the family of linear factor models, we can use an array of statistical tests provided by the empirical asset-pricing literature to evaluate it. In addition, the model suggests that assets with higher exposure to the portfolio of the most volatile stocks (henceforth portfolio V) should obtain lower returns. If the model is true, then assets with high exposure to portfolio V (i.e., assets with high VMM beta) are overpriced relative to asset-pricing models, such as the CAPM, the Fama-French three-factor model (1993) [6], and the Carhart four-factor model (1997) [7], that do not take this negative premium into account. In particular, the model predicts that the CAPM alpha obeys the following relationship:

$$\alpha_{i,CAPM} = \beta^I_{i,MKT}C + \beta^I_{i,VMM}\lambda^I_{VMM}, \tag{20}$$

where $\beta^I_{i,MKT}$ and $\beta^I_{i,VMM}$ are the univariate slopes of the return of asset i on the market and in the VMM respectively, C is a constant, and λ^I_{VMM} is the premium on the VMM factor. For a given $\beta^I_{i,MKT}$, a higher $\beta^I_{i,VMM}$ of an asset leads to lower CAPM alpha because λ^I_{VMM} is a negative number.

We will start by examining, using time-series regression, whether stocks with high exposure to the portfolio of high-volatility stocks (i.e., stocks with high VMM beta) obtain low returns relative to other asset-pricing models. Then we will examine the unconditional version of the two-factor model directly using time-series regressions, Fama-MacBeth (1973) [54] regressions, and GMM-stochastic discount factor tests. We find that VMM beta is positively correlated with idiosyncratic risk across our test assets, and therefore we proceed to examine the explanatory power of VMM beta versus idiosyncratic risk using Fama-MacBeth regressions and GMM-SDF tests. In addition, we form double-sorted portfolios, sorted first by idiosyncratic risk and then by VMM beta, and examine the returns obtained by these portfolios. Finally, we examine the conditional version of the model using GMM.

In testing the asset-pricing model, we first need to create test assets that have sufficient dispersion in their exposure to the market and to VMM. To create such assets successfully, we need to take into account time variation, not only in the volatility of stock returns, but also in the cross-section of stock volatility. In particular, the composition of the most volatile portfolio of stocks may change frequently, and therefore the sensitivity of an individual stock to VMM can change dramatically in a short time. For example, in the second half of 1978, petroleum industry stocks (SIC 1311) constituted only 2.7% of portfolio V, while in the second half of 1979, petroleum industry stocks constituted 28.1% of portfolio V. The dramatic change was caused by the oil crisis of 1979. Hence, to form the V portfolio using the most volatile stocks and to obtain up-to-date VMM beta estimators, short windows with daily data are preferable. However, to obtain more accurate estimators, longer windows are better. Most studies that have estimated betas have used a formation period of more than a year; on the other hand, Ang et al. (2006) [4] used a formation period of 1 month to estimate idiosyncratic volatility. We choose a formation period of 6 months to balance this tradeoff.[3]

Our sample includes daily and monthly data for AMEX, NASDAQ, and NYSE stocks. For the time-series regressions, we use a sample period from January 1945 to December 2008. We do not use earlier data because during and before World War II, there were several periods in which fewer than five stocks satisfied the conditions to be included in portfolio V. For the Fama-MacBeth regressions and for the GMM-SDF tests, we use the period from July 1963 to December 2008. These tests are used to examine the explanatory power of the model versus idiosyncratic risk, which was found to have explanatory power in a cross-section of expected returns in a study by Ang et al. (2006) [4]. To maintain comparability with this earlier study, we start the

---

[3] The results are robust to a formation period of 3 months.

sample period in July 1963. In our tests, we use the Fama-French (1993) [6] factors, MKTRF, SMB, and HML, as well as the momentum factor, UMD, constructed by French.[4]

4.1   Forming the Test Assets

Our model has substantial predictive power regarding the relationship between univariate market betas, univariate VMM betas, and expected stock returns. Higher univariate VMM beta leads to lower expected return, while higher univariate market beta leads to higher expected return. In accordance with the spirit of the model, we construct strategies that select stocks based on their univariate slopes with respect to the market and to VMM. We first form portfolio V as the value-weighted top decile of stocks sorted by total volatility. We then estimate total volatility using daily returns of the past 6 months and sort the stocks into $5 \times 5 = 25$ portfolios. First, we sort the stocks into quintiles according to their univariate market beta as estimated using daily returns for the past 6 months. Next, for every quintile, we sort the stocks into subquintiles based on their univariate VMM beta.

Because a sound estimation of VMM beta is of crucial importance for our tests, we use the method proposed by Pastor and Stambaugh (2003) [55] and forecast the next-period VMM beta using a cross-sectional predictive model that relates the VMM beta of a specific stock in a certain month to the lagged VMM beta and other predictive variables as described below.

4.1.1   Choosing Portfolio V

We use the following procedure to form portfolio V every month:

1. Include only stocks that have daily returns for all trading days in the past 6 months.
2. Exclude the lowest decile of stocks in terms of dollar volume.
3. Rank stocks according to their total volatility as estimated for the previous 6 months according to Eq. 21 and pick the value-weighted top decile as portfolio V.

We use liquidity-based filtering because we want to capture the joint movements across volatile stocks and to measure sensitivities to VMM. Hence, we refrain from using noisy stocks with low-quality daily return data that suffer from microstructural issues and from the problem of zero returns that might obscure our estimates.

---

[4] The data source for these four factors is Kenneth French's web site at Dartmouth.

Table 1 Factor Statistics. The table reports the means, standard deviations, and correlations of VMM and various factors. The factors MKTRF, SMB, and HML are the Fama and French (1993) [6] factors, and the momentum factor, UMD, is as constructed by French. The sample period is from July 1963 to December 2008, and the estimated values relate to monthly returns. VMM is constructed every month using the following procedure. Only stocks with daily returns for every trading day in the previous 6 months are considered as candidates for portfolio V. Next, stocks in the lowest decile in terms of dollar volume (volume times price) are eliminated. Then the monthly return volatility of stocks is estimated, using the 6-month daily returns corrected for one-lag autocorrelation as in French et al. (1987) [56] and in Eq. 21. A value-weighted portfolio is formed from the highest decile of stocks as sorted by total volatility. The monthly return of this portfolio is obtained for the following month. Finally, the Fama and French MKT return is subtracted to obtain the monthly return for VMM

Factor	Mean	StdDev	ρ(i, MKTRF)	ρ(i, SMB)	ρ(i, HML)	ρ(i, UMD)	ρ(i, VMM)
MKTRF	0.38	4.45	1.00	0.30	−0.38	−0.08	0.52
SMB	0.24	3.19	0.30	1.00	−0.26	0.01	0.69
HML	0.43	2.89	−0.38	−0.26	1.00	−0.13	−0.53
UMD	0.86	4.03	−0.08	0.01	−0.13	1.00	−0.06
VMM	−0.86	8.22	0.52	0.69	−0.53	−0.06	1.00

We estimate $Var(r_i)$ using daily returns of the past 6 months. Because asynchronous trading of securities causes daily portfolio returns to be autocorrelated, we follow French et al. (1987) [56] and estimate $Var(r_i)$ as the sum of the squared daily return plus twice the sum of the products of adjacent returns:

$$\hat{\sigma}_{i,t}^2 = \sum_{\tau=1}^{N_t} (r_{i,\tau,t})^2 + 2\sum_{\tau=1}^{N_t-1} (r_{i,\tau,t})(r_{i,\tau+1,t}), \qquad (21)$$

where there are N_t daily stock returns, $r_{i,\tau,t}$, in formation period t. After obtaining the variance for the entire 6 months, we divide by six to obtain an estimate of the monthly variance.

Table 1 provides statistics for VMM and its relationship with other well-known factors. VMM has an average monthly return of −0.86%, and its monthly standard deviation, 8.22%, is not surprisingly the highest among the factors. VMM has a correlation of 0.69 with SMB and a correlation of −0.53% with HML, suggesting that small-growth stocks set the tone within portfolio V. VMM has a low correlation with UMD, suggesting that its return is not driven by momentum effects. Finally, the correlation of VMM with MKT is 0.52. Although the VMM factor has a short position in the market portfolio, the market beta of portfolio V is high enough to make the correlation between VMM and MKT positive.

4.1.2 Forecasting VMM Beta

To forecast the next period β_{VMM} for a specific stock, we start by regressing the daily return of the stock on the daily returns of VMM in the formation period. To account for asynchronous price movements in returns, we follow Lewellen and Nagel (2006) [57], who included four lags of factor returns, imposing the constraint

Table 2 Predictive Regressions of VMM beta. The table summarizes the results of stock-level cross-sectional predictive regressions of VMM beta $\left(\beta^l_{VMM,i,t+1}\right)$ on various lagged variables for the period from July 1963 to December 2008. The dependent variable, $\beta^l_{VMM,i,t+1}$, is estimated using a univariate regression of daily stock returns on VMM in the holding month $(t + 1)$, accounting for asynchronous price movements in returns as in Lewellen and Nagel (2006) [57] and in Eq. 22. The independent variables, $\beta^l_{VMM,i,t}$, $\sigma_{i,t}$, and $\varphi_{i,t}$ are estimated using the 6-month formation period prior to month $(t + 1)$. For each stock, $\beta^l_{VMM,i,t}$ is estimated by a univariate regression of daily stock returns on VMM over the 6-month formation period, accounting for asynchronous price movements in returns as in Lewellen and Nagel (2006) [57] and in Eq. 22. The monthly volatility of a stock, $\sigma_{i,t}$, is estimated using the prior 6-month daily returns corrected for one-lag autocorrelation, as in French et al. (1987) [56] and in Eq. 21. $\varphi_{i,t}$ measures the affiliation of the four-digit SIC industry code of stock i with portfolio V during the 6-month formation period and is constructed for each four-digit SIC industry code as follows. The percentage market-cap proportion of every industry i (denoted by a four-digit SIC code) in the market (denoted by m_i) and the percentage market-cap proportion of every industry i (denoted by a four-digit SIC code) in portfolio V (denoted by v_i) are measured as of the end of the 6-month formation period. A measure of industry affiliation to portfolio V is constructed as $\varphi_i = v_i - m_i$. IVOL is idiosyncratic risk and is estimated as in Ang et al. (2006) [4] relative to the Fama and French (1993) [6] three-factor model, using the daily returns of the 1 month prior to $(t + 1)$. Cross-sectional regressions are then run over all stocks for each month from July 1963 to December 2008. A time-series average of the estimated coefficients is taken to arrive at point estimates. T-statistics are reported in parentheses. The t-statistics are obtained from time series of estimated coefficients and include a GMM correction for heteroscedasticity and serial correlation. The $\bar{R}^2$ column gives the average R^2 over time

const	$\beta^l_{VMM,i,t}$	$\sigma_{i,\,t}$	$\phi_{i,\,t}$	$IVOL_{i,\,t}$	$\bar{R}^2$
0.35 (9.15)	0.38 (11.31)				0.02
0.11 (2.77)		0.04 (7.09)			0.02
0.56 (8.79)			0.05 (14.71)		0.01
0.34 (7.05)				0.09 (5.96)	0.01
0.16 (4.32)	0.22 (11.78)	0.02 (6.23)	0.03 (9.30)		0.03

that lags 2, 3, and 4 have the same slope to reduce the number of parameters. The Lewellen and Nagel method is an extension of that proposed by Dimson (1979) [58], who included current and lagged factor returns in the regression and addressed the finding that small stocks tend to react with a week or greater delay to common news (Lo and MacKinlay 1990), so that a daily beta will miss much of the small-stock covariance with market returns. Specifically, we estimate β^l_X, where X is the excess return either on the market or in VMM, using the following regression in which the dependent variable is an excess return of a stock:

$$r_{i,t} = \alpha_i + \beta_{i,0} r_{X,t} + \beta_{i,1} r_{X,t-1} + \beta_{i,2}[r_{X,t-2} + r_{X,t-3} + r_{Xt-4}] + \varepsilon_{i,t}. \quad (22)$$

The estimated beta is then: $\beta_{i,X} = \beta_{i,0} + \beta_{i,1} + \beta_{i,2}$. The empirical literature has shown that stock level beta estimators are fairly noisy and not persistent (e.g., Blume 1971) [59]. In our case, the problem is exacerbated because we are using a short period to estimate VMM beta and the VMM factor is highly volatile. Table 2 presents cross-sectional predictive regression results for next-month VMM beta $\left(\beta^l_{VMM,t+1}\right)$ on various variables estimated for the previous 6 months. Every month t, we measure the next-month VMM beta using the daily returns of month $t + 1$. On average, a cross-sectional regression of $\beta^I_{VMM,t+1}$ on $\beta^I_{VMM,t}$ yields an R^2 of only 0.02.

To improve the predictive ability of VMM beta, we start by adding volatility—a stock cannot have high exposure to portfolio V without being volatile itself. The reverse argument, however, is not necessarily true. A stock with high volatility can have low exposure to volatile stocks, for example if its volatility is purely idiosyncratic and is driven by factors that are not common with any other stock. Nevertheless, the formation-period volatility has significant predictive power for next-period VMM beta. In fact, as a stand-alone predictor, it is not inferior to the lagged VMM beta, judging by the average R^2 which is 0.02 in both cases. Table 2 also shows that the measure of idiosyncratic risk using the last-month daily returns has significant predictive ability for the next-period VMM beta.

If a certain industry is extremely volatile at a certain point in time, then portfolio V is likely to contain a high proportion of stocks associated with that industry, and the high-volatility stock factor will be dominated by this industry. In such an event, a stock belonging to that industry is likely to have high exposure to portfolio V. To quantify this intuition, we measure the proportion of every industry i (defined by the four-digit SIC code[5]) in the market (denoted by m_i) and the proportion of every industry i (defined by the four-digit SIC code) in portfolio V (denoted by v_i). We then construct a measure of industry affiliation to portfolio V:

$$\varphi = v_i - m_i. \tag{23}$$

A stock of industry i that has the same proportion of market cap in portfolio V and in the market portfolio will have a neutral affiliation $\varphi = 0$. For example, in the period from October 1999 to March 2000, the most volatile industry was SIC 7372, "Prepackaged software," with a market proportion of 7.69%, a portfolio V proportion of 33.19%, and $\varphi = 25.50$. Table 2 shows that higher φ is indeed positively correlated with higher VMM beta in the following period.

Table 2 shows that all three variables are jointly significant in forecasting next-period VMM beta, and therefore we use all three variables to forecast next-period VMM beta:

$$\beta^I_{VMM,i,t+1} = C_0 + C_1\beta^I_{VMM,i,t} + C_2\sigma_{i,t} + C_3\varphi_{i,t}. \tag{24}$$

Each month, we estimate the coefficients in (24) by running 240 monthly cross-sectional regressions over the previous 20 years and estimating the coefficients in (24) as the average of the values obtained in the 240 regressions. It is important to update the predictive regression because the relationships among the variables can change over time. For example, SIC codes have become more accurate and informative over time, and indeed untabulated results show that C_3 is increasing over time.

---

[5] We use the four-digit SIC code to obtain the most informative partition of industries. The results are robust to a specification of three-digit SIC code.

Table 3 Statistics for 5 × 5 portfolios. 25 value-weighted portfolios are constructed, sorted first by univariate market beta, β^I_{MKT}, and then sorted by univariate VMM beta, β^I_{VMM}. Portfolio VMM is formed as described in Table 1. Only stocks with more than 12 days of trading and more than 75 % of trading days in each month in the past 6 months are considered. β^I_{MKT} is estimated by a univariate regression of stock daily returns on the market during the 6-month formation period, accounting for asynchronous price movements in returns as in Lewellen and Nagel (2006) [57] and in Eq. 22. β^I_{VMM} is forecast using a cross-sectional predictive model in which the independent variables are lagged with respect to β^I_{VMM} (estimated during the 6-month formation period), stock volatility, and each stock's industry affiliation to portfolio V, as shown in Table 2. The predictive model is estimated using 240 cross-sectional regressions for each month in the 20 years prior to the holding period. Stocks are then sorted into quintiles according to β^I_{MKT}, and within each quintile, they are sorted into five subquintiles according to β^I_{VMM}. The statistics in the pair of panels in the first row labeled "Raw Returns Mean" and "Std.Dev." are measured in monthly percentage terms and apply to total simple returns. The "Market Share" panel is expressed in percentage points and represents the average market share of each portfolio measured as of the end of the 6-month formation period. The values in the "Book to Market", "IVOL," and "Volatility" panels are calculated for each formation period for each portfolio using a value-weighted average across stocks and then averaged over time. The "Book to Market" panel shows the book-to-market ratio within each portfolio, calculated as proposed by Fama-French. IVOL is idiosyncratic risk, measured as proposed by Ang et al. (2006) [4] relative to the Fama and French (1993) three-factor model, using the daily returns of the last month in the formation period. Volatility is estimated using the daily returns for the previous 6 months corrected for one-lag autocorrelation, as in French et al. (1987) [56] and in Eq. 21. The study period is from January 1945 to December 2008

| | Univariate β^I_{VMM} quintiles | | | | | | | | | |
	Low	2	3	4	High	Low	2	3	4	High
	Mean return					Std.dev return				
Low β^I_{MKT}	0.89	0.79	1.00	0.96	0.95	3.28	3.62	4.50	5.38	7.31
2	0.94	1.05	1.09	0.95	0.81	3.63	4.22	4.54	5.20	6.66
3	1.08	1.06	1.09	0.95	0.78	4.21	4.79	5.41	6.17	7.54
4	1.01	0.96	1.01	1.07	0.90	5.29	5.81	6.52	7.29	8.35
High β^I_{MKT}	1.09	1.10	0.89	0.66	0.37	6.67	8.06	8.44	9.20	10.58
	Market share					Book to market				
Low β^I_{MKT}	0.09	0.05	0.03	0.02	0.01	0.66	0.57	0.59	0.63	0.63
2	0.12	0.06	0.04	0.02	0.01	0.55	0.54	0.58	0.59	0.59
3	0.13	0.05	0.03	0.02	0.01	0.51	0.55	0.57	0.57	0.54
4	0.10	0.04	0.03	0.02	0.01	0.53	0.54	0.56	0.55	0.52
High β^I_{MKT}	0.05	0.02	0.02	0.01	0.01	0.54	0.55	0.54	0.54	0.54
	IVOL (daily)					Volatility (monthly)				
Low β^I_{MKT}	0.88	1.17	1.48	1.91	2.85	4.88	6.26	7.71	9.59	13.01
2	0.95	1.13	1.33	1.62	2.24	5.70	6.65	7.60	8.92	11.62
3	1.04	1.26	1.46	1.74	2.24	6.54	7.53	8.57	9.87	11.99
4	1.21	1.47	1.70	1.97	2.37	7.65	8.88	9.94	11.24	12.78
High β^I_{MKT}	1.59	1.95	2.21	2.53	3.18	9.69	11.46	12.66	14.06	16.21

4.1.3 The 25 Test Assets

Stocks are first sorted into quintiles based on market beta, and then in each quintile, they are sorted again into subquintiles according to the forecast VMM beta. Table 3 presents statistics for the 25 portfolios. For each market beta quintile, the raw returns on the highest-VMM-beta subquintile (the rightmost column) are generally lower than the returns of other portfolios. This result is most pronounced for the (5,5) portfolio—the portfolio with the highest market beta and the highest VMM beta. This portfolio earned an average return of 0.37% per month, which is by far the lowest return among all portfolios. Portfolios with higher VMM beta are more volatile; the standard deviation of portfolio monthly returns increases with VMM beta. In addition, the value-weighted average volatility and idiosyncratic volatility across stocks in each portfolio increase with VMM beta. Idiosyncratic volatility is measured as proposed by Ang et al. (2006) [4] with respect to the Fama-French (1993) [6] three-factor model, using the daily returns of the previous month. Intuitively, a portfolio with higher VMM beta will contain stocks with higher sensitivities to portfolio V, which contains the most volatile stocks, and therefore we expect it to be more volatile as well.

To test a factor model, initial studies must constitute portfolios using pre-formation criteria, but then examine them using post-ranking factor loadings computed over the full sample. To provide a convincing explanation of factor risk, we need to show that the portfolios also exhibit persistent loadings on VMM over the same period used to compute the alphas. The pair of panels in the first row of Table 4 shows the post-formation VMM betas of the 25 portfolios and their t-statistics. Indeed, in each and every row, the post-formation coefficients of VMM follow the pre-formation coefficients in terms of ranking. Moreover, the dispersion in VMM beta among portfolios is fairly high. We then form a high-VMM-beta minus low-VMM-beta portfolio for each market beta quintile and show (Table 4) that the VMM betas of these five portfolios are 0.6, 0.46, 0.52, 0.44, and 0.66.

4.2 Time-Series Analysis

To examine whether other asset-pricing models overprice portfolios with high VMM beta, we examine the Jensen alphas obtained for the 25 portfolios. The pair of panels in the second row of Table 4 shows the CAPM alphas and their t-statistics for each of the 25 portfolios. Indeed, for each market beta quintile, we see that the alphas generally decrease with VMM beta. The portfolio with the highest VMM beta has the lowest CAPM alpha for each and every market beta quintile. Moreover, for each market beta quintile, the alphas of the high-VMM-beta minus low-VMM-beta portfolio are -0.35%, -0.48%, -0.62%, -0.39%, and -1.01% (from the quintile with the lowest market beta to the quintile with the highest market beta). The t-statistic values for these alphas are -1.66, -2.69, -3.31, -1.90, and -4.19 respectively. These findings indeed support the prediction of the model that stocks with higher exposure to portfolio V are overpriced by the CAPM.

The results are qualitatively the same when using the Fama-French three-factor model and the Carhart four-factor model (the panels in the third and fourth rows of Table 4). A joint test for the 25 alphas equal to zero rejects the CAPM, the Fama-French three-factor model, and the Carhart four-factor model with p-values of

Table 4 Post-Formation Regressions. The table shows the results of various post-formation monthly regressions for the 25 portfolios described in Table 3. There are 10 panels in the table. The left panels contain point estimates, and the right panels report robust Newey-West (1987) [60] t-statistics. Each panel contains 25 values corresponding to the 25 portfolios and five values corresponding to five portfolios of high VMM beta minus low VMM beta for each market beta quintile. The first pair of panels shows the post-formation VMM beta estimated using a regression of portfolio monthly returns on VMM monthly returns for each portfolio. The next four pairs of panels contain Jensen alphas with respect to the CAPM, the Fama-French (1993) three-factor model, the Carhart four-factor model, and the MKT + VMM two-factor model proposed in this paper. The MKTRF, SMB, and HML factors are the Fama and French (1993) [6] factors; the momentum factor (UMD) is as constructed by French. For the panels that report point estimates of Jensen's alpha, the last row depicts the p-values obtained for a joint test for the 25 alphas equal to zero. The test is conducted by first estimating all 25 regressions simultaneously using GMM with robust heteroscedasticity and autocorrelation-consistent covariance matrix and then using a Wald test. The sample period is from January 1945 to December 2008

	Univariate β^I_{VMM} quintiles											
	Low	2	3	4	High	H-L	Low	2	3	4	High	H-L
	Post-form β^I_{VMM}						$t(\beta^I_{VMM})$					
Low β^I_{MKT}	0.04	0.11	0.21	0.32	0.64	0.60	1.15	2.37	4.06	5.67	9.45	10.00
2	0.08	0.19	0.22	0.30	0.54	0.46	1.40	3.76	3.48	4.98	8.21	10.72
3	0.18	0.25	0.36	0.47	0.70	0.52	3.51	3.90	5.71	6.98	11.51	15.07
4	0.34	0.42	0.53	0.70	0.77	0.44	6.24	6.73	8.97	17.90	8.11	7.37
High β^I_{MKT}	0.55	0.76	0.85	1.01	1.21	0.66	10.04	16.71	18.22	15.99	14.53	11.16
	Post-form α_{CAPM}						$t(\alpha_{CAPM})$					
Low β^I_{MKT}	0.22	0.05	0.14	0.03	−0.13	−0.35	2.46	0.47	1.24	0.20	−0.70	−1.66
2	0.19	0.19	0.19	−0.03	−0.28	−0.48	2.48	2.28	2.32	−0.30	−2.02	−2.69
3	0.21	0.11	0.06	−0.14	−0.41	−0.62	3.17	1.56	0.78	−1.44	−2.53	−3.31
4	0.00	−0.12	−0.14	−0.12	−0.39	−0.39	−0.03	−1.15	−1.46	−0.79	−2.15	−1.90
High β^I_{MKT}	−0.07	−0.18	−0.42	−0.69	−1.08	−1.01	−0.57	−1.02	−2.40	−3.18	−4.11	−4.19
$P(\alpha=0)$	0.0014											
	Post-form α_{FF3}						$t(\alpha_{FF3})$					
Low β^I_{MKT}	0.07	−0.09	−0.01	−0.14	−0.17	−0.25	0.92	−0.95	−0.14	−1.12	−1.08	−1.41
2	0.09	0.09	0.08	−0.15	−0.30	−0.38	1.25	1.19	1.13	−1.85	−2.43	−2.79
3	0.16	0.06	0.04	−0.14	−0.36	−0.52	2.54	0.77	0.53	−1.55	−2.52	−3.38
4	0.05	−0.04	−0.05	−0.01	−0.32	−0.37	0.68	−0.45	−0.49	−0.06	−1.92	−2.05
High β^I_{MKT}	0.05	0.02	−0.24	−0.50	−0.84	−0.90	0.47	0.13	−1.76	−2.79	−3.58	−3.60
$P(\alpha=0)$	0.0001											
	Post-form α_{CAR4}						$t(\alpha_{CAR4})$					
Low β^I_{MKT}	0.14	−0.04	0.00	−0.15	−0.20	−0.34	1.45	−0.41	0.02	−1.08	−1.11	−1.64
2	0.14	0.14	0.13	−0.15	−0.25	−0.39	1.71	1.80	1.59	−1.66	−1.99	−2.62
3	0.17	0.13	0.13	−0.09	−0.23	−0.40	2.81	1.87	1.44	−0.98	−1.32	−2.23
4	0.09	0.01	0.05	0.05	−0.24	−0.33	0.98	0.07	0.44	0.38	−1.43	−1.83
High β^I_{MKT}	0.09	0.04	−0.19	−0.38	−0.75	−0.84	0.70	0.30	−1.28	−2.17	−2.81	−3.04
$P(\alpha=0)$	0.001											
	Post-form $\alpha_{MKT+VMM}$						$t(\alpha_{MKT+VMM})$					
Low β^I_{MKT}	0.06	−0.08	0.08	0.08	0.28	0.19	0.69	−0.89	0.78	0.53	1.45	1.03
2	0.02	0.09	0.11	−0.05	−0.06	−0.08	0.24	1.15	1.40	−0.54	−0.48	−0.53
3	0.10	0.04	0.09	−0.01	−0.03	−0.12	1.48	0.53	1.08	−0.09	−0.17	−0.73
4	0.00	−0.04	0.03	0.26	0.03	0.03	0.00	−0.37	0.36	2.08	0.17	0.16
High β^I_{MKT}	0.13	0.23	0.08	0.00	−0.16	−0.29	1.13	1.68	0.58	0.01	−1.01	−1.51
$P(\alpha=0)$	0.0953											

Table 5 Statistics for Double-Sorted IVOL and VMM Beta Portfolios. Each month, stocks are sorted into quintiles based on idiosyncratic volatility, measured as proposed by Ang et al. (2006) [4], relative to the Fama and French (1993) [6] three-factor model, using the daily returns of the prior month. Then each quintile is sorted into two deciles by VMM beta, calculated as in Table 3. There are six panels in the table. The first row in each panel corresponds to the five idiosyncratic risk quintile base portfolios. The second row corresponds to the five low-VMM-beta portfolios and the third row to the five high-VMM-beta portfolios. The statistics correspond to those shown in Table 3. The sample period is from July 1963 to December 2008

	Idiosyncratic risk quintiles									
	beta	2	3	4	High	Low	2	3	4	High
	Mean return					Std. dev return				
Base	0.89	0.93	0.95	0.81	−0.01	3.83	4.88	6.02	7.57	8.71
Low β^l_{VMM}	0.85	0.94	0.90	0.86	0.31	3.55	4.40	5.21	6.29	7.47
High β^l_{VMM}	0.96	0.98	1.06	0.69	−0.39	4.91	6.26	7.59	9.43	10.67
	Market share					Book to market				
Base	0.57	0.24	0.11	0.05	0.02	0.52	0.54	0.56	0.58	0.68
Low β^l_{VMM}	0.38	0.15	0.07	0.03	0.01	0.53	0.56	0.58	0.62	0.72
High β^l_{VMM}	0.19	0.09	0.05	0.02	0.01	0.50	0.52	0.53	0.55	0.64
	IVOL (daily)					Volatility (monthly)				
Base	0.92	1.49	2.06	2.84	4.66	6.68	8.76	10.86	13.30	16.28
Low β^l_{VMM}	0.88	1.47	2.04	2.80	4.39	6.07	7.84	9.51	11.52	14.23
High β^l_{VMM}	1.01	1.52	2.09	2.88	4.98	7.95	10.26	12.74	15.49	18.79

0.0014, 0.0001, and 0.0001 respectively. On the other hand, the two-factor beta pricing model proposed in this paper does a significantly better job in pricing these portfolios. A joint test for the 25 alphas equal to zero cannot reject the model at the 5% significance level (the p-value is 0.095).

An important empirical issue is whether our results agree with those of Ang et al. (2006) [4], who found that stocks with high idiosyncratic volatility (IVOL) relative to the Fama and French (1993) [6] model have abysmally low average returns. The cross-sectional correlation between VMM beta and idiosyncratic volatility across the test assets is 0.84, where VMM beta is obtained for each portfolio using a post-formation regression over the sample from July 1963 to December 2008 and idiosyncratic volatility is calculated for each portfolio every month, using the method of Ang et al. (2006) [4] and averaged across the sample from July 1963 to December 2008. The high cross-sectional correlation makes it difficult to disentangle these two effects.

We start to address this problem by sorting stocks into IVOL quintiles, and then for each IVOL quintile, we sort them again into two portfolios based on VMM beta. Tables 5 and 6 show the results of this analysis. For the quintile with the highest idiosyncratic risk, the portfolio with lower VMM beta has a simple return of 0.31% per month, while the portfolio with higher VMM beta has a simple return of −0.39% (Table 5). For the quintile with the highest idiosyncratic risk, the risk-adjusted returns on the high-VMM-beta portfolio are significantly lower than those of the low-VMM-beta portfolio (Table 6). For example, the CAPM alpha for the

Table 6 Double-Sorted IVOL and VMM Beta Portfolios–Post-Formation Regressions. Each month, stocks are sorted into quintiles based on idiosyncratic volatility, measured as proposed by Ang et al. (2006) [4], relative to the Fama and French (1993) [6] three-factor model, using the daily returns of the previous month. Then each quintile is sorted into two deciles by VMM beta, calculated as in Table 3. There are 10 panels in the table. The left panels contain point estimates, and the right panels report robust Newey-West (1987) [60] t-statistics. In each panel, the first row corresponds to the five idiosyncratic-risk quintile base portfolios. The second row corresponds to the five low-VMM-beta portfolios and the third row to the five high-VMM-beta portfolios. The fourth and last row shows results for a high-VMM-beta minus low-VMM-beta portfolios for each idiosyncratic risk quintile. The sixth and last column in each row corresponds to a high-idiosyncratic-risk minus low-idiosyncratic-risk portfolio for each row. The first pair of panels contains the post-formation VMM beta estimated using a regression of portfolio monthly returns on VMM monthly returns for each portfolio. The next four pairs of panels show Jensen's alphas with respect to the CAPM, the Fama-French (1993) [6] three-factor model, the Carhart four-factor model, and the MKT + VMM two-factor model proposed in this paper. The MKTRF, SMB, and HML factors are the Fama and French (1993) [6] factors; the momentum factor (UMD) is as constructed by French. The sample period is from July 1963 to December 2008

	Idiosyncratic risk quintiles											
	Low	2	3	4	High	H-L	Low	2	3	4	High	H-L
	Post-form β_{VMM}						$t(\beta_{VMM})$					
Base	0.14	0.29	0.48	0.71	0.89	0.75	3.43	5.23	8.94	16.99	19.19	23.34
Low β_{VMM}	0.08	0.17	0.33	0.49	0.63	0.55	1.94	3.02	6.56	10.81	11.62	12.30
High β_{VMM}	0.26	0.47	0.68	0.95	1.16	0.90	5.58	8.35	11.76	21.12	23.07	30.49
H-L β_{VMM}	0.19	0.30	0.34	0.46	0.53	0.35	13.85	11.90	12.48	23.03	13.56	8.87
	Post-form α_{CAPM}						α_{CAPM}					
Base	0.12	0.06	0.01	−0.22	−1.07	−1.20	2.14	1.32	0.09	−1.35	−5.19	−4.78
Low β_{VMM}	0.13	0.13	0.02	−0.08	−0.67	−0.80	1.69	1.86	0.25	−0.60	−3.77	−3.55
High β_{VMM}	0.11	0.02	0.02	−0.44	−1.55	−1.65	1.61	0.21	0.14	−2.01	−5.37	−5.36
H-L β_{VMM}	−0.02	−0.11	0.00	−0.36	−0.87	−0.86	−0.21	−0.79	0.01	−2.01	−3.66	−3.78
	Post-form α_{FF3}						α_{FF3}					
Base	0.10	0.06	0.03	−0.16	−1.14	−1.23	2.18	1.15	0.49	−1.27	−7.60	−6.95
Low β_{VMM}	0.06	0.04	−0.05	−0.17	−0.86	−0.92	1.03	0.71	−0.62	−1.62	−6.34	−5.46
High β_{VMM}	0.13	0.13	0.12	−0.26	−1.52	−1.65	2.25	1.38	1.15	−1.50	−6.95	−7.22
H-L β_{VMM}	0.07	0.08	0.17	−0.10	−0.66	−0.73	0.77	0.76	1.29	−0.56	−2.89	−3.15
	Pos-Form α_{CAR4}						α_{CAR4}					
Base	0.08	0.12	0.10	−0.07	−0.88	−0.96	1.54	2.14	1.54	−0.60	−5.45	−4.88
Low β_{VMM}	0.05	0.06	−0.02	−0.07	−0.67	−0.72	0.77	0.98	−0.29	−0.66	−4.41	−3.83
High β_{VMM}	0.10	0.20	0.18	−0.16	−1.21	−1.31	1.51	2.08	1.71	−0.90	−4.74	−4.80
H-L β_{VMM}	0.05	0.14	0.20	−0.09	−0.54	−0.59	0.62	1.12	1.56	−0.45	−1.97	−2.17
	Pos-form $\alpha_{MKT+VMM}$						$\alpha_{MKT + VMM}$					
Base	−0.03	0.04	0.21	0.26	−0.34	−0.32	−0.63	0.69	3.51	2.44	−2.79	−2.21
Low β_{VMM}	−0.07	−0.02	0.05	0.14	−0.28	−0.21	−1.37	−0.24	0.70	1.20	−1.61	−1.04
High β_{VMM}	0.05	0.19	0.42	0.32	−0.47	−0.52	0.82	2.06	3.57	2.71	−3.75	−3.66
H-L β_{VMM}	0.12	0.21	0.37	0.17	−0.19	−0.32	1.41	1.86	2.41	1.20	−1.09	−1.61

high-VMM-beta minus low-VMM-beta portfolio in the quintile with the highest idiosyncratic risk is −0.87% per month, which is statistically significant at the 1% level. The results suggest that the VMM beta has an explanatory power beyond that of idiosyncratic volatility. However, a caveat is in order: the two variables are positively correlated, and therefore sorting by VMM beta creates a detectable difference in IVOL (Table 5). We will revisit this issue using Fama-MacBeth analysis and GMM-SDF tests.

Finally, Table 6 shows that the two-factor model does a better job of pricing the quintile portfolios sorted by idiosyncratic volatility, using the method of Ang et al. (2006) [4]. Although the monthly alphas of the high-idiosyncratic-risk minus low-idiosyncratic-risk portfolio are -1.20%, -1.23%, and -0.96% using CAPM, the Fama-French three-factor model, and the Carhart four-factor model, the monthly alpha of this portfolio using the two-factor model is -0.32%.

4.3 Fama-MacBeth Analysis

The two-factor asset-pricing model suggests that expected returns can be expressed as:

$$E(r_i - r_f) = \beta^I_{i,MKT}\lambda^I_{MKT} + \beta^I_{i,VMM}\lambda^I_{VMM}, \tag{25}$$

where $\beta^I_{i,MKT}$ and $\beta^I_{i,VMM}$ are the univariate slopes of the return of asset i on the market and in the VMM respectively and λ^I_{VMM} and λ^I_{MKT} are the premiums on the VMM factor and the market factor respectively. We can also write the model using the bivariate slopes from a multiple regression of stock return on the excess returns both of the market and of the VMM:

$$E(r_i - r_f) = \beta^{II}_{i,mf}\lambda^{II}_{MKT} + \beta^{II}_{i,VMM}\lambda^{II}_{VMM}. \tag{26}$$

In this form, λ^{II}_{MKT} is the expected excess market return and λ^{II}_{VMM} is the expected return on VMM. Because VMM and the market have a positive correlation of 0.52, and because the model suggests that $\lambda^I_{VMM} < 0$ and $\lambda^I_{MKT} > 0$, the model implies the following relationship among the premiums:

- $\lambda^I_{VMM} < 0$.
- $\lambda^I_{MKT} > 0$.
- $\lambda^{II}_{VMM} > \lambda^I_{VMM}$
- $\lambda^{II}_{MKT} < \lambda^I_{MKT}$.

Naturally, the model suggests that the bivariate premium on each factor equals its expected return. The Fama-MacBeth [54] method is a convenient framework to evaluate the model and its predictions. In addition, it enables us to augment the factors suggested by the model with various factors that have proven to have explanatory power for the cross-section of expected returns, such as the Fama-French SMB and HML factors and the momentum factor, UMD. Finally, the Fama-MacBeth procedure provides a closer look into the pricing relationship between idiosyncratic volatility and VMM beta.

Following Fama-MacBeth (1973) [54], we first perform time-series regressions in which we regress the excess portfolio returns on a constant and on various factors: MKT, SMB, HML, UMD, and VMM. In the second step, the excess portfolio returns are regressed on the estimated factor loadings for each month in the sample. Then a time-series average of the estimated coefficients is calculated to obtain point estimates and statistical significance values for the factor premiums. To examine the role of idiosyncratic risk (IVOL), we calculate the IVOL of each portfolio for each month as proposed by Ang et al. (2006) [4] and use the averaged IVOL value for each portfolio for the entire sample.

Table 7 shows the results of the Fama-MacBeth regressions. The first row shows that the CAPM can account for 16% of the cross-sectional variation in the returns on the 25 portfolios. In contradiction to the theoretical expectation of the CAPM, the market factor (MKT) shows up with an insignificantly negative factor premium. Our two-factor model suggests that the CAPM is wrongly specified. Because the univariate market beta and VMM beta are positively correlated, the CAPM attributes high market beta to portfolios with high VMM beta that obtain low returns. The second row shows that VMM beta on its own also has an insignificantly negative factor premium. In this case, the cross-sectional R^2 is 0.28.

Rows 3 and 4 show the Fama-MacBeth results for our two-factor model. Row 3 contains the results with the univariate betas, while row 4 contains the results with the bivariate betas. In both cases, the R^2 with the two-factor model jumps to 0.61. The predictions of the model regarding risk premiums are therefore supported. The estimated univariate market premium is 1.67%, and the estimated VMM premium is -2.47%. Both premiums are significant at the 1% level. The bivariate market premium is 0.97%, which is significant at the 1% level, and the bivariate VMM premium is -0.86%, which is significant at the 5% level. The bivariate VMM premium, -0.86%, is exactly the mean monthly return of VMM for the sample period.

Row 5 shows the results for the Fama-French three-factor model, and row 6 shows the results for the Fama-French three-factor model augmented with VMM. Adding VMM to the Fama-French three-factor model increases R^2 from 0.47 to 0.73, and VMM has a factor premium of -1.02%, which is significant at the 5% level. In fact, row 6 shows that VMM is the only one of the four factors that is significant at the 5% level. In the absence of VMM, SMB, and HML, the effect of VMM is apparent. The SMB factor, which is positively correlated with VMM, has a negative premium of -0.39%. The HML factor, which is negatively correlated with VMM, has a positive premium of 0.36%. However, adding VMM changes the coefficient of SMB to -0.1% and renders the HML coefficient negative, with a premium of -0.48%. The results are qualitatively the same for the Carhart four-factor model (rows 7 and 8).

Finally, we examine the role of idiosyncratic risk. Row 10 shows that a model with market and idiosyncratic volatility has an R^2 of 0.39, which is significantly lower than the R^2 of the two-factor model, which is 0.61. Nevertheless, because IVOL is positively correlated with VMM beta, the premium on IVOL is negative, -0.28%, and significant at the 5% level. Row 11 shows that when IVOL is added to the univariate market beta and the univariate VMM beta, it becomes economically and statistically insignificant, with a premium of -0.02%. However, VMM is still significant at the 1% level. Hence, these results suggest that VMM drives out idiosyncratic volatility, not the other way around.

Table 7 Fama-MacBeth Analysis. This table shows the estimated Fama-MacBeth (1973) [54] factor premiums on 25 portfolios sorted first by market beta and then by VMM beta, as described in Table 3. Following Fama-MacBeth, in the first step, time-series regressions, in which excess portfolio returns are regressed on a constant and on a set of factors corresponding to each row in the table are run for the entire sample. In the second step, the excess portfolio returns are regressed on the estimated factor loadings for each month in the sample. Then a time-series average of the estimated coefficients is calculated to arrive at point estimates and statistical significance values for the factor premiums. MKT is the market factor, SMB and HML are the Fama-French (1993) [6] factors, and UMD is a momentum factor constructed by French. VMM is constructed as explained in Table 1. IVOL is the value-weighted average of idiosyncratic risk for each portfolio, as calculated by Ang et al. (2006) [4], measured each month using the daily returns for the previous month and then averaged across the entire sample period. The notation [1] means that the beta obtained from a single cross-sectional regression of the average excess returns for each portfolio on the factor loadings. Fama-MacBeth (1973) [54] R^2 and adjusted R^2 are used. A univariate time-series regression was used. The sample period is from July 1963 to December 2008

	c	λ_{MKT}	λ_{SMB}	λ_{HML}	λ_{UMD}	λ_{VMM}	IVOL	R^2	Adj. R^2
1	0.68 (2.76)	−0.24 (−0.80)						0.16	0.13
2	0.56 (3.51)	1.67[1] (3.31)						0.28	0.25
3	−0.54 (−1.67)	0.97 (2.68)				−0.41 (−1.05)		0.61	0.58
4	−0.54 (−1.67)	0.75 (2.01)				−2.47[1] (−3.64)		0.61	0.58
5	−0.33 (−0.99)	0.49 (1.28)	−0.39 (−1.86)	0.36 (1.26)		−0.86 (−2.22)		0.37	0.28
6	−0.02 (−0.06)	0.75 (1.98)	−0.10 (−0.45)	−0.48 (−1.42)		−1.02 (−2.57)		0.69	0.63
7	−0.02 (−0.59)	0.50 (1.32)	−0.40 (−1.92)	0.14 (0.47)	1.85 (2.15)			0.47	0.36
8	0.05 (0.13)	0.18 (0.54)	−0.13 (−0.58)	−0.57 (−1.66)	1.62 (1.90)	−1.11 (−2.75)		0.73	0.66
9	0.77 (3.86)						−0.20 (−1.34)	0.37	0.34
10	0.70 (2.84)						−0.28 (−2.14)	0.39	0.34
11	−0.50 (−1.48)	1.63[1] (3.51)				−2.39[1] (−2.99)	−0.02 (−0.11)	0.61	0.56

4.4   GMM-SDF Tests

Our model provides an explicit stochastic discount factor (SDF) which is linear in the market return and the return on the high-volatility portfolio:

$$M_{t+1} = 1 + (\tilde{\mu}'\Sigma^{-1}\tilde{\mu})_t - (\iota'\Sigma^{-1}\tilde{\mu})_t(r_{MKT,t+1} - r_{f,t+1}) + 2\Psi_t(r_{V,t+1} - r_{MKT,t+1}).$$

The model suggests that the coefficient of excess market return in the SDF is negative, while the coefficient of the return of high-volatility assets minus the market in the SDF is positive. We examine the predictions of the model by estimating the model $E[MR] = 1$ using the GMM as proposed by Hansen (1982) [26]. In the analysis described below, we choose the weighting matrix W to be the asymptotically optimal one given by the inverse of the covariance matrix of the moment conditions. We use the same 25 portfolios as in the previous sections. As Cochrane (2005) [61] has noted, when the factors are correlated, one should test whether the SDF-parameter coefficients equal zero to see whether a certain factor helps to price the assets, rather than testing whether the factor premium obtained from the Fama-MacBeth method equals zero. In our case, the excess market return and the VMM factor indeed have a positive correlation of 0.52.

We start by examining the pricing ability of the unconditional two-factor model versus the CAPM, the Fama-French three-factor model, and the Carhart four-factor model. In particular, we estimate the following moment conditions:

$$1 = E[(B_0 - B'F_{t+1}) \cdot R_{t+1}], \tag{27}$$

where B_0 is a constant, B is the vector of coefficients to be estimated, F_{t+1} is a vector of factors included in the specification of the SDF, and R_{t+1} is the vector of returns on the 25 portfolios. Using this specification, a factor that commands a positive risk premium should have a positive coefficient.

Consistently with the Fama-MacBeth regressions, row 1 of Table 8 documents the failure of the CAPM to price the 25 portfolios. The CAPM is formally rejected by Hansen's (1982) [26] test of overidentifying restrictions with a p-value of 1%, and the coefficient of the market is negative and statistically insignificant. Row 2 shows the results with the unconditional version of the stochastic discount factor included in the model. Adding VMM along with the market excess return to the specification of the stochastic discount factor significantly improves the pricing ability of the SDF. Now the test of overidentifying restrictions cannot reject the two-factor SDF at the 10% significance level (the p-value is 13%). Both the excess market return and the return of the VMM portfolio have the expected signs, and both are statistically significant at the 1% level.

The two-factor SDF performs better than the Fama-French three-factor model (row 3) and the Carhart four-factor model (row 5), both of which are rejected by the test of overidentifying restrictions at the 5% significance level. Adding VMM to the Fama-French three-factor model renders both the SMB and the HML statistically insignificant, while VMM remains significant at the 1% level. Moreover, after adding VMM to the Fama-French three-factor SDF, the test of overidentifying

Table 8 SDF-GMM Tests. This table shows results from estimating the stochastic discount factor M, using the moment conditions $E[MR] = 1$. MKT is the market factor, SMB and HML are the Fama-French (1993) [6] factors, and UMD is a momentum factor constructed by French. IVOL is the value-weighted average of idiosyncratic risk for each portfolio, as calculated by Ang et al. (2006) [4], measured each month using the daily returns from the previous month. The hedging demand term ψ is estimated each month using daily returns for the 6-month formation period and using Eq. 29. The moment conditions for rows 1–6 are $1 = E[(B_0 - B'F_{t+1}) \cdot R_{t+1}]$. The moment conditions for row 7 are $1 = E[(B_0 - B_1(rmkt,t + 1 - rf,t + 1) - B_2(1 + B_3\psi_l)(r_{v,t+1} - r_{mkt,t+1})) \cdot R_{t+1}]$. The moment conditions for rows 8–11 are $1 = E[(B_0 - B'F_{t+1}) \cdot R_{t+1} - \gamma_{IVOL}IVOL_t]$. The parameter estimates are obtained by minimizing the GMM criterion function in which the weighting matrix of moment conditions is the asymptotically optimal one. TJ is Hansen's (1982) [26] test of overidentifying restrictions, and p-val is the corresponding p-value. T-statistics are reported in brackets and include a GMM correction for heteroscedasticity and serial correlation. The sample period is from July 1963 to December 2008

	C	b_{MKT}	b_{SMB}	b_{HML}	b_{UMD}	b_{VMM}	γ_{IVOL}	Ψ	TJ	p-val
1	0.99 (195.93)	−0.16 (−0.13)				−5.34 (−4.86)			41.82	0.01
2	1.10 (38.93)	10.64 (4.91)							29.47	0.13
3	1.04 (29.27)	8.35 (2.92)	−8.62 (−3.23)	6.77 (1.46)		−6.15 (−3.59)			35.47	0.03
4	1.10 (26.86)	9.63 (3.49)	3.83 (0.99)	−2.50 (−0.48)					29.79	0.07
5	1.12 (20.02)	6.71 (2.51)	−8.55 (−3.22)	2.16 (0.49)	12.19 (2.68)	−7.14 (−3.23)			31.85	0.04
6	1.09 (19.21)	4.44 (1.62)	4.24 (0.97)	−16.28 (−2.86)	7.47 (1.64)	−6.19 (−3.66)			29.18	0.06
7	1.10 (36.63)	11.20 (4.84)						127.62 (1.13)	25.88	0.21
8	1.00 (140.32)	3.25 (2.39)					−0.005 (−4.55)		36.05	0.03
9	1.08 (36.99)	9.59 (4.27)				−4.21 (−3.26)	−0.002 (−1.54)		29.41	0.10
10	1.09 (23.48)	8.84 (3.33)	3.48 (0.92)	13.08 (2.71)			−0.007 (−3.62)		28.83	0.09
11	1.18 (16.95)	7.97 (2.38)	3.55 (0.84)	10.08 (1.63)	11.55 (2.07)		−0.007 (−3.07)		27.76	0.09

restrictions cannot reject the SDF at the 5% significance level. The results for the Carhart four-factor models are qualitatively the same (rows 5 and 6).

The conditional SDF model obtained by the model implies that the effect of the covariance between an asset's return and the VMM factor depends on the hedging demand term Ψ. When the hedging demand term is large, covariance with VMM leads to lower expected returns. To estimate the conditional model, we first need to estimate the hedging demand term Ψ. The expression for Ψ in the model, as the number of assets in group V goes to infinity, converges to the following term:

$$\Psi_t = \frac{\rho_{v,t}(k-1)}{\sigma_{V,t}^2(1-\rho_{v,t})},\tag{28}$$

where $\rho_{v,t}$ is the correlation of each pair of assets in portfolio V at time t and $\sigma_{v,t}$ is the volatility of portfolio V at time t. We estimate Ψ_t using daily returns during the 6-month formation period. We estimate $\rho_{v,t}$ as the average correlation between all pairs in portfolio V during the 6-month formation period, and we estimate the monthly total volatility of portfolio V, $\sigma_{V,T}$, using daily returns during the formation period as shown in Eq. 21. Following Ferson and Harvey (1999) [62], we determine the scaling variable Ψ_t. After obtaining an estimate for Ψ_t for every month, we estimate the following moment conditions:

$$1 = E[(B_0 - B_1(r_{MKT,t+1} - r_{f,t+1}) - B_2(1 + B_3\Psi_t)(r_{V,t+1} - r_{MKT,t+1})) \cdot R_{t+1}].\tag{29}$$

The model suggests that the coefficient B_3 should be positive; in times where Ψ_t is high, covariance with VMM leads to lower returns. Row 7 of Table 8 reports the results of this estimation. The conditional model performs better than any other model, including the unconditional one, according to the p-value of the test of overidentifying restrictions, which is 0.21. The coefficients of the market excess return and of VMM remain significant and with the expected sign. The coefficient of Ψ_t has the expected positive sign, but is statistically insignificant.

To examine the role of idiosyncratic volatility, we use the method proposed by Nyberg (2008) [63] to examine whether idiosyncratic volatility has pricing power beyond that of the stochastic discount factors specified above. We estimate the parameters of the stochastic discount factors using the GMM using the following moment conditions:

$$1 = E[(B_0 - B'F_{t+1}) \cdot R_{t+1} - \gamma_{IVOL}IVOL_t].\tag{30}$$

The idiosyncratic volatility for every portfolio is estimated using the previous month's daily returns, as in Ang et al. (2006) [4]. If the stochastic discount factors specified above cannot capture the negative relationship between idiosyncratic volatility and returns, then γ_{IVOL} should have a negative coefficient. Rows 8, 10, and 11 show that idiosyncratic volatility indeed has a pricing ability greater than that of the SDF, whether using CAPM, the Fama-French three-factor model, or the Carhart four-factor model. In all cases, IVOL is significant at the 1% level. In fact, the test cannot reject either the Fama-French three-factor model or the Carhart four-factor model when IVOL is added to the specification. However, when idiosyncratic volatility is added to the two-factor model with market return and VMM, IVOL becomes statistically insignificant. Moreover, the p-value of the test for overidentifying restrictions decreases from 0.13 without IVOL to 0.10 with IVOL.

The GMM-SDF tests agree with the Fama-MacBeth analysis on several results. First, the two-factor model proposed here provides better pricing of the test assets than the CAPM, the Fama-French three-factor model, or the Carhart four-factor model. Controlling for SMB, HML, UMD, and idiosyncratic volatility, the VMM beta has a significant pricing ability for the cross section of the expected returns of the test assets. Nevertheless, idiosyncratic risk and VMM beta are positively correlated, and in the absence of VMM beta, idiosyncratic risk can help in pricing the test assets. Moreover, the GMM-SDF tests provide support to the conditional version of the two-factor model because this model does a better job of pricing the test assets than the unconditional version.

5 Conclusions

A fundamental assumption that underlies the lion's share of portfolio choice and asset-pricing theories is that investors care only about their absolute consumption or wealth. However, both in the social context and in the mutual-fund arena, a growing literature suggests that investors are concerned about their status relative to a reference group of other investors. In this chapter, we examine the implications of such concerns on portfolio choice and asset pricing in an economy with status-conscious investors and traditional Markowitz investors. We devise a model that captures the fundamental features of the concern for social status. Status is inherently positional and therefore network-dependent and gives rise to a strategic interaction among investors. In addition, different investors define their status with respect to different local reference groups. Hence, in each reference group, there must be investors with high relative status and investors with low relative status. Our model introduces many pairs of low-status and high-status investors into an economy populated with traditional Markowitz investors. These status-conscious investors strategically choose their investments to maximize their expected status.

The model provides a rich set of implications. In a general equilibrium, low-status investors hold a single high-volatility asset to move up the status ladder. Because high-status investors are concerned about the risk of losing their status, they demand assets that co-vary with high-volatility assets as a hedge against low-status investors. In equilibrium, the demand for exposure to high volatility leads to a two-factor model in which the first factor is the market and commands a positive premium, while the second factor is a portfolio of high-volatility stocks and commands a negative premium. This model also has dynamic implications. At times when the returns of high-volatility assets co-vary more and the variance of the high-volatility factor is higher, high-status investors are induced to invest more in assets with high exposure to the high-volatility factor, and its premium becomes more negative.

The general-equilibrium asset-pricing model derived in this chapter is novel in at least two important aspects. First, it is not driven by the preferences of a single representative agent, but is rather a result of strategic interactions among heterogeneous investors. Second, the general theme of asset-pricing models is that factor risk premiums arise because risk-averse investors seek to limit their exposure to systematic risk factors. In our proposed model, the high-volatility factor premium arises because status-conscious investors seek exposure to this factor to hedge against their status risk.

We test the asset-pricing implications of the model using stock market data and find significant economic and statistical support. The two-factor model proposed in this chapter does a better job than the CAPM, the Fama-French three-factor model (1993) [6], and the Carhart four-factor model (1997) [7] in pricing assets with dispersion in their exposure to the market and to high-volatility stocks. In particular, the model provides an explanation for the idiosyncratic volatility puzzle posed by Ang et al. (2006) [4] because there is a positive cross-sectional correlation between high exposure to the high-volatility factor and idiosyncratic risk. Nevertheless, we show that our two-factor model has a cross-sectional pricing ability above and beyond that of idiosyncratic risk, suggesting that the empirical results of this chapter cannot be explained solely by the negative discount on idiosyncratic risk documented by Ang et al. (2006) [4].

A Appendix

A.1 Proof of Proposition 2

We will prove the proposition in several steps. First, we examine the best risky strategy of the laggard, given that he invests some wealth in risky assets. The following lemma shows that within any group I, the laggard will not invest in more than one asset. In particular, the risky asset in group I chosen by the laggard is one in which the leader invests the least amount among all her investments in group I.

Lemma 6. *Given a strategy of the leader that satisfies condition (4) for all possible strategies of the laggard, and given that the laggard invests some wealth in risky assets, within each group I the laggard holds at most one risky asset. If the laggard invests in one asset in group I, then that asset belongs to the set Si ($\theta_{I,d}$), where*

$$S_I(\theta_{I,d}) = \underset{j \in \{1,\dots,N_I\}}{\arg\min} \theta_{I,d,j},$$

and where $\theta_{I,d}$ is the length N_I of the leader's group I portfolio and $\theta_{I,d,j}$ is the amount invested by the leader in asset j of group I.

Proof. Because the leader uses a strategy that satisfies condition (4) for all possible strategies of the laggard, minimizing (3) implies that the laggard prefers portfolios with higher expected return, higher variance, and lower covariance with the leader. Let us fix the portfolios that the laggard holds in the non-I groups, fix the amount that the laggard invests in group I, and examine the optimal portfolio within group I. Because all assets have the same distribution within group I, any portfolio yields the same expected return. Therefore, we can focus on how the choice of portfolio within group I affects the laggard's variance and covariance with the leader.

We now show that to maximize the variance of his portfolio, the laggard is strictly better off investing in a single asset of group I. The contribution of the group I portfolio to the total variance of the laggard takes place through the covariance terms of the laggard's group I portfolio with the laggard's other group portfolios and through the variance of the group I portfolio. By fixing the wealth that the laggard invests in group I, it is not difficult to show that the covariance terms of the group I portfolio with his non-group I portfolios do not depend on how he distributes his wealth across the assets in group I. However, the variance of the group I portfolio is maximized by investing in a single asset of group I because the correlation of any pair of assets in group I is less than one according to Eq. 5. Given that the assets across group I have identical distributions, the laggard is indifferent to which asset he holds.

Next, we show that to minimize the covariance of the laggard with the leader, the laggard is strictly better off investing in assets that belong to $S_i(\theta_{I,d})$, the set of assets in group I in which the leader invests the least amount. The covariance of the laggard's group I portfolio with the leader's portfolio depends on the covariance of the laggard's group I portfolio with the leader's non-group I portfolios and the covariance of the laggard's group I portfolio with the leader's group I portfolio. Again, by fixing the amount that the laggard invests in group I, the covariance of his group I portfolio with the leader's non-group I portfolios is kept constant. The covariance between the laggard's group I portfolio and the leader's group I portfolio can be expressed as follows:

$$Cov(r_{I,d}, r_{I,g}) = \theta'_{I,d} \Sigma_I \theta_{i,g},$$

where $r_{I,d}$ is the return on the leader's group I portfolio, $r_{I,g}$ is the return on the laggard's group I portfolio, $\theta_{I,d}$ is the leader's group I portfolio, $\theta_{I,g}$ is the laggard's group I portfolio, and Σ_I is the covariance matrix of group I. Because all assets in group I have the same distribution, Σ_I can be written as follows:

$$\Sigma_I = \sigma_i^2(\rho_I \Omega + (1 - \rho_I)I),$$

where Ω is an $N_I \times N_I$ matrix of ones and I is the $N_I \times N_I$ identity matrix. Now we can express the covariance between the laggard's group I portfolio and the leader's group I portfolio as:

$$Cov(r_{I,d}, r_{i,g}) = \sigma_i^2(\rho_I + (1 - \rho_I)\theta'_{I,d}\theta_{I,g}).$$

Therefore, the laggard can minimize this covariance by investing in group I assets that belong to $S_I(\theta_{I,d})$. From a covariance point of view, it does not matter how the laggard distributes his wealth within the assets in $S_I(\theta_{I,d})$. However, taking into account that the laggard wants to maximize his variance, he is strictly better off investing in a single asset in $S_I(\theta_{I,d})$.

We further examine the best risky strategy of the laggard, given that he invests some wealth in risky assets. The following lemma shows that the laggard will invest in only a single risky asset out of all risky assets in the economy.

Lemma 7. *Given a strategy of the leader that satisfies condition (4) for all possible strategies of the laggard, and given that the laggard invests some wealth in risky assets, then the laggard invests in a single risky asset.*

Proof. Using Lemma 6, the risky strategy of the laggard can be characterized by a length G vector θ_g, $\theta'_g 1 = 1$, that reflects his investment in a single asset of each group.

Let θ_d represent the portion that the leader invests in every group, such that $\theta'_d 1 = 1$. Let w_d be the portion that the leader invests in risky assets, and let w_g be the portion that the laggard invests in risky assets. Let μ be the length G vector of expected returns for groups. Let $\tilde{\Sigma}$ be the $G \times G$ covariance matrix for individual assets across different groups, and let $\hat{\Sigma}$ be the $G \times G$ covariance matrix that reflects the covariance of the G assets chosen by the laggard with the G portfolios chosen by the leader from each group. Finally, let Var_d be the variance of the risky portfolio of the leader. We can then write the laggard's problem as:

$$Min_{\theta_g} U(\theta_g) = \frac{k(w_d \theta'_d \mu + 1 - w_d) - (w_g \theta'_g \mu + 1 - w_g)}{\sqrt{k^2 w_d^2 Var_d - 2k w_g w_d \theta'_d \hat{\Sigma} \theta_g + w_g^2 \theta'_g \tilde{\Sigma} \theta_g}}. \tag{31}$$

Now we will show that the best response of the laggard is not only to invest in a single asset from every group, but also to invest in a specific group among all groups. In other words, $\theta_g = E_i$, where E_i is a vector of zeros except for entry i, which is one. By showing this, we will conclude that given an investment in risky assets, the best response of the laggard is to invest in a single risky asset out of all risky assets in the economy.

Assume by contradiction that the best response of the laggard is not to invest in a single asset. In this case, there must be a pair of groups I and J where he invests a portion of his risky portfolio in w_i^* and w_j^*. Due to the short sales constraint, it must be that $0 < w_i^*, w_j^* < 1$. We can examine strategies in which the laggard transfers wealth z from I to J and invests $w_i = w_i^* + z$ and $w_i = w_j^* - z$ in a single asset of group I and a single asset of group J. Now we can write the objective function of the laggard as $U(z)$ instead of $U(\theta_g)$.

Consider the unconstrained problem of the laggard, when short sales are allowed, and solve for z. First, note that $U(z)$ is continuous for all z because its denominator represents the variance of the wealth difference between the players.

This variance cannot be zero because if the leader chooses a single asset out of every group, Lemma 6 has shown that the laggard will choose a different asset than the leader out of every group. Therefore, it must be that the portfolios of the two players are different. Now the optimality of w_i^* and w_j^* and the fact that $0 < w_i^*$, $w_j^* < 1$ guarantee that $z = 0$ is a local minimum for this problem. At this point, $U(z = 0)$, the value of the objective function of the laggard, is positive because the leader has a higher expected wealth than the laggard. Note that in the unconstrained problem of the laggard, he can increase the weight on the security (either i or j) that has higher expected return, and by doing so, he can obtain negative values for $U(z)$. Alternatively, if both assets have the same expected return, he can increase the weight on one of them, taking the denominator to infinity and the value of the objective function $U(z)$ to zero. Therefore, since $U(z = 0) > 0$ and $z = 0$ is a local minimum, the function $U(z)$ must have at least one maximum point. Hence, $U(z)$ has at least two extremum points. However, it is not difficult to show that the function $U(z)$ is of the form:

$$U(z) = \frac{a + bz}{\sqrt{Az^2 + Bz + C}}. \tag{32}$$

By taking the first derivative of $U(z)$, it is easy to show that each member in this family of functions has at most one extremum point, which leads to a contradiction. Hence, the laggard will invest only in one risky asset.

Next, we will introduce the risk-free asset into the analysis. We will show that if the laggard invests in a risky asset, he will not invest in the risk-free asset as well:

Lemma 8. *Given a strategy of the leader that satisfies condition (4) for all possible strategies of the laggard, the laggard will not invest both in a risky asset and in the risk-free asset.*

Proof. This proof is similar to the previous one. We assume by contradiction that the best response of the laggard is to invest both in a risky asset and in the risk-free asset. We let z be the amount invested in the risky portfolio. Now we observe that $U(z)$ must still obey Eq. 32, and therefore we can use the same line of reasoning to show that the laggard must either invest all his wealth in the risk-free asset or all his wealth in the risky portfolio.

We use Lemmas 7 and 8 to conclude that the best response of the laggard is to invest in a single asset, either a risky asset or the risk-free asset. In the event that the laggard invests in a risky asset of some group I, he is indifferent among the assets in group I that belongs to $S_I(\theta_{I,d})$, and therefore any mixed strategy across $S_I(\theta_{I,d})$ is a best response as well.

A.2 Proof of Proposition 3

In this section, we provide a sketch of the proof of Proposition 3. Let us first consider the leader's investment in non-V groups, and then her investment in group V.

The following discussion will show that if the laggard invests in a single asset chosen uniformly by a mixed strategy over group V, the leader will invest the same amount in each of the assets in the non-V groups. Choosing a portfolio that is different from the equally weighted portfolio for some group $we \neq V$ will not change the leader's expected return and the covariance with the laggard. However, it will increase the variance of the leader's portfolio because the covariance between groups will remain the same, whereas the variance of the group V portfolio will increase. Therefore, not investing in an equally weighted portfolio within a non-V group decreases the value of the leader's objective function.

What is left to show is that for N_v large enough, the leader will invest the same amount in each of the assets in group V. When she chooses a portfolio within group V, the leader faces a tradeoff between a preference for lower variance and a preference for higher covariance with the laggard. Although any portfolio within group V yields the same expected return on the leader's portfolio, choosing the equally weighted portfolio is the best choice for reducing the overall variance of the leader's portfolio. However, the leader might be induced to invest in other portfolios within group v to increase her covariance with the laggard. For example, she could choose only a single asset in group V, hoping that the laggard chooses the same asset. We will show that when N_V is large enough, the leader is better off concentrating on decreasing her variance because the large number of assets makes it impossible for the leader to find a portfolio that yields higher covariance with the laggard in a way that offsets the variance inefficiency resulting from not investing in the equally weighted portfolio. This proof uses only one group in the economy, group V, but it can be generalized to many groups. The presence of more groups in the economy does not change the nature of the covariance-variance tradeoff faced by the leader.

Let w_d be the portion invested in the risky assets by the leader. Let μ be the expected return of asset v, and let θ be the risky portfolio of the leader within group V. Let ρ be the correlation of any pair in group V, and let n be the number of assets in group V. Given the mixed strategy of the laggard, the leader seeks a risky portfolio θ to maximize:

$$U_n(\theta) = \frac{1}{n} \sum_{j=1}^{n} \Phi \left(\frac{k(\mu w_d + 1 - w_d) - \mu}{\sigma \sqrt{1 - 2kw_d(\rho + (1-\rho)\theta_j) + k^2 w_d^2(\rho + (1-\rho)\theta'\theta)}} \right) \quad (33)$$

First, we will characterize the general form of the leader's solution to this problem.

Lemma 9. *The portfolio that maximizes the function $U_n(\theta)$ takes the following form:*

$$\theta = z\frac{1}{n}\iota + (1-z)E_j;\ j \in \{1,\ldots,n\}. \tag{34}$$

In other words, it is a linear combination of the equally weighted portfolio and a single asset j, where z is the amount invested in the equally weighted portfolio.

The leader's response reflects the tradeoff between variance and covariance with the laggard. If the leader wants to minimize variance, she should invest in the equally weighted portfolio. However, if she wants to maximize the covariance with the laggard, then the prospect of a successful bet on the laggard's asset might increase the covariance with the laggard. The solution reflects this tradeoff because it is a linear combination of the equally weighted portfolio and a single asset j.

Lemma 10. *There exists an n_0 such that for every $n > n_0$, the equally weighted portfolio is a local maximum.*

Proof. Now the leader solves for z to find the weight invested in the equally weighted portfolio. Without loss of generality, the leader invests $(1 - z)$ in asset 1. We can express the leader's problem as a function of n, the number of assets in group V, as follows:

$$U_n(z) = \frac{n-1}{n}\Phi\left(\frac{A}{\sqrt{f_n(z)}}\right) + \frac{1}{n}\Phi\left(\frac{A}{\sqrt{g_n(z)}}\right). \tag{35}$$

where the expected value of the wealth difference between the players is A. In addition, the variance of the wealth difference between the players in the event that the laggard chooses an asset other than asset 1 is expressed as a function of z, the weight invested in the equally weighted portfolio is:

$$f_n(z) = 1 - 2kw_d\left(\rho + (1-\rho)\left[\frac{z}{n}\right]\right) + k^2w_d^2$$
$$\times \left(\rho + (1-\rho)\left[\frac{z(2-z)}{n} + (1-z)^2\right]\right), \tag{36}$$

and the variance of the wealth difference between the players in the event that the laggard chooses asset 1 is:

$$g_n(z) = f_n(z) - 2kw_d(1-\rho)(1-z). \tag{37}$$

Algebraic manipulations show that $U_n(z = 1) = 0$. Hence, we conclude that the equally weighted portfolio is an extremum point. Moreover, the second derivative of the objective function at $z = 1$ converges to a negative number as the number of assets in V goes to infinity:

$$\lim Un(z = 1) < 0. \tag{38}$$

We conclude that there is an n_0 such that for all $n > n_0$, the equally weighted portfolio is a local maximum.

Lemma 11. *There exists an n_0 such that for every $n > n_0$, the equally weighted portfolio is a global maximum.*

Proof. Given that the solution for this problem has the form of (34), algebraic manipulations show that any extremum must be a local maximum for n large enough. Because the equally weighted portfolio is a local maximum, for large enough n, there cannot be any other local maxima; if there were, then the continuity of $U_n(z)$ implies that there should also be a local minimum point between these maxima. This contradicts our previous observation that for n large enough, any extremum point must be a local maximum.

A.3 Conditions for Theorem 4

1. N_V should be large enough in the sense of Proposition 3.
2. Conditions to have the laggard not deviate from investing in asset v:

   (a) $\sigma_v > \sqrt{2}\sigma_j \forall j \in \{1, \ldots, g\}$.
   (b) $\sigma_{v,j} > 0 \forall j \neq v$.
   (c) $\sigma_v > 2\sigma_V$.
   (d) $k(\theta'\tilde{\mu} + 1) > (\tilde{\mu}_j + 1)\forall j \in \{1, \ldots, g\}$.

3. Conditions to have the leader refrain from taking a short position in the risk-free asset or in any of the risky assets:

   (a) $0 < \Psi^{-1}\iota'\Sigma^{-1}\tilde{\mu} + 1 < k$.
   (b) $E_j\Sigma^{-1}\tilde{\mu} > 0 \forall j \neq v$.
   (c) $E_v\Sigma^{-1}\tilde{\mu} > -\Psi$.

   where $\sigma_{v,j}$ is the covariance between an asset in group V and an asset in group J, σ_j is the volatility of an individual asset of group J, σ_V is the volatility of group V, Σ is the covariance matrix for groups, $\tilde{\mu}$ is the expected excess return over the groups, E_j is a vector of zeros except for entry j, which is one, N_V is the number of assets in group V, θ is the optimal portfolio of the leader, and $\Psi = \dfrac{k-1}{\sigma_v^2 - \sigma_V^2}$

A.4 Proof of Theorem 4

By setting $A = \tilde{\mu}' \, \Sigma^{-1} \tilde{\mu}$, we can perform the following simplification:

$$\theta' \tilde{\mu} = xA + y_v,$$

$$\theta' \Sigma \theta = x^2 A + 2xy\tilde{\mu}_v + y^2 \sigma_V^2,$$

$$\theta' \Sigma Ev = x\tilde{\mu}_v + y\sigma_V^2.$$

Now we can write the leader's problem as:

$$Max_{(x,y)} \frac{k([xA + y\tilde{\mu}_v] + 1) - (\tilde{\mu}_v + 1)}{\sqrt{k^2 \left[x^2 A + 2xy\tilde{\mu}_v + y^2 \sigma_V^2\right] - 2k\left[x\tilde{\mu}_v + y\sigma_V^2\right] + \sigma_v^2}}. \tag{39}$$

Taking the first-order conditions for x and y and equating both to zero lead to the solution:

$$x = \frac{\sigma_v^2 - \sigma_V^2}{k(k-1)},$$

$$y = \frac{1}{k}.$$

So the leader's risky portfolio over all groups is:

$$\theta = \frac{\sigma_v^2 - \sigma_V^2}{k(k-1)} \Sigma^{-1} \tilde{\mu} + \frac{1}{k} E_v. \tag{40}$$

Given the leader's strategy, we revisit the problem of the laggard and find the conditions required to keep the laggard investing only in group V. Because the laggard invests only in a single risky asset or in the risk-free asset, we examine his utility from investing in asset j (note that the laggard is interested in minimizing U_j):

$$U_j = \frac{k(\theta' \tilde{\mu} + 1) - (\tilde{\mu}_j + 1)}{\sqrt{k^2 \theta' \Sigma \theta - 2k\theta' \Sigma E_j + \sigma_j^2}}. \tag{41}$$

Substituting the investment of the leader, we obtain:

$$U_j = \frac{k\left(xA + \frac{\tilde{\mu}_v}{k} + 1\right) - (\tilde{\mu}_j + 1)}{\sqrt{k^2 \left[x^2 A + 2x\frac{\tilde{\mu}_v}{k} + \frac{\sigma_V^2}{k^2}\right] - 2k\left[x\tilde{\mu}_j + \frac{\sigma_{v,j}}{k}\right] + \sigma_j^2}}. \tag{42}$$

We examine the conditions to guarantee that $U_v < U_j$ for all j. The conditions are algebraically complex, but we can find simple sufficient conditions to satisfy this inequality:

1. $\sigma_{v,j} > 0 \forall j$.
2. $\sigma_v > \sqrt{2}\sigma_j \forall j$.
3. $\sigma_v > 2\sigma_V$.

Restricting the analysis to strategies that are symmetric within each group, Proposition 2 implies that in Nash equilibrium, the laggard must use a mixed strategy in which he invests in a single risky asset chosen uniformly over a specific group or over several groups. The conditions above guarantee that the laggard prefers an asset from group V to an asset from any other group. Therefore, he will use a mixed strategy only over group V. Because the unique best response of the leader is determined by solving her maximization problem, this equilibrium is unique among strategies that are symmetric within each group.

References

1. Liu H (2008) Portfolio insurance, underdiversification, and idiosyncratic risks. Working Paper
2. Kumar A (2009) Who gambles in the stock market? J Finance 64(4):1889–1933
3. Bali TG, Cakici N, Whitelaw RF (2011) Maxing out: stocks as lotteries and the cross-section of expected returns. J Financ Econ 99(2):427–446
4. Ang A, Hodrick RJ, Xing Y, Zhang X (2006) The cross-section of volatility and expected returns. J Finance 61(1):259–299
5. Merton RC (1987) A simple model of capital market equilibrium with incomplete information. J Finance 42(3):483–510
6. Fama EF, French KR (1993) Common risk factors in the returns on stocks and bonds. J Financ Econ 33(1):3–56
7. Carhart MM (1997) On persistence in mutual fund performance. J Finance 52(1):57–82
8. Smith A The wealth of nations. Random House, New York (1776, Reprint 1937)
9. Marx K (1849) Wage-labour and capital. International Publishers, New York
10. Veblen T (1965) The theory of the leisure class. MacMillan, New York (1899, Reprint)
11. Duesenberry JS (1949) Income, saving, and the theory of consumer behavior. Harvard University Press, Cambridge, MA
12. Brown KC, Harlow WV, Starks LT (1996) Of tournaments and temptations: an analysis of managerial incentives in the mutual fund industry. J Finance 51(1): 85–110. http://ideas.repec.org/a/bla/jfinan/v51y1996i1p85-110.html
13. Heffetz O, Frank RH (2008) Preferences for status: evidence and economic implications. Handbook Soc Econ 1:69–91
14. Frank RH (1985) The demand for unobservable and other nonpositional goods. Am Econ Rev 75(1):101–116
15. Robson AJ (1992) Status, the distribution of wealth, private and social attitudes to risk. Econometrica 60(4): 837–857. http://ideas.repec.org/a/ecm/emetrp/v60y1992i4p837-57.html
16. Becker GS, Murphy KM, Werning I (2005) The equilibrium distribution of income and the market for status. J Polit Econ 113(2): 282–310. http://ideas.repec.org/a/ucp/jpolec/v113y2005i2p282-310.html
17. Frank RH (1985) Choosing the right pond: human behavior and the quest for status. Oxford University Press, New York

18. Frank RH Are positional externalities different from other externalities? J Pub Econ (forthcoming)
19. Kempf A, Ruenzi S (2008) Tournaments in mutual fund families. Rev Financ Stud 21 (2):1013–1036
20. Cabral LMB (2002) Increasing dominance with no efficiency effect. J Econ Theory 102 (2):471–479
21. Cabral LMB (2003) R&D competition when firms choose variance. J Econ Manage Strat 12 (1):139–150. http://ideas.repec.org/a/bla/jemstr/v12y2003i1p139-150.html
22. Anderson A, Cabral LMB (2007) Go for broke or play it safe? Dynamic competition with choice of variance. Rand J Econ 38(3):593–609
23. Buunk AP, Gibbons FX (2007) Social comparison: the end of a theory and the emergence of a field. Organ Behav Hum Decis Process 102(1):3–21
24. Blanton H, Gibbons FX, Buunk AP, Kuyper H (1999) When better-than-others compare upward: choice of comparison and comparative evaluation as independent predictors of academic performance. J Pers Soc Psychol 76(3):420–430
25. Schoenberg E, Haruvy E Relative wealth concerns in asset markets: an experimental approach. Working Paper
26. Hansen LP (1982) Large sample properties of generalized method of moments estimators. Econometrica 50(4):1029–1054
27. Krasny Y (2011) The effect of social status on decision making in financial networks. Quart J Finan. 1(3):495–549
28. Friedman M, Savage LJ (1948) The utility analysis of choices involving risk. J Polit Econ 56 (4):279–304
29. Cole HL, Mailath GJ, Postlewaite A (2001) Investment and concern for relative position. Rev Econ Des 6(2):241–261
30. Abel AB (1990) Asset prices under habit formation and catching up with the Joneses. Am Econ Rev 80(2):38–42
31. Demarzo PM, Kaniel R, Kremer I (2004) Diversification as a public good: community effects in portfolio choice. J Finance 59(4):1677–1716
32. Lauterbach B, Reisman H (2004) Keeping up with the Joneses and the home bias. Eur Financ Manage 10(2):225–234
33. Roussanov NL (2010) Diversification and its discontents: idiosyncratic and entrepreneurial risk in the quest for social status. J Finan 65(5):1755–1788. http://ideas.repec.org/a/bla/jfinan/v65y2010i5p1755-1788.html
34. Robson AJ (1996) The evolution of attitudes to risk: lottery tickets and relative wealth. Game Econ Behav 14(2):190–207
35. Barberis N, Huang M (2008) Stocks as lotteries: the implications of probability weighting for security prices. Am Econ Rev 98(5):2066–2100
36. Kahneman D, Tversky A (1979) Prospect theory: an analysis of decision under risk. Econometrica 47(2):263–291
37. Brunnermeier MK, Gollier C, Parker JA (2007) Optimal beliefs, asset prices, and the preference for skewed returns. Am Econ Rev 97(2):159–165
38. Van Nieuwerburgh S, Veldkamp L (2010) Information acquisition and under-diversification. Rev Econ Stud 77(2):779–805
39. DeMarzo P, Kaniel R, Kremer I (2007) Technological innovation and real investment booms and busts. J Financ Econ 85(3):735–754
40. DeMarzo PM, Kaniel R, Kremer I (2008) Relative wealth concerns and financial bubbles. Rev Financ Stud 21(1):19–50
41. Altshuler Y, Pan W, Pentland A (2012) Trends prediction using social diffusion models. In: Proceedings of international conference on social computing, behavioral-cultural modeling, and prediction
42. Brunnermeier MK, Nagel S (2004) Hedge funds and the technology bubble. J Finance 59 (5):2013–2040

43. Elton EJ, Gruber MJ, Blake CR, Krasny Y, Ozelge S (2010) The effect of the frequency of holdings data on conclusions about **mutual** fund management behavior. J Bank Finan 34(5):135–146
44. Chen HL, Pennacchi GG (2009) Does prior performance affect a mutual fund's choice of risk? Theory and further empirical evidence. J Financ Quant Anal 44(4):745–775
45. Chevalier J, Ellison G (1997) Risk taking by mutual funds as a response to incentives. J Polit Econ 105(6):1167–1200
46. Chevalier J, Ellison G (1999) Career concerns of mutual fund managers. Q J Econ 114 (2):389–432
47. Altshuler Y, Aharony N, Fire M, Elovici Y, Pentland A (2011) Incremental learning with accuracy prediction of social and individual properties from mobile-phone data. CoRR
48. Altshuler Y, Fire M, Aharony N, Elovici Y, Pentland A (2012) How many makes a crowd? On the correlation between groups' size and the accuracy of modeling. In: Proceedings of international conference on social computing, behavioral-cultural modeling, and prediction
49. Eagle N, Pentland A, Lazer D (2009) Inferring social network structure using mobile phone data. P Natl Acad Sci (PNAS) 15:274–278
50. Blondel VD, Guillaume JL, Lambiotte R, Lefebvre E (2008) Fast unfolding of communities in large networks. J Statis Mech: Theor Exper 2008:P10008
51. Newman M (2003) The structure and function of complex networks. SIAM Rev 45:167–256
52. Watts D, Strogatz S (1998) Collective dynamics of "small-world" networks. Nature 393 (6684):440–442
53. Fama EF (1996) Multifactor portfolio efficiency and multifactor asset pricing. J Financ Quant Anal 31(4):441–465
54. Fama EF, MacBeth JD (1973) Risk, return, and equilibrium: empirical tests. J Polit Econ 81 (3):607–636
55. Pastor L, Stambaugh RF (2003) Liquidity risk and expected stock returns. J Polit Econ 111 (3):642–685
56. French KR, Schwert GW, Stambaugh RF (1987) Expected stock returns and volatility. J Financ Econ 19(1):3–29
57. Lewellen J, Nagel S (2006) The conditional CAPM does not explain asset-pricing anomalies. J Financ Econ 82(2):289–314
58. Dimson E (1979) Risk measurement when shares are subject to infrequent trading. J Financ Econ 7(2):197–226
59. Blume ME (1971) On the assessment of risk. J Finance 26(1):1–10
60. Newey WK, West KD (1987) A simple, positive semi-definite, heteroscedasticity and autocorrelation-consistent covariance matrix. Econometrica 55(3):703–708
61. Cochrane J (2005) Asset pricing, 2nd edn. Princeton University Press, Princeton
62. Ferson WE, Harvey CR (1999) Conditioning variables and the cross-section of stock returns. J Finance 54(4):1325–1360
63. Nyberg P (2008) The dynamic behavior of the idiosyncratic volatility discount: aggregate idiosyncratic volatility and return reversals revisited. Working Paper
64. Lahart J (2008) Bernanke's bubble laboratory. Wall Street J. http://online.wsj.com/article/SB121089412378097011.html

Stealing Reality: When Criminals Become Data Scientists (or Vice Versa)

Yaniv Altshuler, Nadav Aharony, Yuval Elovici, Alex Pentland, and Manuel Cebrian

Abstract In this paper, we discuss the threat of malware targeted at extracting information about the relationships in a real-world social network as well as characteristic information about the individuals in the network, a type of attack which we dub *Stealing Reality*. We explain how *Stealing Reality* attacks differ from traditional types of attacks against individuals' privacy and discuss why their impact is significantly more dangerous than that of other attacks such as identity theft. We then analyze this new form of attack and show what an optimal attack strategy would look like. Surprisingly, it differs significantly from many conventional network attacks in that it involves extremely slow spreading patterns. We point out that besides yielding the best outcome for the attackers, such an attack may also deceive existing monitoring tools because of its low traffic volumes and the fact that it imitates natural end-user communication patterns.

This chapter is based on a paper that was published in IEEE Journal of Intelligent Systems, 26(6), 2011.

Y. Altshuler (✉) • N. Aharony • A. Pentland
MIT Media Lab, Massachusetts Institute of Technology, Cambridge, MA 02139, USA
e-mail: yanival@media.mit.edu; nadav@media.mit.edu; sandy@media.mit.edu

Y. Elovici
Telekom Innovation Lab, Information Systems Engineering, Ben Gurion University,
P.O.B. 653, Beer Sheva 84105, Israel
e-mail: elovici@bgu.ac.il

M. Cebrian
Department of Computer Science and Engineering, University of California San Diego,
La Jolla, CA 92093, USA
e-mail: cebrian@mit.edu

Y. Altshuler et al. (eds.), *Security and Privacy in Social Networks*,
DOI 10.1007/978-1-4614-4139-7_7, © Springer Science+Business Media New York 2013

1   Introduction

We live in the age of social computing. Social networks are everywhere, are exponentially increasing in volume, and are changing everything about our lives, the way we do business, and how we understand ourselves and the world around us. The challenges and opportunities residing in the social-oriented ecosystem have overtaken scientific, financial, and popular discourse. With the growing emphasis on personalization, personal recommendation systems, and social networking, there is a growing interest in understanding personal and social behavior patterns. This trend is manifested in the growing demand for *"data scientists"* and data-mining experts in the commercial ecosystem, which in turn is derived from the increasing number of social data-driven startup companies as well the social inference-related research sponsored by other commercial entities and various NGOs.

This work is somewhat of a "what-if" exploration. History has shown that whenever something has a tangible value associated with it, there will always be those who will try to steal it for profit. Along this line of thought – based on current trends in the data ecosystem coupled with the emergence of advanced tools for social and behavioral pattern detection and inference – we ask the following question: *What will happen when the criminals become data scientists?*

We conjecture that the world will increasingly see malware that integrates tools and mechanisms from network science into its arsenal, as well as attacks that directly target human-network information as a goal rather than a means. Paraphrasing Marshall McLuhan's *"the medium is the message,"* we have reached the stage where *"the network is the message."*

Specifically, we point out a new type of information security threat: a class of malware, the goal of which is not to corrupt the machines it infects, to take control of them, or to steal explicit information stored on them (e.g., credit-card information and personal records). Rather, the goal of this type of attack is to steal social network and behavioral information through data collection and network science inference techniques. We call this type of attack a *"Stealing Reality"* attack.

After characterizing the properties of this new kind of attack, we analyze how it could be carried out. We reveal the optimal strategy for attackers interested in learning a social network and its hidden underlying social principles. Remarkably, our analysis shows that such an optimal strategy involves in many cases an extremely slow spreading pattern. Counterintuitively, such attacks generate far greater damage in the long term than more aggressively spreading attacks. In addition, such attacks are likely to avoid detection by many of today's network security mechanisms, which tend to focus on detecting network traffic anomalies such as an increase in traffic volume. We demonstrate this surprising new discovery using several real-world social network datasets.

The rest of this chapter is organized as follows: related work is discussed in Sect. 2, after which Sect. 3 describes the threat model of the *Stealing Reality* social network attack. Section 4 presents an analysis of the attack as well as the optimal attack strategy. Section 5 introduces the concept of the "social learnability" of a network, while Sect. 6 summarizes experimental results. Concluding remarks are given in Sect. 7. This chapter is an extended version of a work that was originally published in *IEEE Journal of Intelligent Systems* [1].

2 Background and Related Work

In recent years, the social sciences have been undergoing a digital revolution, heralded by the emerging field of "computational social science." Lazer et al. [2] have described the potential of computational social science to increase our knowledge of individuals, groups, and societies with unprecedented breadth, depth, and scale. Computational social science combines the leading techniques from network science [3-6] with new machine learning and pattern recognition tools that are specialized for understanding people's behavior and their social interactions [7-10].

The pervasiveness of mobile phones the world over has made them ubiquitous social sensors of location, proximity, and communications. The term *"Reality Mining,"* coined in [11], describes the collection of sensor data pertaining to human social behavior. Using call records, cellular-tower IDs, and Bluetooth proximity logs collected from individual mobile phones, the subjects' social network can be accurately detected, as well as their regular patterns of daily activity [9, 11]. Mobile phone records from telecommunications companies have proven to be highly valuable for uncovering individual-level insights: cell-tower location information can be used to characterize human mobility and has revealed that humans follow simple reproducible mobility patterns [12]. Eagle et al. found that the diversity of individuals' relationships is strongly correlated with the level of economic development of communities [13]. On the one hand, data gathered through service providers include information on very large numbers of subjects, but on the other hand, this information is constrained to a specific domain (email messages, financial transactions, etc.), and there is very little if any contextual information on the subjects themselves. The alternative approach of gathering data at the individual level makes it possible to collect many more dimensions of data related to the end user, data which are often not available at the operator level.

Madan [14] expanded the work of Eagle and Pentland [11] to show how mobile social sensing can be used to measure and predict the health status of individuals based on their mobility and communication patterns. They also examined the spread of political opinion within communities [15].

Already, companies like *Sense Networks* are putting such tools to use in the commercial world to understand customer churn, to enhance targeted advertisements, and to offer improved personalization and other services. The technical advancements in mobile phone platforms and the availability of mobile software development kits (SDKs) are making the collection of *Reality Mining* data easier than ever before.

3   *Stealing Reality*: The Threat Model

In our discussion, the term "reality information" refers to inferred information about human personal and social behavior. This includes: (1) information on individuals, which we call "node information" (including any attribute of a node that can be learned from available data, such as occupation, level of income, health state, personality type, etc.); (2) dyadic information, which is information on relationships and other attributes of connections between two nodes (called "edge information"); (3) network-level information, which is information on groups of nodes, communities, and general network properties and information. The full set of network information also includes all data on nodes and edges as well. As mentioned above, we do not here consider explicitly stated information, such as names and social-security or credit-card numbers, that can be found in (and stolen from) existing databases. In the same way that *Reality Mining* is the legitimate collection and analysis of such information, *Reality Stealing* is the illegitimate acquisition of it.

3.1   *Motivation for Attackers*

There already exist secondary markets for resale of stolen identities, such as www.infochimps.com, and black-market sites and chat rooms for resale of other illegal datasets [16]. It is reasonable to assume that the email address of a "social hub" would be worth more to an advertiser than that of a "social leaf" and that personal information matching the profile of a student might be priced differently than information matching that of a corporate executive. There are already companies operating in this area that are engaged in the collection of email and demographic information with the intention of selling it [17]. Methods of social network analysis and trend recognition have already been published in many leading venues [18]. Why work hard when one can release automatic agents that can collect the same, and possibly much higher-quality, information? *Stolen Reality* information could be used for several malicious goals:

- Selling to the highest bidder (both "legitimate" bidders such as advertisers, etc., or in the black market to other attackers) [19].
- Bootstrapping other attacks as part of a complex *"Advanced Persistent Threats"* (APT) attack [20–22].
- Business espionage, e.g., analyzing a competitor's customer base and profiling high-yield customers for targeted marketing [23] or producing high-quality predictions [24].

3.2   Why Are Reality Stealing Attacks So Dangerous?

Communication network topologies and network device identifiers can be modified with the press of a button. The same goes for passwords, usernames, and credit-card numbers. Email and online accounts can be easily replaced, and the user's contacts can be quickly warned of the breach. However, it is much harder to change one's social network, person-to-person relationships, friendships, or family ties. If a chronic health condition is uncovered through such an attack, this discovery cannot be undone. The victim of a "behavioral pattern" theft cannot change her behavior and life patterns. This type of information, once out, is very hard to contain.

A second component that accentuates this danger is that real-life information can be deduced from seemingly "safe" data, like accelerometer and location information, which users already freely allow many mobile applications to access.

Because we believe that this threat is concrete, the goal of this paper is to analyze potential attacks from the attackers' perspective so that such attacks can be better understood and proper defenses can be developed. We primarily discuss attacks performed on mobile phones.

3.3   Past Attacks on Real-World Information

To help understand the risk in attacks on inferred real-world information, we here review past attacks on explicit data. In 2008, real identity information on millions of Korean citizens was stolen in a series of malicious attacks and posted for sale [25]. In 2007, the Israel Ministry of the Interior's database, with information on every Israeli citizen, was leaked and posted on the Web [26]. More recently, a court ruling is awaited on whether the database of a bankrupt gay dating site for teenagers will be sold to raise money to repay its creditors (the site includes personal information on over a million teenage boys [27]). In all these cases, once the information is out, there is no way back, and the damage will be felt for a long time thereafter. In a recent *Wall Street Journal* interview, former *Google* CEO Eric Schmidt referred to the possibility that people in the future might choose to change their names legally to detach themselves from embarrassing "reality" information publicity exposed on social networking sites. This demonstrates the sensitivity of this problem and the challenges in recovering from leakage of real-life information, whether by youthful carelessness or by malicious extraction through an attack [28, 29].

Many existing viruses and worms use primitive forms of *"social engineering"* [30] as a means of spreading to gain the trust of their next victims and cause them to click on a link or install an application. For example, *Happy99* was one of the first viruses to attach itself to outgoing emails, thus increasing the chances of having the recipient open an attachment to a seemingly legitimate message sent by a known acquaintance. Contemporary malware still uses similar techniques for seeding attacks, a recent example being *Operation Aurora*, a sophisticated attack originating in China against dozens of U.S. companies during the first half of 2009; the attack was initiated by links spread through a popular Korean instant messaging application [25] which has been associated with the idea of "*Advanced Persistent Threats*," or APTs [20, 21]. Further information on security and privacy leakage in social networks can be found in [31, 32].

4   Social Attack Model

We shall model the social network as an undirected graph $G(V,E)$. A *Stealing Reality* attacker's first goal is to inject a single malware agent into one of the network's nodes. Upon injection, the agent starts to "learn" this node and its interactions with its neighbors. Periodically, the agent tries to copy itself into one of the original node's neighbors. The probability that an agent tries to copy itself to a neighboring node at any given time step is called the *aggressiveness* of the attack and is denoted as ρ. Aggressive agents have higher value of ρ (and hence take shorter periods of time between any two spreading attempts), whereas less aggressive agents are less likely to try to spread at any given time and will wait longer on average between attempts to copy themselves to one of the neighbors of their current host.

As information about the network itself has become a worthy cause for an attack, the attacker's motivation has become to steal as many properties as possible related to the network's social topology. We shall denote the percentage of vertex-related information acquired at time t by $\Lambda_V(t)$ and the percentage of edge-related information acquired at time t by $\Lambda_E(t)$.

The duration of the learning process of the *Stealing Reality* attack is the time it takes the attacking agent to identify with high probability the properties of a node's behaviors or of some of its social interactions. We model this process using a standard *Gompertz function* in its parametric form $y(t) = ae^{be^{ct}}$ (with parameters a, b, and c). This model is flexible enough to fit various social learning mechanisms while providing the following important features: (a) sigmoidal advancement: the longer such an agent operates, the more precise its conclusions will be; (b) the rate at which information is gathered is lowest at the start and end of the learning process; (c) asymmetry of the asymptotes, which is implied by the fact that for any value of T, the amount of information gathered in the first T time steps is greater than the amount of information gathered in the last T time steps.

The applicability of the Gompertz function to model the evolution of local "learning" of the preferences and behavior patterns of users was demonstrated in [33], where a prediction of which applications mobile users will choose to install on their phones was generated using an ongoing learning process. This experiment showed that this process can be best modeled using the function $1-e^{-x}$. Because we know that $1-t < e^{-t}$ (with very tight results for most $t < 1$), we can clearly see that: $1-e^{-x} \approx e^{-e^{-x}x}$, which is an instance of the Gompertz function for $a = 1$, $b = c = -1$. The Gompertz function is frequently used to model a great variety of

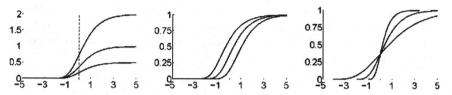

Fig. 1 Illustration of the Gompertz function. The charts represent the following functions (from *left* to *right*): $y = ae^{-e^t}$, $y = e^{-ae^t}$, and $y = e^{e^{-at}}$, for $a = \frac{1}{2}$, $a = 1$, and $a = 2$

processes due to the flexible way that it can be controlled using the parameters a, b, and c. Applications include mobile phone uptake [34], population growth in a confined space [35], and growth of tumors [36] (see illustration in Fig. 1).

An aggressive spreading pattern is more likely to be detected by users or administrators, resulting in the subsequent blocking of the attack. On the other hand, attacks that spread slowly may evade detection for a longer period of time, but the amount of data they gather will be limited. To predict the detection probability of the attack at time t, we shall use *Richard's Curve*, a generalized logistic function often used to model the detection of security attacks [37]:

$$P_{detect}(t) = \frac{1}{(1 + e^{-\rho(t-M)})^{\frac{1}{\rho}\sigma}} \tag{1}$$

where ρ is the *attack aggressiveness*, σ is a normalizing constant for the detection mechanism, and M denotes the normalizing constant for the system's initial state.

Let $I_u(t)$ be the infection indicator of u at time t, T_u be the initial infection time of u, and $p(u,t)$ the Gompertz function. Defining $\Lambda_V(t) = \frac{1}{|V|} \sum_{u \in V} I_u(t) \cdot p(u, t - T_u)$, we get:

$$\Lambda_V(\rho) = \int_0^\infty \left(\frac{\partial \Lambda_V(t)}{\partial t} \cdot \left(1 - p_{detect}(t) \right) \right) dt \tag{2}$$

5 *"Social Learnability"* – Obtaining the Social Essence of a Network

In this section, we define a mathematical measure that predicts the ability of an attacker to "steal," or acquire, a given social network, which we call the *social learnability* of a network. The measure reflects both the information contained in the network itself and the broader context from which the network was derived. After presenting the mathematical formulation of this measure, we demonstrate its importance by showing how it can sort several real-world social networks according to their complexity (which is known) and even group two very different social networks that were generated by the same group of people. We conclude by showing that the optimal learning process with respect to this new measure involves in many cases extremely nonaggressive attacks.

5.1 Information Complexity of Social Networks

This discussion of the information complexity of social networks can be best viewed as an extension of the line of research which studies various aspects of the complexity of reality. Among the most interesting works on this topic are those of Bennett [38, 39], which discuss concepts such as *logical depth, mutual information,* and *long-range order* of complex physical systems using a combination of thermodynamic and computational considerations.

In [40], the analysis and measurement of organization and complexity in nature is summarized as follows:

> The observed complexity of nature is often attributed to an intrinsic propensity of matter to self-organize under certain (e.g., dissipative) conditions. In order better to understand and test this vague thesis, we define complexity as "logical depth," a notion based on algorithmic information and computational time complexity. Informally, logical depth is the number of steps in the deductive or causal path connecting a thing with its plausible origin.

We believe that the structure and complexity of social networks derived through a similar self-organization tendency should be analyzed using similar methods.

Let us denote by K_E the *Kolmogorov complexity* [41] of the network, namely, the minimal number of bits required to "code" the network in such a way that it could later be completely restored. The Kolmogorov complexity of a network represents in fact the basic amount of information contained in a social network. For example, a military organization's network consists of highly homogeneous links and hierarchical structures repeated many times over. We would expect it to require a much shorter minimal description than, say, the social network of the residents of a metropolitan suburb. In the latter case, we would expect to see a highly heterogeneous network composed of many types of relationships (such as work relationships, physical proximity, family ties, and other intricate types of social relationships and group affiliations). For a given resident, some of his network connections will be primarily due to work relationships, while other connections will exist because of physical proximity to next-door neighbors, status as parents of friends of the person's children, and many other intricate types of social relationships and group affiliations of the person. We expect that the minimal amount of information required to describe this network will be much larger than in the first homogeneous network example.

5.2   Social Entropy of Social Networks

At this point, let us recall that every social reality network belongs to (one or more) "*social families*," each of which has its own consistency (or versatility). Some families may contain a great variety of possible networks, each having roughly a similar probability of occurrence, while another may consist of a very limited number of possible networks.

Note that the complexity of each network does not necessarily correlate with its entropy. Some families may consist of a low variety of highly complex networks, while other families may contain a great variety of relatively simple networks.

For example, let us assume that a country has three distinct types of urban cities as defined by planning laws (e.g., metropolitan centers, rural areas, and small towns). Each of the networks that are generated by these three types of cities may be highly complex. However, knowing the type of city under discussion can significantly assist in the reconstruction of its network (based on the fact that there are only three types of networks allowed).

Alternatively, we can imagine a military organization that by its nature tends to generate networks that are highly hierarchical and usually possess low randomness. However, because there are significantly large numbers of subgroups and functionalities in an army, each having its own network structure, having prior knowledge of the variety of networks one may encounter provides little help in the reconstruction of networks based on partial information (although the networks themselves can be expected to have low Kolmogorov complexity).

Let us define $\mathcal{G}_n$ to contain n random instances of networks of $|V|$ nodes that belong to the same *social family* as G. Let X_n be a discrete random variable with possibility values $\{x_1, x_2, \ldots, x_{n^{1/2}|V||V|-1}\}$ (corresponding to all possible graphs over $|V|$ nodes), taken according to the distribution of $\mathcal{G}_n$. The normalized social entropy of the network G can then be calculated by dividing the entropy of the variable X_n by the maximal entropy for graphs of $|V|$ nodes:

$$\lambda_n(G) \overset{\Delta}{=} \frac{H(X_n)}{\log_2 \zeta_{|V|}} \qquad (3)$$

where $\zeta_{|V|}$ denotes the number of distinct nonisomorphic simple graphs of $|V|$ nodes and can be obtained by applications such as *Nauty* [42] or calculated analytically using the Pólya enumeration theorem [43]. $\lambda(G)$ is then defined as: $\left|\lim_{n\to\infty}\lambda_n(\bar{G})\right.$.

Taking n to infinity, we get:

$$\lambda(G) \overset{\Delta}{=} \lim_{n\to\infty} \lambda_n(G)$$

The value of $\lambda(G)$ can be approximated for finite values of n using either a priori knowledge about the composition of G's social family or empirically by analyzing an artificially constructed set of networks of the same family. Such networks can be synthesized (if a generative model for this family is available) or taken from small subnetworks sampled from G.

5.3   Stealing the Social Essence of a Network

At this point, let us recall *Reed's Law* [44], which asserts that the utility of large networks (particularly social networks) can scale exponentially with the size of the network. This observation is derived from the fact that the number of possible subgroups of network participants is exponential in N (where N is the number of participants) and extends far beyond the N^2 scaling embodied in *Metcalfe's Law* [45] that was used to represent the value of telecommunication networks.

Extending this notion, we assert that a strong value emerges from learning the $2.\mathscr{I}$ "social principles" behind a network, denoting by $\mathscr{I}$ the amount of *information* that is encapsulated in a network.

Note that $2^{O(\mathscr{I})}$ is also an upper bound for the *value* that can be obtained from a structure of size $\mathscr{I}$ if we mathematically define a structure's value as the deepest state to which a Turing-equivalent computation system of $\mathscr{I}$ states can relax (which is also identical to the *Poincaré recurrence time* of a system with $\mathscr{I}$ degrees of freedom).

Assuming that at time t an attacker has stolen $|E|\Lambda_E(t)$ edges, then taking K_E as the maximal amount of information that can be coded in network G, we normalize it by the fraction of edges acquired thus far. Because K_E is measured in bits, the appropriate normalization should maintain this scale. By multiplying by $\lambda(G)$, the *normalized social entropy* of the network G, the amount of information in the network can be written as follows:

$$\mathscr{I} = \lambda(G) \cdot K_E \cdot \frac{\log_2\left(|E|\Lambda_E(t)\right)}{\log_2 |E|}$$

After normalizing by the overall "social essence" of the network (received for $\Lambda_E = 1$), the following expression results for the social essence of the acquired subnetwork:

$$\Lambda_S(t) = \frac{2^{\lambda(G)\cdot K_E \cdot \frac{\log_2(|E|\Lambda_E(t))}{\log_2|E|}}}{2^{\lambda(G)\cdot K_E}} = 2^{\lambda(G)\cdot K_E \cdot \frac{\log_2 \Lambda_E(t)}{\log_2|E|}}$$

which after some arithmetic yields:

$$\Lambda_S(t) = \Lambda_E(t)^{\frac{\lambda(G)\cdot K_E}{\log_2|E|}} \tag{4}$$

Note that K_E represents the *network* complexity, whereas $\lambda(G)$ represents the complexity of its *social family*.

At this point, we assert that our *social learnability measure* presented above is indeed a valuable property for measuring network attacks. To support this assertion, we demonstrate the values of this measure for several different real-world networks. Figure 2 presents an analysis of the networks derived from the *Social Evolution* experiment [14, 46], the *Reality Mining* network [9], and the *Friends and Family* [47] experiment. One can easily see the logic behind the predictions

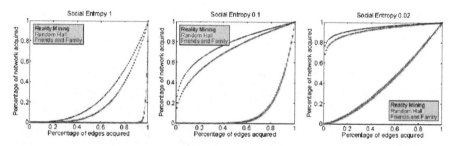

Fig. 2 An illustration of the reality stealing process for three different values of social entropy $h(G)$ (0.02, 0.1, and 1) for four different networks: the *Random Hall* network [14, 46], the *Reality Mining* network [9], the *Friends and Family* [47] self-reporting network, and the *Friends and Family* Bluetooth network [47]. Using this example, we can see that the *Reality Mining* network is easier to steal from than the *Random Hall* network, which in turn is easier to steal from than the *Friends and Family* networks

generated using the *social learnability measure* about the difficulty of learning each of these networks. Specifically, the *Social Evolution* network is predicted to be harder to steal than the *Reality Mining* network, but easier to steal than the *Friends and Family* networks. This can be explained by looking closely at the details of the three experiments. Whereas the *Reality Mining* experiment tracked people within a relatively static work environment, the *Social Evolution* experiment took place in an MIT undergraduate dormitory, involving students with (apparently) much more complex mobility and interaction patterns. The *Friends and Family* dataset involved even more complicated interactions because it consisted of a heterogeneous community of couples, which increased the amount of information encapsulated within the network.

In addition, note how the *social learnability measure* places the two *Friends and Family* networks directly on top of each other, despite the fact that the two networks contain significantly different information on volume, meaning, and network information dimensions. Still, because these two networks essentially represent the same social group of people, their *social learnability* measures have highly similar values.

The importance of the social entropy of a network is illustrated in Fig. 4, which shows an analysis of the *Reality Mining* network [9] for various possible values of social entropy. The value for the Kolmogorov complexity of the network was approximated using an *LZW* compression of the network.

Figure 3 demonstrates the progress of the network-essence stealing process for various network complexity values. Note that as the amount of information contained in a network increases (in other words, as the network represents more complex social structures), the network becomes much more difficult to acquire.

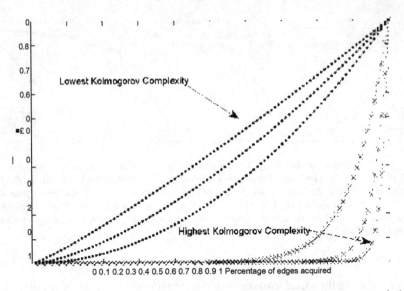

Fig. 3 Analytic illustration of the evolution of Λ_S as a function of the overall percentage of edges acquired for networks with the same number of edges ($|E| = 1{,}000{,}000$), assuming the same social entropy $\lambda(G) = 0.1$ and with different levels of Kolmogorov complexity

5.4 Easily Learnable Networks

As more and more *reality edges* are stolen by the attacker, the amount of information that the attacker possesses increases. However, looking at Eq. 4 and its illustrations in Figs. 2, 3, and 4, we can clearly see that this increase is not monotonic. In fact, for some networks, the first few edges enable the attacker to construct a relatively small portion of the *social reality* they represent, whereas for other networks, the benefit that an attacker would gain from a relatively small portion of the network's edges would be much greater. We refer to the latter as *easily learnable networks*, a term denoting networks for which stealing the first $x\%$ of edges enables the reconstruction of $\omega(x)$ of the social reality that the network encapsulates. From Eq. 4, we can derive the following criterion for *easily learnable networks*:

$$\lambda(G) < \frac{\log_2 |E|}{K_E} \tag{5}$$

Note that for networks that are not easily learnable, the amount of information that can be constructed from the first few stolen social edges is very limited. However, for every network that is not easily learnable, there is a threshold value of the number of stolen edges after which the network becomes easily learnable and

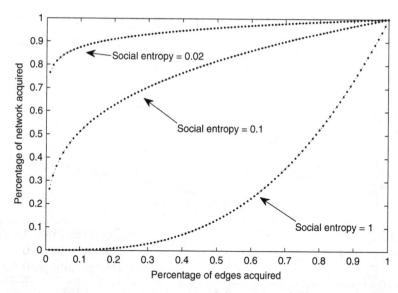

Fig. 4 Demonstration of the importance of a network's social entropy $\lambda(G)$, illustrated for the *Reality Mining* network [9]. The curves represent an approximation of the social essence measure calculated using an LZW compression of the *Reality Mining* network. It can be seen that if the network is assumed to be derived from a family of maximum entropy (namely, having a uniform distribution of all possible networks), the evolution of the *Stealing Reality* attack differs significantly than for networks derived from a family of a lower social entropy. In fact, even for $\lambda(G) = 0.1$, stealing the network would be materially easier because additional information could be obtained from any edge acquired

$\omega(1)$ information can be obtained from every new stolen edge. From Eq. 4, we can calculate this threshold as:

$$\frac{\partial \Lambda_S(t)}{\partial \Lambda_E(t)} > 1$$

Let us denote by $\widehat{\Lambda_E}$ the *critical learning threshold* above which the process of learning a network accelerates as described above (with each new learned edge contributing a steadily growing amount of information concerning the network's structure) to be defined as follows:

$$\widehat{\Lambda_E} > \left(\frac{\log_2 |E|}{\lambda(G) \cdot K_E} \right)^{\frac{\log_2 |E|}{\lambda(G) \cdot K_E - \log_2 |E|}} \tag{6}$$

Consequently, to provide as strong a protection as possible for the network, we should make sure that for every value of t:

$$\sum_{e_i \in E} I_{e_i}(t) \cdot e^{-\alpha e^{-r_i(t - T_{e_i})}} < \left(\frac{\log_2 |E|}{\lambda(G) \cdot K_E} \right)^{\frac{\log_2 |E|}{\lambda(G) \cdot K_E - \log_2 |E|}}$$

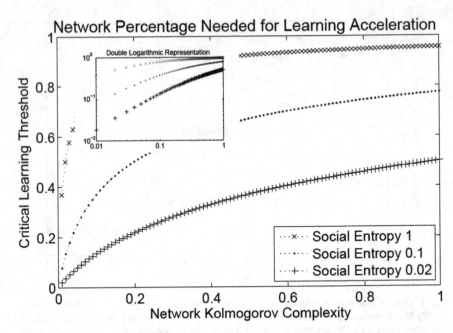

Fig. 5 Analytic illustration of the *easily learnable* network concept and the critical learning threshold as expressed in Eq. 6. The graph illustrates the critical learning threshold $\widehat{\Lambda_E}$ for networks of 1,000 nodes as a function of increasing Kolmogorov complexity for three different values of the social entropy $\Lambda(G)$. The critical learning threshold is the portion of the network that needs to be stolen for the network to become easily learnable (from that point), or in other words, to enable an attacker to obtain $\omega(1)$ information from any additional single stolen edge. For example, for a network with a social entropy value of 0.02 and with a Kolmogorov complexity of 0.6 of the network size, an attacker would have to obtain 40% of the network to reach the stage of accelerated learning

Otherwise, the attack will prevail when a time t is reached for which the above inequality no longer holds.

The notion of an *easily learnable* network is illustrated in Fig. 5, which analytically presents the critical learning threshold $\widehat{\Lambda_E}$ for networks of 1,000 nodes as a function of the network's Kolmogorov complexity for three possible values of social entropy.

6   Experimental Results

We evaluate our model on data derived from a real-world cluster of mobile phone users drawn from the call records of a major city within a developed western country and made up of approximately 200,000 nodes and 800,000 edges.

Figure 6 demonstrates the attack efficiency (namely, the maximum amount of network information acquired) as a function of the attack's "aggressiveness" (i.e., its infection rate). The two curves represent the overall amount of information

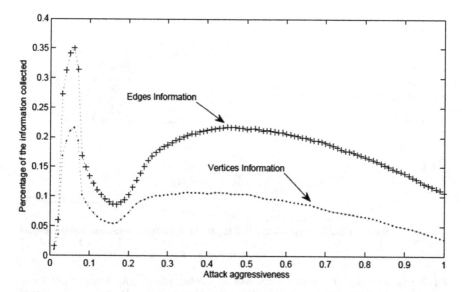

Fig. 6 Results of an analysis of the overall amount of data that can be captured by a *Stealing Reality* attack, illustrating the phenomenon that the most successful attack possible (namely, an attack that is capable of stealing the maximum amount of information) is associated with a very low value of the attack aggressiveness, ρ. The upper curve represents $\Lambda_E(\rho)$, the overall percentage of edge-related information stolen. The lower curve represents $\Lambda_V(\rho)$, the overall percentage of vertex-related information stolen. Note the local maximum around $\rho = 0.5$, which is, however, outperformed by the global maximum at $\rho = 0.04$

(both edge-related and vertex-related) that can be obtained as a function of the aggressiveness value ρ. It can be seen that although a local optimum exists for an aggressiveness value of slightly less than $\rho = 0.5$ (a relatively aggressive attack), this value is exceeded by the global optimum achieved by a much more "subtle" attack with an aggressiveness of $\rho = 0.04$.

To perform an extensive further validation of our analytic model for predicting the success of *Stealing Reality* attacks, we have simulated attacks for random subnetworks of a real-world 200,000-node mobile network using a wide range of attack aggressiveness values and numerous sets of values for the attack properties. For each combination, we have empirically determined the overall expected amount of information that is stolen by the attack.

Although the actual percentage of stolen information varied significantly among the various simulations, demonstrating the influence of changes to the attack properties, many of the simulations displayed the same interesting phenomenon: a global optimum of the attack performance located around a very low value of ρ. Some of these scenarios are presented in Fig. 7. The values of α and β which demonstrated this behavior were between 10 and 500. Values of r_i were between 0.1 and 100, whereas the values of σ were between 0.1 and 12. The values of M were between 0.1 and 30. It is interesting to mention that for high values of α and β, low values of M exhibited this phenomenon, but high values of M did not.

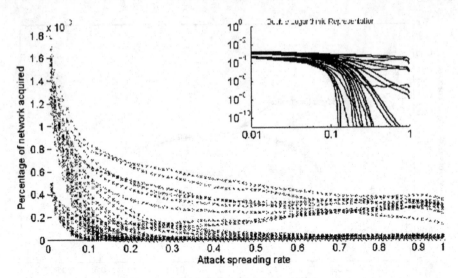

Fig. 7 Extensive study of a real-life mobile network simulating *Stealing Reality* attacks. Different curves represent different sets of values for the attack parameters α, β, σ, M, and r_i. Performance of each scenario is measured as the percentage of information acquired, as a function of the infection rate ρ. The scenarios that are presented in this figure demonstrate a global optimum of the attack performance at very low values of ρ, stressing the fact that in many cases an extremely non-aggressive attack yields the maximum amount of stolen information

To perform further validation of our theoretical attack model, we used a small-scale real-world social network obtained from the *Friends and Family* study [47] and containing data derived from a multitude of mobile-mounted sensors (e.g., call logs, accelerometers, Bluetooth and WiFi interactions). Using these data, we have confirmed our assumptions about the learning process [33]. The authors are currently working on a paper which will focus on the empirical implementation and validation of the model presented in this work.

7   Discussion and Concluding Remarks

This paper has presented the concept of a *Stealing Reality* attack, which is an attack aimed at acquiring implicit social information rather than explicit personal data. We have proposed a novel social network measure called *social learnability* and demonstrated its importance by validating it using several real-world social networks. We then showed that to maximize this measure, an attack must often resort to slow and subtle spreading patterns rather than aggressive ones, thus achieving maximum learning of the network while remaining undetected. We then validated this theoretical result experimentally using a real-world mobile-based social network.

The new concept of *Stealing Reality* attacks might provide an explanation for evidence observed in the process of investigating recent *Advanced Persistent Threats* (APT) attacks and might further suggest that such attacks might have happened in the past and gone undetected. The reason for the "stealthiness" of the *Stealing Reality* attack is the focus of most existing network monitoring methods on detecting "noisy" attack attempts. Systems such as *Network Telescope* [48] are designed to detect activity in IP segments that are supposed to contain no activity. Other widely used methods rely on the detection of anomalies in network activity [49, 50], which requires a considerable amount of data. As a result, a nonaggressive attack can be expected to "stay below the radar" and to avoid detection by such systems.

Finally, it is interesting to note the sensitivity of the attack to the accuracy of the selection of the optimal aggressiveness value (Fig. 6), which further hints at the usefulness of this type of attack for entities such as global hacking organizations or national defense agencies that have the resources needed to gather the information required for such accurate estimation.

References

1. Altshuler Y, Aharony N, Pentland A, Elovici Y, Cebrian M (2011) Stealing reality: when criminals become data scientists (or vice versa). IEEE Intell Syst 26(6):22–30. doi:10.1109/MIS.2011.78
2. Lazer D, Pentland A, Adamic L, Aral S, Barabasi AL, Brewer D, Christakis N, Contractor N, Fowler J, Gutmann M, Jebara T, King G, Macy M, Roy D, Alstyne MV (2009) Social science: computational social science. Science 323(5915):721–723
3. Altshuler Y, Pan W, Pentland A (2012) Trends prediction using social diffusion models. In: Proceedings of the international conference on social computing, behavioral-cultural modeling, and prediction. Lecture notes in computer, Springer, pp 97–104
4. Barabasi AL, Albert R (1999) Emergence of scaling in random networks. Science 286 (5439):509–512
5. Newman M (2003) The structure and function of complex networks. SIAM Rev 45:167–256
6. Watts D, Strogatz S (1998) Collective dynamics of "small-world" networks. Nature 393 (6684):440–442
7. Altshuler Y, Aharony N, Fire M, Elovici Y, Pentland A (2011) Incremental learning with accuracy prediction of social and individual properties from mobile-phone data, CoRR
8. Altshuler Y, Fire M, Aharony N, Elovici Y, Pentland A (2012) How many makes a crowd? On the correlation between groups' size and the accuracy of modeling. In: Proceedings of the international conference on social computing, behavioral-cultural modeling, and prediction. Lecture notes in computer science, Springer, pp 43–52
9. Eagle N, Pentland A, Lazer D (2009) Inferring social network structure using mobile phone data. Proc Natl Acad Sci (PNAS) 106:274–278
10. Yeung CA, Noll C, Meinel M, Gibbins C, Shadbolt N (2011) Measuring expertise in online communities. IEEE Intell Syst 26(1):26–32. doi:10.1109/MIS. 2011.18
11. Eagle N, Pentland A (2006) Reality mining: sensing complex social systems. Pers Ubiquit Comput 10(4):255–268
12. Gonzalez MC, Hidalgo CA, Barabasi AL (2008) Understanding individual human mobility patterns. Nature 453(7196):779–782. URL http://dx.doi.org/10.1038/nature06958

13. Eagle N, Macy M, Claxton R (2010) Network diversity and economic development. Science 328(5981):1029–1031
14. Madan A, Cebrian M, Lazer D, Pentland A (2010) Social sensing for epidemiological behavior change. In: Proceedings of the 12th ACM international conference on ubiquitous computing (Ubicomp '10). ACM, New York, pp 291–300. DOI http://doi.acm.org/10.1145/1864349.1864394, URL http://doi.acm.org/10.1145/1864349.1864394
15. Madan A, Farrahi K, Perez DG, Pentland A (2011) Pervasive sensing to model political opinions in face-to-face networks. In: Pervasive computing. Springer, Berlin, pp 214–231
16. Herley C, Florencio D (2010) Nobody sells gold for the price of silver: dishonesty, uncertainty and the underground economy. In: Moore T, Pym D, Ioannidis C (eds) Economics of information security and privacy. Springer, New York, pp 33–53. URL http://dx.doi.org/10.1007/978-1-4419-6967-5_3
17. Flexo (2007) I won't sell e-mail addresses. www.consumerismcommentary.com
18. Barbieri D, Braga D, Ceri S, Valle ED, Huang Y, Tresp V, Rettinger A, Wermser H (2010) Deductive and inductive stream reasoning for semantic social media analytics. IEEE Intell Syst 99 (Preprints). DOI http://doi.ieeecomputersociety.org/10.1109/MIS.2010.111
19. Krishnamurthy B, Wills CE (2009) On the leakage of personally identifiable information via online social networks. In: Proceedings of the 2nd ACM workshop on online social networks (WOSN '09). ACM, New York, pp 7–12. DOI http://doi.acm.org/10.1145/1592665.1592668, URL http://doi.acm.org/10.1145/1592665.1592668
20. Binde BE, McRee R, O'Connor TJ (2011) Assessing outbound traffic to uncover advanced persistent threat. Technical report. Sans Institute
21. Solutionary: White paper (2011) The advanced persistent threat (APT), 22 Apr 2011. http://resources.idgenterprise.com/original/AST-0056724_Advanced-Persistent-Threat-Solutionary.pdf
22. Svensson P (2011) Possible e-mail theft from Epsilon slams banks, retailers. USA Today, April 2011
23. Brunner M, Hofinger H, Krauss C, Roblee C, Schoo P, Todt S (2010) Infiltrating critical infrastructures with next-generation attacks. Technical report. Fraunhofer Institute for Secure Information Technology (SIT), Munich
24. Tang L, Liu H (2010) Toward collective behavior prediction via social dimension extraction. IEEE Intell Syst 99:1–17
25. AFP (2010) S. Korea to probe huge online data leak. www.enews.ma/korea-probe-huge_i165401_7.html
26. Jeffay N (2009) Israel poised to pass national ID database law. Jewish Daily Forward. www.forward.com/articles/112033/
27. Emery D (2010) Privacy fears over gay teenage database. http://www.bbc.co.uk/news/10612800
28. Perez JC (2007) Facebook's beacon more intrusive than previously thought. PC World, 30
29. Stana RM, Burton DR (2002) Identity theft: prevalence and cost appear to be growing. Technical report, GAO-02-363. U.S. General Accounting Office, Washington, DC
30. Granger S (2001) Social engineering fundamentals, Part I: Hacker tactics. www.securityfocus.com, Symantec
31. Gross R, Acquisti A (2005) Information revelation and privacy in online social networks. In: Proceedings of the 2005 ACM workshop on privacy in the electronic society (WPES '05). ACM, New York, pp 71–80. DOI http://doi.acm.org/10.1145/1102199.1102214, URL http://doi.acm.org/10.1145/1102199.1102214
32. Korolova A, Motwani R, Nabar SU, Xu Y (2008) Link privacy in social networks. In: Proceedings of the 17th ACM conference on information and knowledge management (CIKM '08). ACM, New York, pp 289–298. DOI http://doi.acm.org/10.1145/1458082.1458123, URL http://doi.acm.org/10.1145/1458082.1458123
33. Pan W, Aharony N, Pentland A (2011) Composite social network for predicting mobile apps installation. In: Proceedings of the 25th conference on artificial intelligence (AAAI), San Francisco, pp 821–827

34. Rouvinen P (2006) Diffusion of digital mobile telephony: are developing countries different? Telecommun Policy 30(1):46–63

35. Erickson G, Currie P, Inouye B, Winn A (2006) Tyrannosaur life tables: an example of Nonavian dinosaur population biology. Science 313(5784):213–217

36. D'Onofrio A (2005) A general framework for modeling tumor-immune system competition and immunotherapy: mathematical analysis and biomedical inferences. Physica D 208:220–235

37. Christakis NA, Fowler JH (2010) Social network sensors for early detection of contagious outbreaks. PLoS ONE 5(9). doi:10.1371/journal.pone.0012948

38. Bennett CH (1987) Dissipation, information, computational complexity and the definition of organization. In: Emerging syntheses in science. Addison-Wesley, Redwood City, pp 215–231

39. Bennett CH (1990) How to define complexity in physics, and why. In: Complexity, entropy, and the physics of information, vol 8, SFI studies in the science of complexity. Addison-Wesley, Redwood City, pp 137–148

40. Bennett C (1986) On the nature and origin of complexity in discrete, homogeneous, locally-interacting systems. Found Phys 16:585–592. URL http://dx.doi.org/10.1007/BF01886523. 10.1007/BF01886523

41. Kolmogorov A (1965) Three approaches to the quantitative definition of information. Probl Inf Transm 1(1):1–7

42. McKay BD (1981) Practical graph isomorphism. Congressus Numerantium 30:45–87

43. Harary F (1973) Enumeration of graphs. Graph Theory, 185–187

44. Reed D (2001) The law of the pack. Harv Bus Rev 79(2):23–24

45. Metcalfe B (1995) Metcalfe's law: a network becomes more valuable as it reaches more users. Infoworld 17(40):53–54

46. Madan A, Moturu ST, Lazer D, Pentland AS (2010) Social sensing: obesity, unhealthy eating and exercise in face-to-face networks. In: Proceedings of the wireless health 2010 (WH '10). ACM, New York, pp 104–110. DOI http://doi.acm.org/10.1145/1921081.1921094, URL http://doi.acm.org/10.1145/1921081.1921094

47. Aharony N, Pan W, Ip C, Khayal I, Pentland A (2011) The social fMRI: measuring, understanding and designing social mechanisms in the real world. In: Proceedings of the 13th ACM international conference on ubiquitous computing (Ubicomp '11). ACM, New York

48. Moore D, Paxson V, Savage S, Shannon C, Staniford S, Weaver N (2003) Inside the slammer worm. IEEE, Security Privacy 1(4):33–39. doi:10.1109/MSECP.2003.1219056

49. Apap F, Honig A, Hershkop S, Eskin E, Stolfo S (2002) Detecting malicious software by monitoring anomalous Windows registry accesses. In: Recent advances in intrusion detection. Springer, Berlin/Heidelberg, pp 36–53

50. Moskovitch R, Pluderman S, Gus I, Stopel D, Feher C, Parmet Y, Shahar Y, Elovici Y (2007) Host based intrusion detection using machine learning. In: Proceedings of the IEEE intelligence and security informatics, New Jersey, pp 107–114

Applications of k-Anonymity and ℓ-Diversity in Publishing Online Social Networks

Na Li and Sajal K. Das

Abstract Many online social network (OSN) owners, such as Facebook and Twitter, regularly publish data they have collected from their users' online activities to third parties, such as sociologists and commercial companies. These third parties mine these data and extract information for their particular purposes. This data-sharing elicits users' concerns regarding disclosures of their privacy. This chapter takes a systematic look at the applications of some classical privacy preservation models, including k-anonymity and ℓ-diversity, which were originally developed to protect tabular data privacy to secure users' privacy contained in OSN data.

Keywords k-anonymity • ℓ-diversity • Relation privacy • Online social networks • Utility loss • Topology-based attack

1 Introduction

In recent years, the popularity of online social networks (OSNs) like Facebook and Linkedin has grown exponentially because they facilitate networking between people and their family and friends. These OSN sites allow their users to create online profiles and share personal information with a huge number of friends, which is also available to strangers. The authors [1] have pointed out that users' private information is seriously exposed in these online social networks. Furthermore, users' privacy may also be threatened when OSN site owners share data with third parties, such as commercial companies and sociologists, who exploit the data collected by OSN websites to serve their particular purposes.

N. Li (✉) • S.K. Das
Center for Research in Wireless Mobility and Networking (CReWMaN), Computer Science
and Engineering, The University of Texas at Arlington, Arlington, TX, USA
e-mail: na.li@mavs.uta.edu; das@uta.edu

Y. Altshuler et al. (eds.), *Security and Privacy in Social Networks*,
DOI 10.1007/978-1-4614-4139-7_8, © Springer Science+Business Media New York 2013

The data collected by OSN sites are quite valuable to these third parties, as they can analyze these data to extract the information they need. For example, a company may use the data that form the basis of customer profiles to promote its products to these customers through an online recommendation system. Sociologists may analyze these data to better understand the evolution of social communities in the physical world. These third parties usually obtain these data either by crawling an OSN website through the public interface provided by the OSN owner, or by requesting these data from the OSN owner who routinely publishes the OSN data. This information sharing may elicit users' concerns regarding disclosures of their privacy. The failure to protect users' privacy can result in serious consequences, not only by severely undermining the popularity of OSNs, but by restricting the amount of data that OSN owners are willing to share with third parties.

Basically, there are two types of attacks that can compromise users' privacy on OSNs: passive attacks and active attacks. During a passive attack, an adversary only leverages data analysis to infer users' private information, while during an active attack, an adversary takes actions beyond static data mining and analysis. In an example given by Backstrom et al. [2], an adversary creates a subgraph with a special topology in the OSN by creating dummy users and relationships prior to data publishing. Then, after he re-identifies himself from the published OSN by searching for the subgraph with this special topology, he can further re-identify other normal users with whom he already established connections.

Another active attack, called a stealing-reality attack [3], is part of a complex advanced persistent threats (APT) attack [4]. The first goal of such an attacker is to inject a single malware agent into one of the network's nodes and begin learning about this node and its interactions with neighboring nodes. Gradually, the agent mimics being one of the original node's neighbors and continues to compromise the neighbor's neighbors. As the information collected from the network is sufficient to launch an attack, the attacker will steal as many of a social network's topological properties (i.e., relationships) as possible. The authors [5] have even shown the possibility of compromising a significant fraction of users' relationships in an OSN by subverting a small group of users. Thus, there are various forms of active attacks, which are more complex than static data analysis.

In this chapter, we focus on passive attacks against users' privacy in publishing OSN data to third parties and discuss privacy preservation techniques from the viewpoint of OSN owners. Apparently, simply removing users' information from the data before publishing will ensure the preservation of users' privacy. If this is done, it will hide all users' information, but it will completely destroy the utility of the published data that is needed by third parties. For example, a sociologist who is interested in researching the evolution of group dynamics cannot garner much practical insight from the OSN data published with no details regarding users' relationships. Therefore, the challenge for an OSN owner is how best to handle the dilemma presented by preserving privacy and maintaining data utility for third parties.

We model OSNs as undirected graphs, where the vertices and edges represent users and their relations, respectively. We define all information relevant to a user, such as his/her email or affiliation, as node attributes. Additionally, we can weigh each edge to indicate different strengths of users' relationships.

There is a substantial literature on protecting users' privacy in publishing OSN data, which primarily addresses users' identity privacy and relationship privacy. In this chapter, we will primarily discuss the applications of classical privacy preservation models that were originally developed to protect tabular data privacy, such as k-anonymity and ℓ-diversity, to preserve users' privacy when publishing OSN data. For some other related work, including preserving weight privacy of relationships [6, 7], we refer readers to our survey article [8], in which we proposed a novel taxonomy of anonymization techniques for preserving users' relationship privacy in publishing OSN data. Note that to identify a user from a published OSN, an adversary can leverage unique attributes associated with that user. However, we will discuss *topology-based attacks,* in which we assume the attacker is equipped with some topological properties associated with a target user to identify the user; for example, the degree or one-hop neighborhood of the vertex that corresponds to the user.

This chapter is organized as follows. In Sect. 2 we discuss some work that employed k-anonymity to protect users' privacy when publishing OSN data. In Sect. 3, we focus on our previous work that applied ℓ-diversity model to preserve users' relationship privacy. In Sect. 4 we provide some experimental examples. Finally, we summarize this chapter in Sect. 5.

2 k-Anonymity

The k-anonymity model [9] was proposed in order to make any object indistinguishable from at least $k-1$ others using prior knowledge. In general, such prior knowledge is called a quasi-identifier that includes several pieces of information, each of which is not unique for an object, while their combination helps to distinguish an object from others. If the prior knowledge is solely relevant to a user's attributes in a graph model, we can directly apply the anonymization techniques developed for preserving tabular data privacy to protecting user's attribute privacy so that a malicious third party cannot infer the values of sensitive attributes of a target user.

However, the main difference between tabular data and OSN data is that the latter contain some relational data (e.g., users' relations), which creates a particular challenge for preserving users' privacy. The reason is that one relation is usually associated with more than one user. Thus, changing it (i.e., removing/inserting) for anonymization can affect other users whose relation privacy may have been previously well preserved. Under this condition, we have to rehandle privacy preservation for these associated users after changing the currently focused relation.

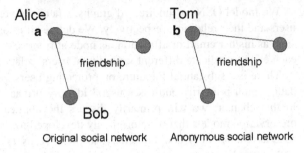

Fig. 1 Topology-based attack

Original social network   Anonymous social network

There has been extensive work on how to apply a k-anonymity model to preserve users' identity privacy, in which the prior knowledge mastered by an attacker varies from a node's degree (i.e., the number of direct neighbors of a user) to any arbitrarily given subgraph that covers a target user. It would seem that removing users' identifiers from OSN data to be published or using pseudo-identities should effectively preserve users' identity privacy. However, Fig. 1 illustrates its ineffectiveness. In this example, so long as the attacker knows that Alice has two friends, he can tell the node with degree of two in the anonymized graph corresponds to Alice. In the following, we will detail various k-anonymity-based techniques to preserve not only users' identity privacy, but also user's relationship privacy in publishing OSN data.

2.1 k-Degree Anonymity

Liu and Terzi [10] first applied k-anonymity to preserve users' identity privacy, where the prior knowledge assumed to be mastered by an attacker was the node degree. Specifically, an attacker intends to identify a target user from the published OSN graph using his knowledge of that user's degree. We again use the example illustrated in Fig. 1. In this example, simply adding an edge between Bob and Tom before releasing OSN data can sufficiently preserve Alice's identity, as this makes all nodes have the same degree of two in the published graph. Therefore, knowing that Alice has two neighbors no longer helps the attacker to identify Alice.

The anonymization technique [10] includes two steps. First, in an arbitrarily given graph, G(V, E), a sequence of node degrees are generated based on the original node degrees, which satisfy k-degree anonymity defined in Definition 1 (see below). The sequence generation is subject to one constraint that requires minimizing the distance between the degree sequence to be generated and the original one, where the distance is denoted in Definition 2 (see below). The intention to require this constraint is to minimize the change of the original nodes and edges in the graph manipulation-based anonymization technique in order to maintain as much utility in the published data as possible. To achieve this goal, the authors designed a dynamic programming algorithm to generate the anonymous degree sequence.

Second, a new graph, $\hat{G}(V, \hat{E})$, is formed based on the newly generated degree sequence, where $\hat{E} \cap E = E$ (or $\hat{E} \cap E \approx E$ in the relaxed version). The authors evaluated the performance of their anonymization technique with respect to anonymization cost, including the degree sequence distance, cluster coefficient (a measure of degree to which nodes in a graph tend to cluster together), and average path length. This demonstrates that their k-degree anonymity technique not only protects user identities against node-degree based attack, but also maintains data utility well.

Definition 1. k-degree anonymity. A graph $G(V, E)$ is k-degree anonymous if each vertex in V shares the same degree with at least $k-1$ other vertices.

Definition 2. Degree sequence distance. Given two degree sequences, $\check{d}$ and d, their distance is defined as $L(\check{d}-d) = \sum_{v_i}|\check{d}(v_i)-d(v_i)|$, where $d(\cdot)$ is the original degree and $\check{d}(\cdot)$ is the revised degree.

2.2   k-Neighborhood Anonymity

The authors [11] modeled an attack stronger than the aforementioned degree-based attack, called neighborhood based attack. In this case, the attacker is assumed to have extra knowledge of the 1-hop neighborhood structure of a target user in the original OSN graph. Under this new attack model, depending only on the k-degree anonymity technique cannot effectively defend users' identity privacy against the neighborhood-associated topology-based attack. As shown in Fig. 2, by knowing Ada's neighborhood structure, an attacker can identity her from a 2-degree anonymous graph. Therefore, a stronger anonymization technique [11] was designed based on a k-neighborhood anonymity model, as defined below in Definition 3.

There are three steps in this anonymization technique [11]. First, the neighborhood of each vertex is extracted and encoded based on its topology. The intention of coding the neighborhood is to easily compare the neighborhoods of vertices to find isomorphic neighborhoods, where graph isomorphism is defined below in Definition 4. Second, vertices are grouped into small groups with sizes of at least k. The vertices in each group are required to have similar neighborhood codes. Finally, graph manipulation techniques, such as edge insertion/deletion, are applied to the graph to ensure that all vertices in each group have the same 1-hop neighborhood topology with the intention to achieve k-neighborhood anonymity.

Definition 3. k-neighborhood anonymity. A vertex v is k-neighborhood anonymous if there are at least $k-1$ other vertices for each of which its immediate neighbors form a subgraph isomorphic to the subgraph constructed by the immediate neighbors of v. A graph is k-neighborhood anonymous if and only if all vertices are k-neighborhood anonymous.

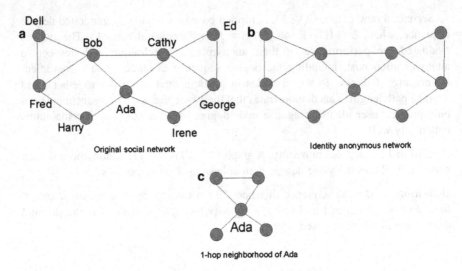

Fig. 2 2-degree anonymous graph with the failure of defending against neighborhood based attack

Definition 4. Graph Isomorphism. Given two graphs, $G_1(V_1, E_1)$ and $G_2(V_2, E_2)$, G_1 is isomorphic to G_2 if and only if there exists at least one bijective function f: $V_1 \rightarrow V_2$, such that for any edges $(u, v) \in E_1$, there is an edge $((f(u), f(v)) \in E_2$.

2.3 k-Automorphism

The k-automorphism anonymization model [12] provides for even stronger identity preservation than the k-neighborhood anonymity model. Specifically, k-automorphism anonymization guarantees the security of a target user's identity privacy, even when an attacker knows a priori of any arbitrary-hop neighborhood topology of the target user. Given graph automorphism in Definition 5 below, the authors [12] first defined a k-automorphic graph: given a graph G, if (a) there exist $k-1$ automorphic functions F_a (a = 1,..., k-1) in Gand (b) for each vertex v in G, F_{a_1} (v) $\neq F_{a_2}$ (v) ($1 < a_1 \neq a_2 < k-1$), then G is a k-automorphic graph. The goal of privacy preservation [12] is that given any graph G and any sub-graph query Q, publishing a graph G* that must satisfy two constraints: (1) there are at least k matches of Q in G*, where *match* is introduced in Definition 6 below; and (2) any two of the k matches are different matches according to Definition 7 below, where no attacker can identify the target user with a probability higher than 1/k.

Definition 5. Graph Automorphism. An automorphism of a graph G(V, E) is an automorphic function f of the vertex set V, such that for any edge e = (u, v), f(e) = (f(u), f(v)) is also an edge in G. If there exist k automorphisms in G, this means that there exist $k-1$ different automorphic functions.

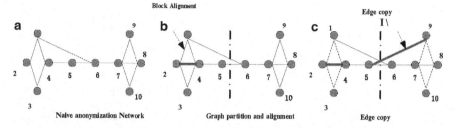

Fig. 3 Graph partition and edge copy

Definition 6. Match. Given two graphs Q and G, if there exists at least one subgraph X in G such that Q is isomorphic to X under the bijective function f, then Q is subgraph isomorphic to G and X is called a subgraph match of Q in G.

The anonymization technique [12] involves three steps. First, the original graph is partitioned into several groups of subgraph blocks each of which contains at least k subgraphs and any two subgraphs do not share any vertices or edges. Second, graph manipulation is used to ensure that the subgraphs in each group are isomorphic to each other. Finally, if any edges cross different isomorphic blocks in the original graph, then some dummy edges will be inserted across the blocks for publishing to achieve the complete isomorphism of subgraph blocks. The authors proved that graph G^* anonymized by their proposed algorithm achieved k-automorphism, thereby defending users' identity privacy against any topology-based attack. An example is illustrated in Fig. 3. Ten nodes are first grouped into two blocks. To make the two blocks isomorphic, an edge is inserted between v_2 and v_4. In addition, an edge connecting v_5 and v_9 is inserted to compensate for the block-crossing edge (v_1, v_6). The final published graph is a 2-automorphic graph.

Definition 7. Different Matches. Given a sub-graph query Q and two matches m_1 and m_2 of Q in a social network G', where m_1 and m_2 are isomorphic to Q under functions f_1 and f_2, respectively, if there exists no vertex v (in query Q) whose match vertices in m_1 and m_2 are identical, m_1 and m_2 are called different matches.

2.4   *k-Isomorphism*

The k-automorphism techniques [12] can effectively preserve users' identity privacy, although users' relation privacy is only weakly protected. In the example illustrated in Fig. 4, an attacker who knows that Alice has two friends and that Tom has three can infer that Alice and Tom are friends in the social network graph, although he cannot pinpoint Alice and Tom. This successful inference results from the full connection between the vertices of degree 2 and the vertices of degree 3, which causes a lack of *structure-diversity* of edges in the published graph. This problem was also noted by the authors [13]. Moreover, the authors [13] were concerned with users' privacy in an

Fig. 4 2-automorphism anonymous graph with the failure of protecting users' relationship privacy

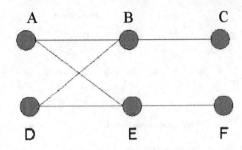

Fig. 5 Attack against relationship privacy in a 4-automorphism anonymous graph

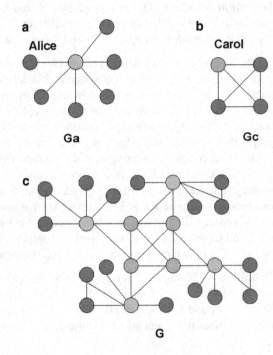

indirect relationship, which is represented by a path between two nodes in the graph. This relationship privacy may not be preserved, even in a *k*-automorphic graph. An example is illustrated in Fig. 5, where *G* is a 4-automorphism anonymous graph.

Suppose the adversary knows G_a for Alice and G_c for Carol. Although the attacker cannot distinguish individual users, he is convinced that there exists a path of length 2 between Alice and Carol, which indicates the close relationship between them.

To preserve users' indirect relationship privacy, a *k*-isomorphism model was proposed [13]. A *k*-isomorphism requires a graph *G* contain *k* disjoint subgraphs that are isomorphic to each other. This privacy preservation model guarantees that an attacker cannot infer whether the two users are linked by a path of (at most) a certain length in the original graph with a probability of more than $1/k$. Correspondingly, the authors proposed an anonymization technique to achieve the k-isomorphism privacy preservation. As compared to the k-automorphism technique [12], the improvement in the k-isomorphism technique is to partition the original graph G in to k *disjointed subgraphs,* which ensures the complete isomorphism of all k subgraphs.

3 ℓ-Diversity

The ℓ-diversity model [14] was originally proposed to preserve tabular data privacy after researchers became aware of the weakness of the k-anonymity model. Specifically, even though k-anonymity can ensure that any object will be indistinguishable from at least $k-1$ others based on the values of quasi-identifier attributes, thus forming a group, the values of a sensitive attribute for objects in one group may be the same. In this case, although the attacker cannot identify a target object, he can still successfully infer the value of the sensitive attribute associated with the target object. To counteract such an attack, the ℓ-diversity model was proposed to ensure the value diversity of any sensitive attribute in each group.

In this section, we primarily address how to apply the ℓ-diversity concept to preserving users' relationship privacy in publishing OSN data [15]. We will first introduce an attack model and a privacy preservation model and then will discuss two corresponding anonymization techniques in detail.

3.1   Attack Model and Privacy Guarantee

In our attack model, the attacker attempts to infer a sensitive relationship between two target users. However, we are still focused on topology-based attacks. Therefore, we assume that the extra knowledge that the attacker has is the number of friends of each target user, which is represented by the vertex degree in the OSN graph. This common information is publicly available on many OSN sites (e.g., LinkedIn). Furthermore, in the worst case scenario, one of the target users can even be identified by the attacker based on some background knowledge that may be collected from the user's blog.

Under this attack model, a k-degree anonymization technique is insufficient to guarantee the relationship privacy we desire. A simple example is illustrated in Fig. 6a, where nodes are grouped in terms of their degrees. Suppose the attacker intends to infer the relationship between user A and user B. In this 4-degree anonymous graph, if the attacker only knows that the two users have degrees of four and one, respectively, he cannot successfully infer their relationship. However, if the attacker can somehow identify user A, even though he cannot identify user B based solely on the knowledge of his degree, the sensitive relationship between user

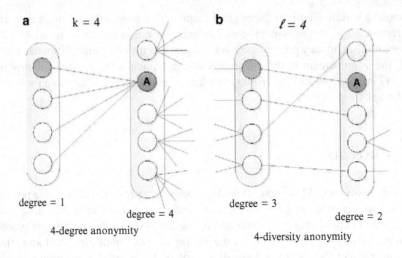

Fig. 6 Anonymous social network graphs against disclosure of users' relationship

A and user B can be disclosed due to the full connection of all vertices of degree one with user A. To defend against this attack, we propose a new privacy anonymization model in Definition 8, which was adapted from the ℓ-diversity concept [14].

Definition 8. A published network is ℓ-diversity anonymous (ℓ-diversified) if and only if given the degrees of any two users, the attacker cannot successfully infer the existence of a relationship between them from the anonymized graph with a probability of greater than $1/\ell$, even when one of them is identifiable from the published data.

Definition 8 is stricter than k-degree anonymity, as we first need to ensure that a user cannot be identified by his/her degree information, which is exactly the degree anonymity. If a published graph satisfies ℓ-diversity, there must be at least ℓ vertices with any unique degree. Moreover, our ℓ-diversity model guarantees the relationship diversity between any two groups of vertices. An example of a 4-diversity anonymous graph is given in Fig. 6b. In this graph, suppose user B has degree of three and user A is exposed; the probability of inferring the relationship between them is just 1/4, as the node connecting with A has a probability of 1/4 of being user B.

3.2 Insights from an ℓ-Diversified Graph

Given an ℓ-diversified graph, we know from Definition 8 that the group size for vertices with a unique degree must not be < ℓ; that is, if we suppose V_a is the set of vertices with degree of d_a, then $|V_a| \geq \ell$. Furthermore, the point of preventing the attacker from inferring relationship between two users with confidence $>1/\ell$ can be interpreted by noting that in each group the ratio of vertices that share a neighboring vertex to the total vertices in that group must not be $>1/\ell$. Suppose in V_a vertices linking to v_n (any vertex in the graph) form a set V_a'; then $|V'_a/V_a| \leq 1/\ell$.

In each group, if we continue partitioning vertices until each smaller group has a size of $|V_a*|$, where $\ell <= |V_a*| < 2\,\ell$, then the second point in Definition 8 can be interpreted as $|V_a*| <= 1$. This indicates that the ℓ-diversity model does not allow any two vertices in the same small group to share any vertex. In other words, edges across any pair of small groups should not share any vertices at their ends, which is exactly the *matching* concept in Graph Theory.

The features of small groups and matching guided us in our designs of relation anonymization techniques. However, these features form a sufficient, but unnecessary condition to judge whether a given graph is ℓ-diversified. Sufficiency is quite obvious. If the vertices in a graph can be partitioned into small groups each of which has vertices of the same degree, and the edges across any small groups also form a matching, then the graph is ensured to be ℓ-diversified. However, not all ℓ-diversified graphs can be partitioned into such small groups holding such a matching property. Yet, because our focus is on converting a graph to an ℓ-diversity anonymous graph, the features we observed at least provide a direction for graph conversion.

3.3   Our Anonymization Techniques

We design solutions for preserving users' relationship privacy using an ℓ-diversity model from two directions. Given an arbitrary social network graph, G: $\langle V, E \rangle$, we intend to make the graph ℓ-diversified using graph-manipulation by (1) finding a subgraph G: $\langle V', E' \rangle$, where $V' = V$ and $E' \subseteq E$, and (2) creating a supergraph G^*: $\langle V^*, E^* \rangle$, where $V^* \supseteq V$ and $E^* \supseteq E$. In addition to the privacy concerns in the published graph, utility loss should be minimized. This is defined as the number of changed vertices/edges as compared to the original graph. In the following, we will discuss two techniques that effectively ℓ-diversify a graph for relation anonymization based on these two directions.

3.3.1   Max-Subgraph Algorithm (MaxSub)

Given an arbitrary graph, G: $\langle V, E \rangle$, the basic idea of MaxSub is to start from a graph G_0: $\langle V_0, E_0 \rangle$, where $V_0 = V$ and $E_0 = \emptyset$. Then, we iteratively add back a subset of the original edges for publishing, while ensuring the ℓ-diversity anonymity at any iteration in the process of edge recovery. MaxSub comprises two main steps: *Internal Matching-Partition* (IMP) and *External Matching-Partition* (EMP), with their pseudocodes in Algorithm 1 and Algorithm 2, respectively.

Step 1. Internal Matching-Partition (IMP): We first arbitrarily select from the original graph a maximal matching. A maximal matching is referred to as a maximal set of edges without any common end-vertex. Specifically, we start by randomly selecting an original edge, and then remove its two end-vertices and their associated edges from the original graph. We continue to pick up edges until no edge remains. All edges selected form a maximal matching which partitions all vertices into groups. Two of these are called "matched" groups, which respectively contains one of the end-vertices of each edge in the matching. If there remain unmatched vertices, they constitute a third group designated an "unmatched" group.

Note that all vertices in each of the two (or three) groups have the same degree, while not sharing any neighboring vertex through the edges in the matching. Thus, in the general case, as long as each group contains at least ℓ vertices, the constraint of ℓ-diversity anonymity will be satisfied and the matching will succeed. In addition to the general case, there are some other situations where, although not all groups have sizes $>\ell$, by adjusting the matching we can still partition the vertices into groups that comply with the ℓ-diversity constraint.

One special situation is when the size of the unmatched group is $<\ell$. In this case, we adjust the matching by removing the minimum number of matched edges, such that the number of unmatched vertices is at least ℓ. Note that at the same time as this adjustment is made, the number of matched vertices in each group decreases. Therefore, we allow the matching adjustment only when we can ensure the ℓ-diversity constraint on matched groups will not be violated. In particular, each matched group has at least ℓ vertices if they form separate groups. Or, matching has to ensure that the total number of vertices in both of the matched groups is not $<\ell$, where the two groups will merge into one and halt further iterative matching.

The other special situation is when each matched group has fewer than ℓ vertices, while their sum has more than ℓ vertices. In this case, similar to the restraint in the matching adjustment of the first special case, we combine the two matched groups into one, after which we terminate their matching. For all other situations, matching fails and is aborted.

Given a successful matching, we publish all edges in it. The process of matching-partition will continue internally in each of the groups that are newly formed and are not terminated until no matching can be found to further split the group into smaller groups with sizes of not less than ℓ. In fact, the procedure of splitting the original vertices into smaller groups by iteratively matching and partitioning can be thought of as the growth of an upside-down tree that is rooted at the original vertex set. The leaf-nodes of the tree are groups that have sizes $\geq\ell$, but are not divisible by additional maximal matchings.

To illustrate the IMP process of executing MaxSub, an example is given in Fig. 7a–d, where $\ell = 2$. Based on a maximal matching $\{(1, 2), (3, 4), (5, 6), (7, 8)\}$, all vertices are partitioned into three groups: $match_1$ $\{v_1, v_3, v_5, v_7\}$, $match_2$ $\{v_2, v_4, v_6, v_8\}$, and $unmatch$ $\{v_9, v_{10}\}$, as shown in Fig. 7b. Because each group has at least ℓ vertices, all edges in the matching are published. For $match_1$ and $match_2$, because they contain vertices $>\ell$, we continue looking for a maximal matching in each of them. For $match_1$, all vertices can be matched further, which leads to another partition, $\{v_1, v_3\}$ and $\{v_5, v_7\}$. For $match_2$, because no matching exists, the iteration terminates without additional edges being published. The graph manipulated by IMP is given in Fig. 7c. Note that the procedure of splitting the

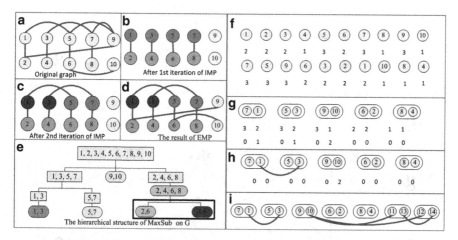

Fig. 7 An example for *ℓ*-diversity based techniques

original vertices into smaller groups by iteratively matching and partitioning can be presented as the growth of an upside-down tree that is rooted at the original vertex set. The leaf-nodes of the tree are groups that have sizes $\geq \ell$, but are not divisible by additional maximal matchings. The corresponding tree to the illustrated example is shown in Fig. 7e without the branches circled in bold. Each leaf-node of the tree forms a set of equal-degree vertices in the graph published by the IMP phase in the MaxSub algorithm.

We observe that although IMP can ensure any published graph to be *ℓ*-diversity anonymous, the utility of the published graph that is defined as the number of original edges published is not well maintained. The reason is that the design of IMP never recovers any additional edges between two groups of vertices after they have been split. For example, given the graph published by the IMP step of MaxSub in Fig. 7c, we could actually find another maximal matching, $\{(v_2, v_9), (v_6, v_{10})\}$, between two leaf-node groups, $\{v_2, v_4, v_6, v_8\}$ and $\{v_9, v_{10}\}$. This matching leads to an additional splitting of a leaf-node group, as marked by a rectangle in Fig. 7e, which results in publishing one more original edge without violating the *ℓ*-diversity constraint. This additional matching is taken care of by the following step in MaxSub, namely, *External Matching-Partition*.

Step 2. External Matching-Partition (EMP): EMP checks for the possibility of adding back more edges that cross those leaf-node groups formed by IMP. In this way, the leaf-node groups may be further split into smaller groups due to the degree differentiation of vertices in each group by edge addition. EMP checks any pair of leaf-node groups, g_i and g_j say, to seek more edges for further publishing.

Specifically, an arbitrary maximal matching is first selected between g_i and g_j subject to a single constraint: if some of the vertices have been previously matched together across the two groups, they are not considered in the new matching. This constraint guarantees that the final published edges across any pair of groups are

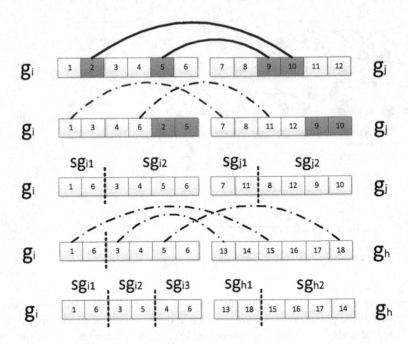

Fig. 8 An example for EMP in MaxSub

still matched, thereby satisfying ℓ-diversity anonymity. An example is illustrated in Fig. 8, where $\ell = 2$. Suppose that (v_2, v_{10}) and (v_5, v_9) are two edges published in IMP. So, the four vertices are marked as "unmatched" vertices and excluded from the new matching between g_i and g_j.

Based on this new matching, g_i and g_j are further partitioned into smaller groups that contain matched and unmatched vertices, respectively. If necessary, partition adjustments can be made by removing edges from the matching to ensure that each newly formed group does not have fewer than ℓ vertices. As shown in Fig. 8, due to the matching of the two edges (v_1, v_7) and (v_6, v_{11}), both g_i and g_j are divided into two smaller groups. Later, after checking the possibility of publishing edges between g_i and some other group, g_h say, if a maximal matching is found between g_h and the entire group g_i after excluding matched vertices in IMP, we then check each small group in g_i to see whether the new matching can split the small group further. In our example, three edges, (v_1, v_{15}), (v_3, v_{13}), and (v_5, v_{18}), form the new matching between g_i and g_h. However, because only one vertex is matched in sg_{i1}, splitting sg_{i1} further will violate the constraint of group size in ℓ-diversity anonymity. Therefore, we abort this edge in this matching. For sg_{i2}, two edges are matched; thus, we further split sg_{i2} into two smaller groups. Meanwhile, vertices in g_h are partitioned into two groups. This procedure for group-crossing matching needs to be done between any pair of leaf-node groups formed by IMP.

Theorem 1. *Given an arbitrary graph, its subgraph published by MaxSub is ℓ-diversity anonymous.*

Proof. We prove Theorem 1 based on two aspects of *ℓ*-diversity anonymity: (1) degree anonymity – each final group contains at least *ℓ* vertices of the same degree; and (2) relationship diversity – neither of two vertices in a group share a neighboring vertex in the published graph. One can see that the combination of these two properties guarantees *ℓ*-diversity anonymity (as defined by Definition 8).

Degree anonymity: Based on the algorithm design, we can see in both IMP and EMP groups are formed by matchings; thus, vertices in each group have the same degree at all times. Furthermore, matching (including matching after successful adjustment) succeeds only if each of the newly formed groups has at least *ℓ* vertices. Therefore, MaxSub achieves degree anonymity.

Relationship diversity: We prove that each of leaf-node groups formed by IMP satisfies relationship diversity by contradiction. Suppose that two vertices in the same group share a neighbor, *v*. Then, both of their edges that connect with the common neighbor must be added during the same iteration when *v* is separated from these two vertices by a matching. This contradicts that all added-back edges in one iteration form a matching. Thus, all leaf-node groups published by IMP satisfy the relationship diversity requirement.

Now we prove that the small groups published by EMP also meet relationship diversity by contradiction. Suppose that two vertices in the same small group *s* have a common neighbor, *v*, in the small groups'. Because EMP only does matching one time between any pair of leaf-node groups generated by IMP, one of these two edges must have been added in IMP. However, this contradicts the design of EMP, where vertices that have been matched together in IMP are excluded from any new matching across the two groups. Thus, the small groups resulting from EMP achieve relationship diversity.

Theorem 2. *Accordingly, the graph that is finally published by MaxSub is ℓ-diversity anonymous. The time complexity for MaxSub is* $O(n^2)$ *for a graph of* n *vertices.*

Proof. The complexity of finding a maximal matching is basically $O(|g|^2)$ in a group with |g| vertices. In the worst IMP case, all vertices can be matched in each group, such that each matched group has the maximum number of vertices to participate in the next matching iteration. Thus, the procedure of iteratively matching and partitioning can be presented as a binary tree, as shown in Fig. 9. The time complexity of the IMP step can be calculated by summing the time consumption on partitioning each tree-node on all tree levels, as formalized in Eq. 1, where *n* is the number of original vertices.

$$T(n) = \sum_{r=0}^{r=\lfloor \log_2 n/\ell \rfloor} (n/2^r)^2 \times 2^r = O(n^2) \tag{1}$$

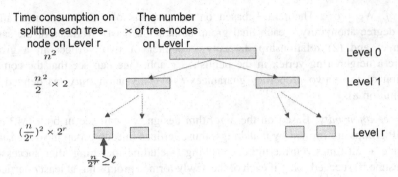

Fig. 9 Worst case for IMP in MaxSub

For each EMP step, suppose that h is the maximum size of a leaf-node group generated by IMP, where $h > \ell$. The time complexity for EMP to process each pair of leaf-node groups is $O(h^2)$. Because the size of each leaf-node group is at least ℓ, the number of pair-wise matchings across groups is, at most, $(n/\ell)(n/\ell-1)/2$. Thus, EMP assumes $O(n^2 h^2/\ell^2)$ for time complexity.

Consequently, taking these two steps into consideration, the overall time complexity for MaxSub is $O(n^2)$.

Algorithm 1 IMP – MaxSub

Input: G(S,Es) - an arbitrary graph as the original graph

Output: E_G: published edges, where $E_G \subseteq E_s$

1 Find a maximal matching in S

2 Partition S into S_{match1}, S_{match2} and $S_{unmatch}$

3 **if** $|S_{match1}|+|S_{match2}| \geq 2 \ell$ **then**

4   **if** $|S_{unmatch}| < \ell$ **then**

5   Adjust the matching

6   **if** Adjustment succeeds then

7          $E_G = \{$edges maintained in the matching$\}$

8   **if** $|S^{adjust}_{match1}| \geq \ell$ **then**

9   **IMP-MaxSub**$(G_1, S^{adjust}_{match1})$ and **IMP-MaxSub**$(G_2, S^{adjust}_{match2})$

10 **else** $E_G = \emptyset$

11 **else**   **if** $|S_{match1}|+|S_{match2}| \geq \ell$ **then**

12   **if** $|S_{unmatch}| < \ell$ **then**

13   Adjust the matching

14   **if** Adjustment succeeds **then**

15             $E_G = \{$edges maintained in the matching$\}$

16   **else** $E_G = \emptyset$

17   **else** $E_G = \emptyset$

Algorithm 2 EMP - MaxSub

Input: The result graph published by IMP in MaxSub and the original graph G

Output: a heuristic maximum ℓ-diversity anonymous subgraph of G

1 **for** any pair of leaf-node groups, g_i and g_j, from IMP **do**

2   Mark vertices matched between g_i and g_j by IMP

3   Find a maximal matching among vertices without marks

4   **for** each SmallGroup sg_k in g_i and g_j **do**

5   Split sg_k into sg^{match}_k and $sg^{unmatch}_k$

6   **if** $sg^{match}_k < \ell$ or $sg^{unmatch}_k < \ell$ **then**

7   Adjust the matching for sg_k

8   **if** Adjustment is successful or ($sg^{match}_k \geq \ell$ or $sg^{unmatch}_k \geq \ell$) **then**

9   Add back edges associated with sg^{match}_k in the new matching

10   **else**

11   Abort the maximal matching

3.3.2 Min-Supergraph Algorithm (MinSuper)

MinSuper is a two-step algorithm for expanding a graph, G, to its supergraph of ℓ-diversity anonymity: (1) forming ℓ-non-conflicting groups, where an ℓ-non-conflicting group is referred to as a group of ℓ vertices without sharing any neighboring vertex in G; (2) equalizing vertex degrees in each ℓ-non-conflicting group. To illustrate MinSuper, we shall use the same example (with $\ell = 2$) as that for MaxSub, as shown in Fig. 7f–i. The pseudocode for MinSuper is given in Algorithm 3.

Step 1. (Forming ℓ-non-conflicting groups: All vertices in G are first sorted in a non-ascending order of their degrees, as shown in Fig. 7f. From the first vertex in the ordered sequence, MinSuper looks for ℓ vertices with no common neighbors to form an ℓ-non-conflicting group by sequentially checking and skipping the conflicting ones. If a group includes only fewer than ℓ non-conflicting vertices after going through the entire sequence, then dummy vertices with degrees of zero are padded to ensure group sizes not less than ℓ. For the running example, the final groups are listed in Fig. 7g.

Step 2. (Equalizing each ℓ-non-conflicting group): Each vertex is first labeled with the difference between its degree and the maximum vertex degree in its group, as shown in Fig. 7g. Then, dummy edges are inserted across any pair of groups, particularly between vertices with non-zero degree differences that have not been linked with any other vertex in each other's group. This constraint in the procedure for injecting dummy edges essentially requires that both the original and dummy edges across any pair of groups do not share vertices at their ends; thus, they meet the feature of matching for ℓ-diversity anonymity.

For a group that still has at least one vertex with a non-zero degree difference after pairing up with any other group, dummy vertices and edges will be inserted into the graph to equalize vertex degrees in that group. In particular, dummy edges will be constructed between those dummy vertices and real vertices with non-zero degree differences in order to reduce the degree differences to zero. For example, as shown in Fig. 7h, a dummy edge is inserted between v_1 and v_3. In order to equalize the degree of v_9 and v_{10}, we create two dummy vertices v_{11} and v_{12}. We cannot simply put the two dummy vertices in one non-conflicting group as they both connect v_{10}, we introduce two more dummy vertices v_{13} and v_{14} to form two non-conflicting groups as shown in Fig. 7i. The final published graph is the one with all original edges plus the dummy edges and vertices introduced. One can see that the procedure of sorting during the first step ensures that vertices in the same ℓ–non-conflicting group have similar degrees, thus minimizing the number of dummy edges required for degree equalization.

Algorithm 3 MinSuper

Input: G(V, E) the original graph, and its vertex set T, where T = V
Output: a heuristic minimum ℓ-diversity anonymous supergraph of G
1 Sort vertices in T in non-ascending order of their degrees
2 *groupnum* = 0
3 **while** T $\neq \emptyset$ **do**
4   t = next non-grouped node in T; Remove t from T
5   *counter* == 0
6   **while** *counter* $< \ell$ and not reach the end of T **do**
7   Find a non-conflicting node v_{nc}; Remove v_{nc} from T
8   *counter++*;
9   **if** *counter* == ℓ **then**
10   An ℓ-group is formed.
11   **else** An ℓ-group is formed with (ℓ- counter) fake nodes
13   *groupnum++*
14 Calculate degree difference $\Delta\, d_v$ for each node v
15 **for** i = 1: *groupnum*-1 **do**
16   **for** j = i : *groupnum* **do**
17   Create fake edges across g_i and g_j
18   **if** g_i still has a set of nodes with nonzero $\Delta\, d_v$, S_i **then**
19   **while** $S_i \neq \emptyset$ do
20   s = next node in S_i
21   Remove s from S_i; Create $\Delta\, d_s$ fake nodes
22   Construct $\Delta\, d_s$ fake edges linking s with fake nodes

---

We start by demonstrating the necessity of inserting dummy vertices in MinSuper to create a supergraph with ℓ-diversity anonymity by Theorem 3.

Theorem 3. *Relying only on the insertion of dummy edges may not work to expand an arbitrary graph to its ℓ-diversity anonymous supergraph.*

Proof. We know that given an *ℓ*-diversity anonymous graph with $\alpha\ell$ vertices, no vertices can have degrees greater than α; otherwise, the graph would require more than αi vertices to ensure there are at least *ℓ* vertices with degrees greater than α. Therefore, if an arbitrary graph with α vertices, *G*, originally has at least one vertex of degree greater than α, depending solely on dummy edges will not help to convert the graph so as to become *ℓ*-diversity anonymous.

Theorem 4. *Given an arbitrary graph, its supergraph published by MinSuper is ℓ-diversity anonymous.*

Proof. First, forming *ℓ*-non-conflicting group guarantees the size of each group to be *ℓ*. Second, because of the degree equalization procedure, all vertices in each group share the same degree. Finally, because of conflict-checking while forming groups, as well as the group-crossing matchings when equalizing vertex degrees in each group, we ensure that no vertices in the same group share any neighboring vertex. Therefore, the graph published by MinSuper is guaranteed to be *ℓ*-diversity anonymous.

Theorem 5. *The time complexity for MinSuper is $O(n^3)$ for a graph of n vertices.*

Proof. The time complexity for vertex sorting is $O(n\log(n))$ by a Merge Sort Algorithm. In the worst case of forming *ℓ*-non-conflicting groups, where each vertex conflicts with all other vertices in a complete graph, it takes each vertex $O(n^2)$ time for checking, and thus $O(n^3)$ for all vertices. For degree equalization, each group requires, at worst, to be checked with all other groups for edge construction. In the worst case for a complete graph, the total number of groups is *n*, and the checking between any pair of groups requires $O(\ell^2)$. Therefore, the time complexity for normalizing degrees is $O(\ell^2 n^2) \approx O(n^2)$. Therefore, the time complexity for MinSuper is $O(n^3)$.

4 Experimental Study

We conducted a comprehensive set of experiments for both synthetic and real-world social network data sets to evaluate our algorithms' performances. In particular, we measured the utility loss of the published data that was caused by our anonymization techniques. We implemented both MaxSub and MinSuper algorithms in MATLAB. In addition, we used a software package called Pajek[1] to measure the topological properties of the original graph and the graphs anonymized by our algorithms.

We conducted our experiments using three data sets. **Co-author data set:** The Co-author data set consists of 7,955 authors of papers in a database and theory conferences that are available at the collection of Computer Science Bibliographies

---

[1] http://vlado.fmf.uni-lj.si/pub/networks/pajek/

(http://liinwww.ira.uka.de/bib-liography). The Co-author graph is constructed by inserting an undirected edge between any pair of authors who have co-authored at least one paper. In total, there are 10,055 edges in this graph. **SIGMOD data set:** The SIGMOD data set was crawled from DBLP (http://dblp.uni-trier.de/xml/) on December 5, 2009; it contains co-authorship information for all previous SIGMOD conferences. In its corresponding graph, there are 3,791 vertices (i.e., authors) and 10,003 edges (i.e., co-authorship). **R-MAT data set:** We used the R-MAT graph model [16] to generate a synthetic data set. The basic idea behind R-MAT is to recursively subdivide the adjacency matrix of a graph into four equally-sized partitions, and then distribute edges within these partitions with unequal probabilities of a, b, c, and d. Using the R-MAT model can generate graphs characterized by scale-free and small-world features, the two most important properties for many real-world social networks. We followed the configuration found in [11], and set the input parameters to $a = 0.45$, $b = 0.15$, $c = 0.15$, and $d = 0.25$ to generate social network graphs with 5,000 vertices and average vertex degree of 5.

4.1 Experimental Results

We studied the utility loss of the anonymized data from the topological measurements of graphs, including: the number of deleted or inserted edges/vertices; the number of pairs of unreachable vertices; the average distance of reachable vertices (i.e., the length of the shortest path between each pair of vertices); the distribution of vertex degrees; and the distance distribution of pairs of reachable vertices.

Number of vertices/edges: Fig. 10a–c show that in our three data sets, as compared with the number of original vertices, the number of dummy vertices created by MinSuper is quite small. As shown in Fig. 10d–f, the number of edges changed by MaxSub is more than that by MinSuper. For MinSuper, as compared with the large number of original edges, only a few dummy edges are inserted.

In addition, we can also observe *the tradeoff between privacy preservation and utility loss*. According to Definition 8, the larger the value of ℓ is, the higher is the level of privacy preservation. However, a small value of ℓ will reduce the utility loss in the published graph in terms of our algorithm design. The reason is that a small value of ℓ leads to groups of smaller size, which creates more chances to add edges across groups. This experimental result is shown in Fig. 10d–f. With increasing ℓ, the plot from MaxSub decreases slightly. Because the value of ℓ is relatively small, ranging only from 2 to 7, the plot does not decline dramatically. For MinSuper, the plot increases with ℓ. This is because increasing ℓ leads to forming ℓ-non-conflicting groups of larger size. Hence, the difference between the maximum and minimum degrees in each group becomes greater, which requires more dummy edges to be created for the purpose of degree equalization.

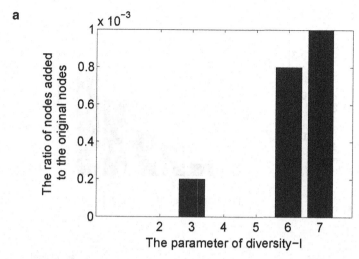

R-MAT nodes

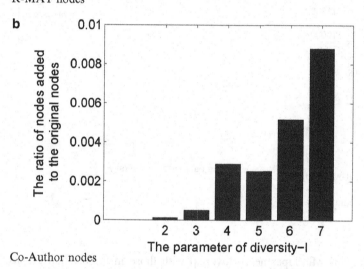

Co-Author nodes

Fig. 10 Experimental study of utility loss

Degree distribution: In Fig. 10g–i, the degree distribution in the graph anonymized by MinSuper is more similar to the original than that in the graph published by MaxSub.

Distance distribution: We discuss the distance distribution only for reachable vertices in the graphs. As shown in Fig. 10j–l, the distance distributions in graphs

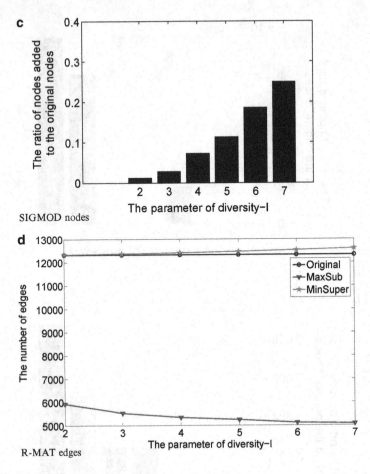

Fig. 10 (continued)

published by MinSuper nearly overlap with those in the original graphs, which reflects less utility loss. Additionally, we observe that there are far more reachable pairs of vertices in the graphs by MinSuper than those in the graphs anonymized by MaxSub, which indicates the better connectivity of the graphs published by MinSuper. The reason is given the fact that MaxSub and MinSuper achieve ℓ-diversity anonymity for an arbitrary graph from two different directions: seeking a subgraph and a supergraph, MinSuper primarily relies on inserting dummy edges, therefore it results in better connectivity of the anonymized graph than MaxSub.

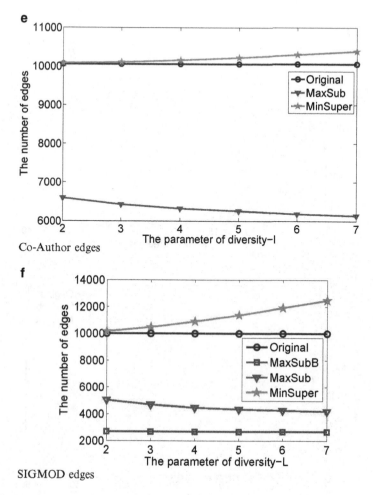

Co-Author edges

SIGMOD edges

Fig. 10 (continued)

5 Conclusions

In this chapter, we have discussed the applications of some classical privacy preservation models that were developed for tabular data to preserve users' privacy when publishing OSN data. In particular, we introduced some *k*-anonymity based techniques developed not only to preserve users' identity privacy, but also to

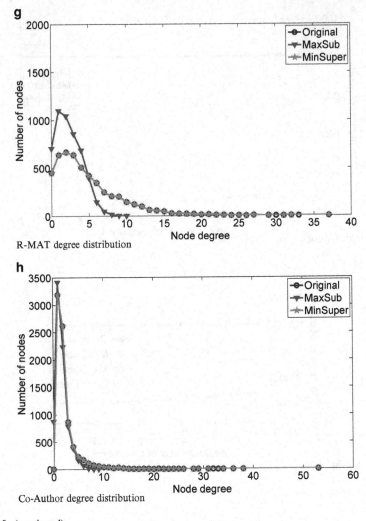

g

R-MAT degree distribution

h

Co-Author degree distribution

Fig. 10 (continued)

protect users' relationship privacy. We also detailed our previous work that employed the ℓ-diversity model to preserve users' relationship privacy.

There are some other models in the traditional fields of data mining and databases for preserving tabular data privacy, such as t-closeness [17], which have not been considered much in the context of publishing OSN data. In addition, a new concept, *differential privacy* [18], has entered the field of preserving data privacy. However, it has not been well explored for handling relational data, like

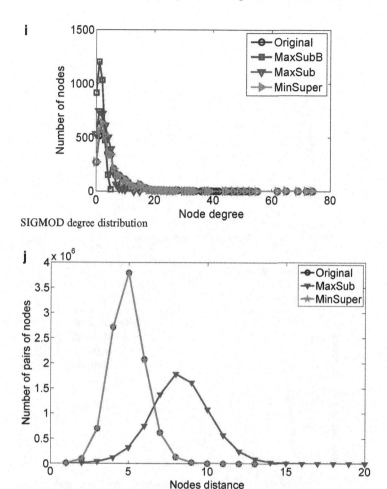

i SIGMOD degree distribution

j R-MAT distance distribution

Fig. 10 (continued)

OSN data, which merits more research efforts. We believe that without securing user's privacy, the reputation of OSNs will be jeopardized and their user population will decrease dramatically. Therefore, more attention should be paid to developing techniques to preserve users' privacy on OSNs.

To the best of our knowledge, this is the first work that addresses the application of the ℓ-diversity model for preserving relational data in publishing OSNs. We believe that it can be applied to some other relevant scenarios, such as preserving group membership, which will become potential research possibilities.

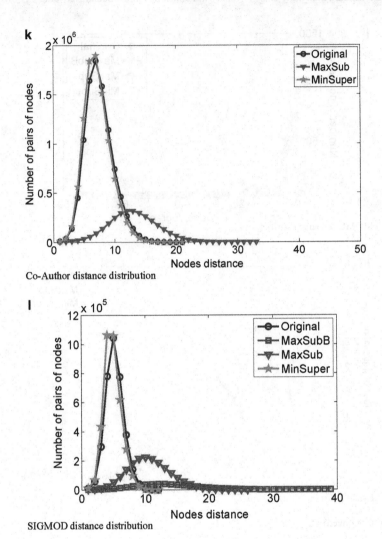

Co-Author distance distribution

SIGMOD distance distribution

Fig. 10 (continued)

References

1. Gross R, Acquisti A (2005) Information revelation and privacy in online social networks. In: Proceedings of the 2005 ACM workshop on privacy in the electronic society (WPES '05), November 7, 2005, Alexandria, Virginia, USA, pp 71–80
2. Backstrom L, Dwork C, Kleinberg J. Wherefore art thou r3579x?: anonymized social networks, hidden patterns, and structural steganography. In: WWW '07, May 8–12, 2007, Banff, Alberta, Canada, pp 71–80

3. Altshuler Y, Aharony N, Pentland A, Elovici Y, Cebrian M (2011) Stealing reality: when criminals become data scientists (or vice versa). IEEE Intell Syst 26(6):22–30
4. Solutionary. http://www.solutionary.com/index/intelligence-center/white-papers/apt-white-paper-reg/apt-white-paper-lp.php
5. Korolova A, Motwani R, Nabar SU, Xu Y (2008) Link privacy in social networks. In: Proceeding of the 17th ACM conference on information and knowledge management (CIKM '08), Napa Valley, pp 289–298
6. Das S, Egecioglu O, Abbadi AE (2009) Anonymizing edge-weighted social network graphs. In: Technical report CS-2009-03, Department of Computer Science, The University of California, Santa Barbara
7. Liu L, Wang J, Liu J, Zhang J (2008) Privacy preserving in social networks against sensitive edge disclosure. In: Technical report CMIDA-HiPSCCS 006-08, Department of Computer Science, University of Kentucky, Kentucky
8. Li N, Zhang N, Das SK (2011) Preserving relation privacy in online social network data. Internet Comput IEEE 15(3):35–42, May–June 2011
9. Sweeney L (2002) K-anonymity: a model for protecting privacy. Int J Uncertain Fuzz Knowl-Based Syst 10(5):557–570
10. Liu K, Terzi E. Towards identity anonymization on graphs. In: SIGMOD '08, June 9–12, 2008, Vancouver, BC, Canada, pp 71–80
11. Zhou B, Pei J. Preserving privacy in social networks against neighborhood attacks. In: ICDE '08, April 7–12, 2008, Cancún, México, pp 506–515
12. Zou L, Chen L, Ozsu MT. K-automorphism: a general framework for privacy preserving network publication. In: Proceedings of the VLDB Endowment (VLDB) 2(1):946–957, August 2009
13. Cheng J, Fu AW-C, Liu J (2010) K-isomorphism: privacy preservation in network publication against structural attack. In: SIGMOD '10, June 6–11, 2010, Indianapolis, Indiana, USA, pp 459–470
14. Machanavajjhala A, Kifer D, Gehrke J, Venkitasubramaniam M (2007) *ℓ*-diversity: privacy beyond k-anonymity. ACM Trans Knowl Discov Data 1(1), March 2007
15. Li N, Zhang N, Das S (2011) Relationship privacy preservation in publishing online social networks. In: Proceedings of the 3rd IEEE international conference on social computing (SocialCom '11), MIT, Boston
16. Chakrabarti D, Zhan Y, Faloutsos C. R-mat: a recursive model for graph mining. In: SIAM DM '04
17. Li N, Li T (2007) t-closeness: privacy beyond k-anonymity and *ℓ*-diversity. In: Proceedings of IEEE 23rd international conference on data engineering, Istanbul
18. Dwork C (2006) Automata, languages and programming lecture notes in computer science, 2006, Vol 4052/2006, 1–12, DOI: 10.1007/11787006_1
19. Bugliesi M et al. (2006) ICALP 2006, Part II, LNCS 4052, pp 1–12

Links Reconstruction Attack

Using Link Prediction Algorithms to Compromise Social Networks Privacy

Michael Fire, Gilad Katz, Lior Rokach, and Yuval Elovici

Abstract The explosion in the use of social networks has also created new kinds of security and privacy threats. Many users are unaware of the risks involved with exposing their personal information, which makes social networks a "bonanza" for identity thieves. In addition, it has already been proven that even concealing all personal data might not be sufficient for providing protection, as personal information can be inferred by analyzing a person's connections to other users. In attempts to cope with these risks, some users hide parts of their social connections to other users. In this paper we present "link reconstruction attack", a method that can infer a user's connections to others with high accuracy. This attack can be used to detect connections that a user wanted to hide in order to preserve his privacy. We show that concealing one's links is ineffective if not done by others in the network. We also provide an analysis of the performances of various machine learning algorithms for link prediction inside small communities.

Keywords Social networks • Social networks privacy • Social networks analysis • Inference attack • Link prediction • Community link prediction

M. Fire • G. Katz • L. Rokach
Deutsche Telekom Laboratories at Ben-Gurion University of the Negev, Department of
Information Systems Engineering, Ben Gurion University, Be'er Sheva, 84105, Israel
e-mail: mickyfi@bgu.ac.il; katzgila@bgu.ac.il; liorrk@bgu.ac.il

Y. Elovici (✉)
Telekom Innovation Lab, Information systems engineering, Ben-Gurion University,
P.O.B. 653, Beer-Sheva, Israel
e-mail: elovici@bgu.ac.il

Y. Altshuler et al. (eds.), *Security and Privacy in Social Networks*,
DOI 10.1007/978-1-4614-4139-7_9, © Springer Science+Business Media New York 2013

1   Introduction

In recent years there has been a surge in the use of social networks, smartphones, and other internet-enabled devices. Because of this trend, ever-growing amounts of data – both personal and financial – are available online. These data can be and are being collected by third parties. Companies can collect users' data by various methods, including social web crawlers [31], website logs [15], social network applications [38], and smart phone applications [3]. In today's technological world, the loss of personal data is not only a financial risk, but can also lead to criminal charges. This problematic situation in which sensitive personal information is exposed to third parties has become worse in recent years due to the explosion in use of online social networks. The amount of personal information contained in such networks is enormous. For example, an analysis of the Facebook social network determined that it had more than 845 million registered users. According to recent statistics published by Facebook [14], 50% of Facebook users log onto this site on a daily basis via laptop or other mobile devices, and 30 billion pieces of content are shared each month (web links, news stories, blog posts, notes, photo albums, etc.). The average Facebook user has 130 friends and creates 90 pieces of content each month. Many Facebook users expose personal details, such as dates of birth, email addresses, high school names, and even their phone numbers [2, 8].

Usually, online social networks like Facebook provide their users with means to protect their personal information. This is done by allowing only one's "friends" (those who the user trusts and defines as such) to access one's personal information. However, limiting access to specific trust groups is not a perfect solution for privacy protection due to the fact that some users tend to accept unfamiliar users into their trust group. In so doing, they expose their personal data to third parties [8, 32]. Furthermore, even if a person takes almost every precaution and reveals nothing except links to other users in the social network, her personal data can still be inferred from her friends. This holds true for different types of social networks, including online social networks [28], mobile phone social networks [7], and real world student cooperation social networks [15]. Therefore, as suggested by Jianming et al. [24] and Lindamood et al. [28], in order to better protect their privacy, users should also conceal their links to other users, or at least make them accessible only to their "friends".

In this paper, we present a method for inferring hidden links within small communities that are part of large social networks. Our method is based on the link prediction algorithm that was first described by Fire et al. [16]. This new algorithm is based on a machine learning classifier trained on a small set of easy-to-compute topological features. We then use the classifier to predict hidden links inside different types of social network communities, each containing up to several hundred links: a Facebook group of people who work in the same company; an SMS social network from the Friends and Family study; the real world Students' Cooperation Network; and groups of researchers with the same affiliation that were collected from the Academia.edu social network. We demonstrate that, although our classifiers were trained only on small training sets, they can still infer hidden links within different types of communities with high rates of F-measure and AUC (Area under the ROC curve). Using our methods, it is possible, with a high degree of accuracy, to infer and reconstruct users' social links and personal information.

The remainder of this paper is organized as follows. In Sect. 2, we provide a brief overview of previous studies on privacy protection in social networks and on different link prediction algorithms. In Sect. 3, we describe the methods and experiments that were used during the construction and evaluation of our classifiers. In Sect. 4, we describe the different social network communities that were used throughout this study. In Sect. 5 we present our experimental results. Finally, in Sect. 6, we present our conclusions and offer future research directions.

2 Related Work

In this section we describe previous work in the fields of social networks privacy and link prediction.

2.1 Privacy in Social Networks

In recent years, online social networks use has grown exponentially. Online social networks, such as Facebook [13], Twitter [37], LinkedIn [29], Flickr [17], YouTube [39], and LiveJournal [30], serve millions of users on a daily basis. With this increased use, new privacy concerns have been raised. These concerns results from the fact that online social network users publish personal information both about themselves and their friends; all of this information can be collected by a third party. Research by Acquisti and Gross [2] in the area of social network privacy attempted to evaluate the amount of personal information that was exposed by users on Facebook. They concluded that many Facebook users disclose personal information about themselves, including dates of birth, email addresses, relationship statuses, and even phone numbers.

Another interesting fact is that around 55% of users accept friend requests from people they do not know. By accepting these friend requests, users disclose their private information to strangers [32]. Moreover, studies on trust levels in social networks showed that 27.5% of Facebook users who participated in the study had met face-to-face with people who they had initially met through Facebook [11]. Recently, Boshmaf et al. [8] collected 250 GB of inbound traffic from Facebook using Socialbots. These Socialbots succeeded in harvesting data from Facebook users by using friend requests that originated from fake Facebook profiles. Another privacy related concern is that one's personal information can be inferred from one's links. Jianming et al. [24] and Lindamood et al. [28] demonstrated methods for inferring users' personal information by using that of their friends. This was done for social networks like Facebook and LiveJournal.

Similar privacy problems also exist in other types of social networks. In smartphones social networks, various applications were identified as collecting users' personal information. This personal information included data on such things as one's location [5] and user keystrokes [12]. An even greater threat was described by Altshuler et al. [6], who showed that attacks could steal one's social network and behavioral information. Moreover, Altshuler et al. demonstrated that other information, such as ethnicity, religion, origin and age could be inferred from social network links that were created through SMS messages [7]. Recently, Fire et al. showed that even complex attributes like academic course final test grades could be inferred from a student's links to other people who took the course. The social network that was used for this analysis was created by analyzing the course's assignments and the course web log [15].

2.2 Link Prediction

The link prediction problem (i.e., inferring the existence of unknown links based on known ones), has many applications outside the domain of social networks. In the bioinformatics domain, link prediction is used to identify interactions among proteins [4], while in the e-commerce domain it is used to provide recommendations to customers [22]. It is even applied in the area of homeland security, where its application attempts to detect terrorist cells [21]. The popularity of this method has generated a wide variety of possible solutions. However, in spite of their diversity, most algorithms rely on supervised machine learning and feature selection. A thorough review of previous work can be found in Hasan and Zaki [20].

In this paper, we focus on the common approach of using supervised learning algorithms to solve the Link Prediction problem. This approach was introduced by Liben-Nowell and Kleinberg in 2003 [27]. They studied the utility of graph topological features by testing them on five co-authorship networks data sets, each containing several thousands of authors. In 2006, Hasan et al. [21] extended their work on the DBLP and BIOBASE coauthorship networks (each containing several hundreds of thousands of papers). Since its publication, the supervised learning approach has been implemented by several research groups [10, 26, 34]. Most solutions that these researchers proposed were tested on bibliographic or co-authorship data sets [10, 21, 27]. In 2009, Song et al. used matrix factorization to estimate the similarity of nodes in large scale social networks, such as Facebook and MySpace [36]. In 2011, several papers were published after the IJCNN social network challenge was issued [23]. Each of these papers proposed a different method for predicting links in social networks. Narayanan et al. won the challenge by using a method that combined machine-learning algorithms and de-anonymization [33]. Cukierski et al. [9] won second place by extracting 94 distinct graph features and using the Random Forest algorithm to analyze the training data (consisting of several thousands of edges). Recently, Fire et al. published a method for predicting links in large scale online social networks using easy-to-compute topological features. Their method used 50,000 links as a training set for the classifiers [16].

In this paper, we use the link prediction algorithm presented by Fire et al. [16] and test it on different types of social network communities in order to reconstruct users' links. We show that reconstructing users' links can compromise their privacy and render them vulnerable to inference attacks, as described by Jianming et al. [24] and Lindamood et al. [28].

3 Methods and Experiments

To identify hidden links inside different communities, we applied methods from the machine learning domain. For each community, we developed a dedicated link classifier capable of predicting the likelihood of the existence of a link between two members. For each community, we extracted a "positive" training set of links that exist in the communities' graphs and a set of "negative" links that do not exist in the graph.

Due to the small sizes of the communities, our "positive" links training set consisted almost entirely of links that connected members inside the community. Our "negative" links training set consisted of two types of links. The first was random links, where both nodes were chosen randomly (hereafter referred to as the "easy" train set). The second type of "negative" links was generated so that the two connected nodes were within a distance of two from each other (hereafter referred to as the "hard" train set).

Subsequently, for each positive and negative link we extracted a small set of easy-to-compute topological features, as suggested by Fire et al. [16]. We then used these extracted topological features to train several supervised learning classifiers. This was done using WEKA [19], a popular suite of machine learning. Finally, we used WEKA to evaluate the performance of each classifier.

The remainder of this section describes the small sets of features that were extracted to train our classifiers and the different machine learning algorithms used in our experiments.

3.1 Feature Extraction

This section describes the different features that were extracted in order to build our community link prediction classifiers. The extracted features are primarily based on the Friends-features subset, as suggested by Fire et al. [16].

Let $G = <V,E>$ be the graph representing the topological structure of a general social network community. Links in the graph are denoted by $e = (u, v) \in E$ where $u, v \in V$ are nodes in the community graph. Our goal is to construct simple classifiers capable of computing the likelihood of $(u, v) \in E$ or $(u, v) \notin E$ for every two nodes $u, v \in V$. To achieve this goal, we extracted the following features for each link, (u, v), from our training sets.

1. **Vertex degree**: Let be $v \in V$, we can define the neighborhood of v by:

$$\Gamma(v) := \{u | (u, v) \in E \text{ or } (v, u) \in E\} \tag{1}$$

If G is a directed graph we can also define the following neighborhoods:

$$\Gamma_{in}(v) := \{u | (u, v) \in E\}$$
$$\Gamma_{out}(v) := \{u | (v, u) \in E\} \tag{2}$$

Using the above defined neighborhoods, we can define the following degree feature:

$$degree(v) := |\Gamma(v)| \tag{3}$$

If G is a directed graph, we can also define the following degree features:

$$degree_{in}(v) := |\Gamma_{in}(v)| \tag{4}$$

$$degree_{out}(v) := |\Gamma_{out}(v)| \tag{5}$$

The degree features are used to measure the number of friends v has inside the community. If we look at a directed graph of a community such as Twitter, the meaning of the degree feature is how many other members of the community v follows (out-degree), and how many members of the community follow v (in-degree).

2. **Common friends**: Let $u, v \in V$; we define the common friends of u and v to be all the members in the community that are friends both of u and v. The formal definition of the number of common friends is: Let be $u, v \in V$ then

$$common - friends(u, v) := |\Gamma(v) \cap \Gamma(u)| \tag{6}$$

The common-friends feature was widely used in previous work in to predict links in different datasets [9, 16, 22, 27, 34, 36].

3. **Total friends**: Let $u, v \in V$; we can define the number of distinct friends of u and v by:

$$total - friends(u, v) := |\Gamma(u) \cup \Gamma(v)| \tag{7}$$

4. **Jaccard's coefficient**: Jaccard's-coefficient is a well-known feature for link prediction [9, 16, 22, 27, 34, 36]. This feature, which measures the similarity among sets of nodes, is defined as the size of the intersection divided by the size of the union of the sample sets. The formal definition of Jaccard's coefficient can be written in the following way.

$$Jaccards'-coefficient(u,v) := \frac{|\Gamma(u) \cap \Gamma(v)|}{|\Gamma(u) \cup \Gamma(v)|} \tag{8}$$

In our approach, this measure indicates whether two community members have a significant number of common friends regardless of their total number of friends. A higher value of Jaccard's-coefficient indicates a stronger connection between two nodes in the community.

5. **Preferential-attachment-score**: The preferential-attachment score is defined as the multiplication of the number of friends of u and v.

$$preferential-attachment-score(u,v) := |\Gamma(u)| \cdot |\Gamma(v)| \tag{9}$$

The Preferential-attachment score is a well-known concept in social networks. It measures how "connected" each user is and also provides a strong indication of how likely (and at what rate) the user is likely to create additional connections [16, 21].

6. **Opposite direction friends**: For a directed graph G, we created a specific measure that indicates whether reciprocal connections exist between each pair of nodes

$$opposite-direction-friends(u,v) := \begin{cases} 1 & \text{if } (v,u) \in E \\ 0 & \text{otherwise} \end{cases} \tag{10}$$

7. **Shortest path**: We define the shortest path measure between nodes u and v in the following manner: $shortest-path(u,v)$. This measure represents the length of the shortest path between u and v inside the community. If the community graph is directed, this measure will not necessarily be symmetrical. The shortest path feature has been explored in several papers [16, 21] and found to be one of most significant features for the predicting hidden links.

8. **Friends measure**: The friends measure is a private case of the Katz measure [25], and was first presented by Fire et al. [16]. The formal definition of the friends measure is: Let be $u, v \in V$, then

$$friends - measure(u,v) := \sum_{x \in \Gamma(u)} \sum_{y \in \Gamma(v)} \delta(x,y) \tag{11}$$

Where $\delta(x,y)$ is defined as:

$$\delta(x,y) := \begin{cases} 1 & \text{if } x = y \text{ or } (x,y) \in E \text{ or } (y,x) \in E \\ 0 & \text{otherwise} \end{cases}$$

The friends measure represents the number of u's friends who also know v's friends. The higher the number of connections between u and v's friends, the greater the chance that u and v know each other.

3.2 Experimental Setup

To build community link prediction tools, we created an easy training set and a hard training set for each community. The easy training set for each community contained 50% positive and 50% negative links. As mentioned previously, the positive links are those that exist within the community, while the negative links are those that, to the best of our knowledge, do not exist.

In the easy training set, each of the negative links was created by randomly choosing two nodes in the community that did not have a link between them, while in the hard training set, negative links were created by choosing two nodes in the community that were at a distance of two from each other. Due to the small size of each community, the size of each training set would have been twice the size of the number of existing links in each community had all of the existing links in each community been included in our training sets.

Once the training set links were selected, a Python code was developed using the Networkx package [18]. This code was used to extract the topological features mentioned above for each of the links (8 features for an undirected network and 14 features for a directed network). Our next step was to evaluate different link prediction methods created by different supervised learning algorithms. We used WEKA's C4.5 (J48), IBk, NaiveBayes, SMO, MultilayerPerceptron, Bagging, AdaBoostM1, RotationForest, and RandomForest implementations of the corresponding algorithms. For each of these algorithms, most of the configurable parameters were set to their default values, with the following exceptions: for C4.5, the minimum number of instances per leaf parameter was between the values of 2, 6, 8 and 10; for IBk, its k parameter was set to 10; for SMO, the NormalizedPolyKernel with its default parameters was used. The ensemble methods were configured as follows: The number of iterations for all ensemble methods was set to 100. The Bagging, AdaBoostM1, and RotationForest algorithms were evaluated using J48 as the base classifier with the number of instances per leaf set to 4, 6, 8, and 10.

4 Communities Datasets

We evaluate our community link prediction classifiers using four communities from different types of social networks datasets: Facebook [13], Academia.edu [1], Friends and Family study [3], and Students' Cooperation Social Network [15] (Table 1).

Facebook. Facebook is a website and social networking service that was launched in February 2004 [13]. As of January 2012, Facebook had more than 800 million registered users [14]. Facebook users may create a personal profile, add other users as friends, and interact with other members. Because the friendship link between two members must be reciprocal, the existence of a link between member A and member B induces a mutual connection. Therefore, we refer to Facebook's underlying friendship graph undirected. We evaluated our classifiers for a small

Table 1 Communities datasets

Community	Is directed	Nodes number	Links number	Obtained by	Date
Facebook coworkers	No	410	635	Web crawler	2012
Academia.edu researchers community	Yes	207	702	Web crawler	2011
Friends and family SMS network	Yes	103	281	Smartphone application	2010–2011
Students' cooperation network	No	185	311	Web log and assignments analysis	2011

Fig. 1 Facebook coworker community social network

community of co-workers that according to their Facebook profile pages worked for the same well-known high-tech company. These co-workers' community network graph contained 410 nodes and 635 links, it was obtained using a web crawler at the beginning of January 2012 (see Fig. 1[1]).

Academia.edu. Academia.edu is a platform for academics to share and follow research that is underway in a particular field or discipline [1]. Members upload and share their papers with other researchers in over 100,000 fields and categories. An Academia social network member may choose to follow any of the network's

---

[1] All the social networks figures in this paper where created by Cytoscape software [35].

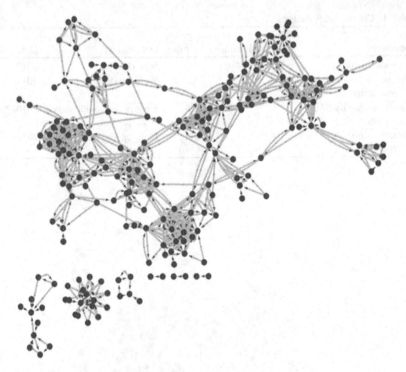

Fig. 2 Academia.edu researchers community social network

members; hence, the directed nature of the links within this network. We evaluated our classifiers for a small community of researchers who, according to their Academia.edu profiles, belonged to the same Ivy League University. The researchers' community network graph contained 207 nodes and 702 links (see Fig. 2) and was obtained using a web crawler.

Friends and family. The Friends and Family dataset contains rich data signals gathered from the smartphones of 140 adult members of a young-family residential community. The data were collected over the course of 1 year [3]. We evaluated our classifiers for members of a social network that was constructed based on SMS messages sent and received by the members. The SMS messages social network directed graph contained 103 nodes and 281 links (see Fig. 3).

Students' cooperation social network. The students' cooperation social network was constructed from the data collected during a "Computer and Network Security" course; a mandatory course taught by two of this paper's authors at Ben-Gurion University [15]. The social network contains data collected from 185 participating students from two different departments. The course's social network was created by analyzing the implicit and explicit cooperation among the students while doing their homework assignments. The students' cooperation graph contained 185 nodes and 311 links (see Fig. 4).

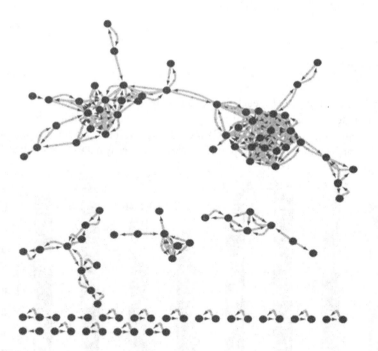

Fig. 3 Friends and family SMS messages social network

Fig. 4 Students' cooperation
social network

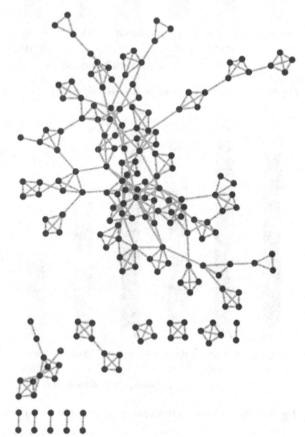

5   Results

For each community and for each easy and hard training set, we evaluated our list of
different machine learning classifiers by using a tenfold cross-validation approach.
We used an area-under-curve (AUC) measure to evaluate our results. In Figs. 5
and 6, we present the classifiers' performances for the easy dataset for the Facebook

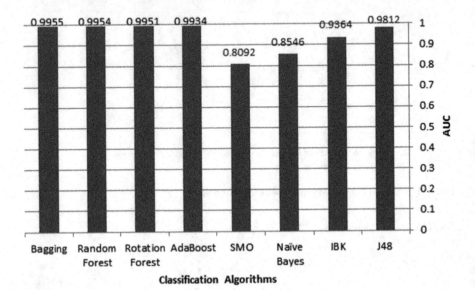

Fig. 5 AUC results – Facebook coworkers' community

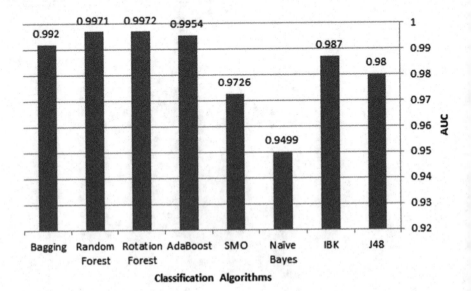

Fig. 6 AUC results – Academia.edu researchers' community

Table 2 Easy training set – classifiers' highest results

Dataset	Classifier	Train set size	TP	F-measure	AUC
Facebook	Rotation forest	1,270	0.9983	0.9667	0.9951
Academia.edu	AdaBoost	1,445	0.969	0.9746	0.9954
Friends and family	AdaBoost	563	0.9818	0.9745	0.9946
Student's cooperation	Bagging	623	0.9643	0.9398	0.9775

Table 3 Hard training set – classifiers' highest results

Dataset	Classifier	Train set size	TP	F-measure	AUC
Facebook	Rotation forest	1,270	0.9835	0.9686	0.9981
Academia.edu	Rotation forest	1,445	0.9127	0.9213	0.9756
Friends and family	Rotation forest	563	0.9537	0.9471	0.9831
Student's cooperation	Rotation forest	623	0.999	0.9883	0.9998

coworkers' community and for the Academia.edu researchers' community, respectively. The best results for each of our datasets are presented in Tables 2 and 3.

As expected, the ensemble methods fared best, especially the Rotation Forest algorithm. In contrast to previous link prediction ensemble classifiers that require large amounts of resources [9, 16], our community link prediction ensemble classifiers were quick to build and train due to the small size of the required training sets. For example, the average time for extracting link features in the Facebook community was 0.002 s, both for negative and positive links.[2]

To obtain an indication of the usefulness of the various features in different communities and datasets, we analyzed their respective importance using Weka's information gain attribute selection algorithm. Our results are presented in Tables 4 and 5. Based on these results, it should be noted that a feature's importance varies among the different communities.

6 Conclusions and Future Work

In today's world, many people use different types of social networks in order to communicate with each other and to share knowledge. One of the main problems with using and participating in social networks is that one's privacy can be easily become compromised. Even if the social network user does not expose information to other users in the network, and even hides all of his personal information, he may still be exposed to inference attacks due to his connections to other users [24, 28]. One can defend oneself against these types of inference attacks by hiding some of one's links in the network. In this study, we presented a method for reconstructing a

---

[2] We ran our algorithm using Python 2.7, on a regular Dell Latitude E6420 laptop with i7 core, and 8 GB RAM.

Table 4 Easy training set – information gain value of different features

Feature	Friends and Family	Academia.edu	Students' cooperation	Facebook
Degree(u)	0.137	0.204	0.015	0.206
Degree(v)	0.13	0.086	0.019	0.095
Common-Friends(u,v)	0.364	0.486	0.588	0
Total-Friends(u,v)	0.121	0.082	0.272	0.244
Jaccard's-Coefficient(u,v)	0.364	0.473	0.598	0
Preferential-attachment-score(u,v)	0.282	0.256	0.106	0.309
Friends-Measure(u,v)	0.667	0.607	0.54	0.088
Shortest-path(u,v)	0.053	0.166	0.289	0.1071
Shortest-path(v,u)	0.105	0.174	-	-
In-degree(u)	0.113	0.106	-	-
In-degree(v)	0.136	0.113	-	-
out-degree(u)	0.162	0.278	-	-
out-degree(v)	0.112	0.048	-	-
Opposite Direction(u,v)	0.701	0.392	-	-

Table 5 Hard training set – information gain value of different features

Feature	Friends and Family	Academia.edu	Students' cooperation	Facebook
Degree(u)	0	0.052	0	0.198
Degree(v)	0	0.015	0.029	0
Common-Friends(u,v)	0.262	0.232	0.544	0.753
Total-Friends(u,v)	0.018	0.014	0.332	0.121
Jaccard's-Coefficient(u,v)	0.217	0.206	0.712	0.753
Preferential-attachment-score(u,v)	0.097	0.061	0.241	0.193
Friends-Measure(u,v)	0.102	0.158	0.4	0.447
Shortest-path(u,v)	0.028	0.057	0.056	0.563
Shortest-path(v,u)	0.537	0.021	-	-
In-degree(u)	0.015	0.012	-	-
In-degree(v)	0	0.014	-	-
out-degree(u)	0	0.064	-	-
out-degree(v)	0	0.007	-	-
Opposite Direction(u,v)	0.589	0.253	-	-

user's hidden links to other users by creating a link prediction community classifier for different types of social networks.

The classifiers presented in this paper were created by using only a handful of graph topological features for each link and a small amount of training data for each data set. Despite these limitations, the tested classifiers succeeded in achieving high results both in terms of F-Measures and AUC measures (also referred to as ROC Areas) for all tested community data sets. While most of the tested classifiers produced positive results, the best results were obtained using ensemble supervised learning algorithms, with the Rotation Forest algorithm achieving the highest AUC rates. We also demonstrated that the presented classifiers could perform well even on the hard training set (See Table 3). These types of link prediction classifiers can assist attackers in reconstructing the hidden user links.

Several possibilities for future research are currently under consideration. The first direction is attempting to reconstruct cross-community hidden links. Another possibility is creating a method to accurately predict and measure one's exposure to inference attacks. A third possible direction is creating a recommender system that would advise users to connect to other users in order to foil link reconstruction attacks.

References

1. Academia.edu (2011) http://academia.edu/
2. Acquisti A, Gross R (2006) Imagined communities: awareness, information sharing, and privacy on the Facebook, privacy enhancing technologies. Springer, Berlin/New York
3. Aharony N, Pan W, Ip C, Khayal I, Pentland A (2011) The social fMRI: measuring, understanding and designing social mechanisms in the real world. In: Proceedings of the 13th ACM international conference on Ubiquitous computing. ACM, New York
4. Airoldi EM, Blei DM, Fienberg SE, Xing EP (2006) Mixed membership stochastic block models for relational data with application to protein-protein interactions. In: Proceedings of ineterational biometric society-ENAR annual meetings, Montréal
5. Allan A, Warden P (2011) Got an iphone or 3g ipad? Apple is recording your moves. http://radar.oreilly.com/2011/04/apple-location-tracking.html
6. Altshuler Y, Aharony N, Pentland A, Elovici Y, Cebrian M (2011) Stealing reality: when criminals become data scientists (or vice versa). Intell Syst IEEE 26:22–30
7. Altshuler Y, Fire M, Aharony N, Elovici Y, Pentland A (2012) How many makes a crowd? On the correlation between groups' size and the accuracy of modeling. Social computing behavioral modeling and prediction(SBP), University of Maryland, College Park
8. Boshmaf Y, Muslukhov I, Beznosov K, Ripeanu M (2011) The socialbot network: when bots socialize for fame and money. ACM Int Conf Proc Ser 93–102
9. Cukierski WJ, Hamner B, Yang B (2011) Graph-based features for supervised link prediction. In: International joint conference on neural networks (IJCNN), San Jose
10. Doppa JR, Yu J, Tadepalli P, Getoor L (2009) Chance-constrained programs for link prediction. In: Proceedings of workshop on analyzing networks and learning with graphs at NIPS conference, Whistler
11. Dwyer C, Hiltz SR, Passerini K (2007) Trust and privacy concern within social networking sites: a comparison of Facebook and MySpace. In: Proceedings of the Americas conference on information systems, Keystone
12. Eckhart T (2011) What is carrier IQ? http://androidsecuritytest.com/features/logs-and-services/loggers/carrieriq/
13. Facebook (2012) http://www.facebook.com
14. Facebook Statistics (2011) https://www.facebook.com/press/info.php?statistics
15. Fire M, Katz G, Elovici Y, Shapira B, Lior R (2011) Predicting student exam's scores by analyzing social network data
16. Fire M, Tenenboim L, Lesser O, Puzis R, Rokach L, Elovici Y (2011) Link prediction in social networks using computationally efficient topological features, SocialCom, MIT, Boston
17. Flickr (2012) http://www.flickr.com
18. Hagberg AA, Schult DA, Swart PJ (2008) Exploring network structure, dynamics, and function using networkx. In: Proceedings of the 7th Python in science conference (SciPy2008), Pasadena
19. Hall M, Frank E, Holmes G, Pfahringer B, Reutemann P, Witten IH (2009) The weka data mining software: an update. SIGKDD Explor Newsl 11:10–18
20. Hasan MA, Zaki MJ (2011) A survey of link prediction in social networks. In: Aggarwal CC (ed) Social network data analytics. Springer, New York

21. Hasan MA, Chaoji V, Salem S, Zaki M (2006) Link prediction using supervised learning. In: Proceedings of SDM workshop of link analysis, counterterrorism and security, Washington
22. Huang Z, Li X, Chen H (2005) Link prediction approach to collaborative filtering. In: Proceedings of the 5th ACM/IEEE-CS joint conference on digital libraries, Denver
23. IJCNN Social Network Challenge (2011) http://www.kaggle.com/c/socialNetwork/Data
24. Jianming H, Wesley WC, Zhenyu L (2006) Inferring privacy information from social networks. IEEE international conference on intelligence and security informatics, San Diego
25. Katz L (1953) A new status index derived from sociometric analysis. Psychometrika 18 (1):39–43 [Online]. Available: http://ideas.repec.org/a/spr/psycho/v18y1953i1p39-43.html
26. Leskovec J, Huttenlocher D, Kleinberg J (2010) Predicting positive and negative links in online social networks. In: Proceedings of the 19th international conference on World Wide Web, WWW '10, Raleigh
27. Liben-Nowell D, Kleinberg J (2007) The link-prediction problem for social networks. J Am Soc Inf Sci Technol 58(7):1019–1031
28. Lindamood J, Raymond H, Kantarcioglu M, Thuraisingham B (2009) Inferring private information using social network data. In: Proceedings of the 18th international conference on World Wide Web, Madrid
29. LinkedIn (2012) http://www.linkedin.com/
30. LiveJournal (2012) http://www.livejournal.com/
31. Mislove A, Marcon M, Gummadi KP, Druschel P, Bhattacharjee B (2007) Measurement and analysis of online social networks. In: Proceedings of the 5th ACM/Usenix Internet measurement conference (IMC'07), San Diego
32. Nagle F, Singh L (2009) Can friends be trusted? Exploring privacy in online social networks. In: International conference on advances in social network analysis and mining, Athens
33. Narayanan A, Shi E, Rubinstein BIP (2011) Link prediction by de-anonymization: how we won the kaggle social network challenge. In: The 2011 international joint conference on neural networks (IJCNN), San Jose
34. Sa HR, Prudencio RBC (2010) Supervised learning for link prediction in weighted networks. III international workshop on web and text intelligence, São Bernardo do Campo, Brazil
35. Shannon P et al (2003) Cytoscape: a software environment for integrated models of biomolecular interaction networks. Genome Res 13(11):2498–2504
36. Song HH, Cho TW, Dave V, Zhang Y, Qiu L (2009) Scalable proximity estimation and link prediction in online social networks. In: Proceedings of the 9th ACM SIGCOMM conference on internet measurement, Chicago
37. Twitter (2012) http://www.twitter.com
38. Wang N, Xu H, Grossklags J (2011) Third-party apps on Facebook: privacy and the illusion of control. In: Proceedings of the ACM symposium on computer-human interaction for management of information technology (CHIMIT), Boston
39. YouTube (2012) http://www.youtube.com/

An Analysis of Anonymity in the Bitcoin System

Fergal Reid and Martin Harrigan

Abstract Anonymity in Bitcoin, a peer-to-peer electronic currency system, is a complicated issue. Within the system, users are identified only by public-keys. An attacker wishing to de-anonymize users will attempt to construct the one-to-many mapping between users and public-keys, and associate information external to the system with the users. Bitcoin tries to prevent this attack by storing the mapping of a user to his or her public-keys on that user's node only and by allowing each user to generate as many public-keys as required. In this chapter we consider the topological structure of two networks derived from Bitcoin's public transaction history. We show that the two networks have a non-trivial topological structure, provide complementary views of the Bitcoin system, and have implications for anonymity. We combine these structures with external information and techniques such as context discovery and flow analysis to investigate an alleged theft of Bitcoins, which, at the time of the theft, had a market value of approximately US$500,000.

Keywords Network analysis • Anonymity • Bitcoin

1 Introduction

Bitcoin is a peer-to-peer electronic currency system first described in a paper by Satoshi Nakamoto (a pseudonym) in 2008 [19]. It relies on digital signatures to prove ownership and a public history of transactions to prevent double-spending. The history of transactions is shared using a peer-to-peer network and is agreed upon using a proof-of-work system [3, 11].

F. Reid (✉) • M. Harrigan
Clique Research Cluster, Complex and Adaptive Systems Laboratory,
University College Dublin, Dublin, Ireland
e-mail: fergal.reid@gmail.com; martin.harrigan@ucd.ie

Y. Altshuler et al. (eds.), *Security and Privacy in Social Networks*,
DOI 10.1007/978-1-4614-4139-7_10, © Springer Science+Business Media New York 2013

Fig. 1 Screen capture of
a tweet from WikiLeaks
announcing their acceptance
of 'anonymous Bitcoin
donations'

 @wikileaks
WikiLeaks

WikiLeaks now accepts anonymous
Bitcoin donations on
1HB5XMLmzFVj8ALj6mfBsbifRoD4miY36v

15 Jun via web

The first Bitcoins were transacted in January 2009, and by June 2011 there were
6.5 million Bitcoins in circulation among an estimated 10,000 users [27]. In recent
months, the currency has seen rapid growth in both media attention and market
price relative to existing currencies. At its peak, a single Bitcoin traded for more
than US$30 on popular Bitcoin exchanges. At the same time, U.S. Senators
and lobby groups in Germany, such as Der Bundesverband Digitale Wirtschaft
(the Federal Association of Digital Economy), raised concerns regarding the
untraceability of Bitcoins and their potential to harm society through tax evasion,
money laundering and illegal transactions. The implications of the decentralized
nature of Bitcoin with respect to the authorities' ability to regulate and monitor the
flow of currency is as yet unclear.

Many users adopt Bitcoin for political and philosophical reasons, as much as
pragmatic ones. There is an understanding amongst Bitcoin's more technical users
that anonymity is not a primary design goal of the system; however, opinions vary
widely as to how anonymous the system is in practice. Jeff Garzik, a member of
Bitcoin's development team, is quoted as saying that it would be unwise "to attempt
major illicit transactions with Bitcoin, given existing statistical analysis techniques
deployed in the field by law enforcement".[1] However, prior to the present work,
no analysis of anonymity in Bitcoin was publicly available to substantiate or
refute these claims. Furthermore, many other users of the system do not share this
belief. For example, WikiLeaks, an international organization for anonymous
whistleblowers, recently advised its Twitter followers that it now accepts *anonymous* donations via Bitcoin (see Fig. 1) and states the following[2]:

> Bitcoin is a secure and anonymous digital currency. Bitcoins cannot be easily tracked back
> to you, and are [sic] safer and faster alternative to other donation methods.

They proceed to describe a more secure method of donating Bitcoins that
involves the generation of a one-time public-key but the implications for those
who donate using the tweeted public-key are unclear. Is it possible to associate a
donation with other Bitcoin transactions performed by the same user or perhaps
identify them using external information? The extent to which this anonymity holds
in the face of determined analysis remains to be tested.

---

[1] http://www.theatlantic.com/technology/archive/2011/06/libertarian-dream-a-site-where-you-
buy-drugs-with-digital-dollars/239776 –Retrieved 2011-11-12.

[2] http://wikileaks.org/support.html – Retrieved: 2011-07-22.

This chapter is organized as follows. In Sect. 2 we consider some existing work relating to electronic currencies and anonymity. The economic aspects of the system, interesting in their own right, are beyond the scope of this work. In Sect. 3 we present an overview of the Bitcoin system; we focus on three features that are particularly relevant to our analysis. In Sect. 4 we construct two network structures, the transaction network and the user network using the publicly available transaction history. We study the static and dynamic properties of these networks. In Sect. 5 we consider the implications of these network structures for anonymity. We also combine information external to the Bitcoin system with techniques such as flow and temporal analysis to illustrate how various types of information leakage can contribute to the de-anonymization of the system's users. Finally, we conclude in Sect. 6.

1.1   A Note Regarding Motivation and Disclosure

Our motivation for this analysis is not to de-anonymize individual users of the Bitcoin system. Rather, it is to demonstrate, using a passive analysis of a publicly available dataset, the inherent limits of anonymity when using Bitcoin. This will ensure that users do not have expectations that are not being fulfilled by the system.

In security-related research, there is considerable disagreement over how best to disclose vulnerabilities [7]. Many researchers favor full disclosure wherein all information regarding a vulnerability is promptly released. This enables informed users to promptly take defensive measures. Other researchers favor limited disclosure; while this provides attackers with a window in which to exploit uninformed users, a mitigation strategy can be prepared and implemented before public announcement, thus limiting damage (e.g. through a software update). Our analysis illustrates some potential risks and pitfalls with regard to anonymity in the Bitcoin system. However, there is no central authority that can fundamentally change the system's behavior. Furthermore, it is not possible to prevent analysis of the existing transaction history.

There are also two noteworthy features of the dataset when compared to contentious social network datasets (e.g. the Facebook profiles of Harvard University students) [18]. First, the delineation between what is considered public and private is clear: the entire history of Bitcoin transactions is publicly available. Secondly, the Bitcoin system does not have a usage policy. After joining Bitcoin's peer-to-peer network, a client can freely request the entire history of Bitcoin transactions; no crawling or scraping is required.

Thus, we believe the best strategy to minimize the threat to user anonymity is to be descriptive about the risks of the Bitcoin system. We do not identify individual users apart from those in the case study, but we note that it is not difficult for other groups to replicate our work. Indeed, given the passive nature of our analysis, other parties may already be conducting similar analyses.

2 Related Work

2.1 Electronic Currencies

Electronic currencies can be technically classified according to their mechanisms for establishing ownership, protecting against double-spending, ensuring anonymity and/or privacy, and generating and issuing new currency. Bitcoin is particularly noteworthy for the last of these mechanisms. The proof-of-work system [3, 11] that establishes consensus regarding the history of transactions also doubles as a minting mechanism. The scheme was first outlined in the B-Money Proposal [10]. We briefly consider some alternative mechanisms in this section. Ripple [12] is an electronic currency wherein every user can issue currency. However, the currency is only accepted by peers who trust the issuer. Transactions between arbitrary pairs of users require chains of trusted intermediaries between the users. Saito [24] formalized and implemented a similar system, i-WAT, in which the chain of intermediaries can be established without their immediate presence using digital signatures. KARMA [28] is an electronic currency wherein the central authority is distributed over a set of users that are involved in all transactions. PPay [30] is a micropayment scheme for peer-to-peer systems in which the issuer of the currency is responsible for keeping track of it. However, both KARMA and PPay can incur large overhead when the rate of transactions is high. Mondex is a smart-card electronic currency [26]. It preserves a central bank's role in the generation and issuance of electronic currency. Mondex was an electronic replacement for cash in the physical world whereas Bitcoin is an electronic analog of cash in the online world.

The authors are not aware of any studies of the network structure of electronic currencies. However, there are such studies of physical currencies. The community currency Tomamae-cho was introduced into the Hokkaido Prefecture in Japan for a 3-month period during 2004–2005 in a bid to revitalize the local economy. The Tomamae-cho system involved gift-certificates that were re-usable and legally redeemable into yen. There was an entry space on the reverse side of each certificate for recipients to record transaction dates, their names and addresses, and the purposes of use, up to a maximum of five recipients. Kichiji and Nishibe [16] used the collected certificates to derive a network structure that represented the flow of currency during the period. They showed that the cumulative degree distribution of the network obeyed a power-law distribution, the network had small-world properties (the average clustering coefficient was high whereas the average path length was low), the directionality and the value of transactions were significant features, and the double-triangle system [22] was effective. Studies have also been performed on the physical movement of currency: "Where's George?" [29] is a crowd-sourced method for tracking U.S. dollar bills in which users record the serial numbers of bills in their possession, along with their current location. If a bill is recorded sufficiently often, its geographical movement can be tracked over time. Brockmann et al. [6] used this dataset as a proxy for studying multi-scale human mobility and as a tool for computing geographic borders inherent to human mobility.

Grinberg [13] considered some of the legal issues that may be relevant to Bitcoin in the United States. For example, does Bitcoin violate the Stamp Payments Act of 1862? The currency can be used as a token for "a less sum than $1, intended to circulate as money or to be received or used in lieu of lawful money of the United States". However, the authors of the act could not have conceived of digital currencies at the time of its writing and therefore Bitcoin may not fall under its scope. Grinberg believes that Bitcoin is unlikely to be a security, or more specifically an "investment contract", and therefore does not fall under the Securities Act of 1933. He also believes that the Bank Secrecy Act of 1970 and the Money Laundering Control Act of 1986 pose the greatest risk for Bitcoin developers, exchanges, wallet providers, mining pool operators, and businesses that accept Bitcoins. These acts require certain kinds of financial businesses, even if they are located abroad, to register with a bureau of the United States Department of the Treasury known as the Financial Crimes Enforcement Network (FinCEN). The legality of Bitcoin is outside the scope of our work, but is interesting nonetheless.

2.2 Anonymity

Previous work has shown the difficulty in maintaining anonymity in the context of networked data and online services that expose partial user information. Narayanan and Shmatikov [21] and Backstrom et al. [4] considered privacy attacks that identify users using the structure of networks, and showed the difficulty in guaranteeing anonymity in the presence of network data. Crandall et al. [9] infer social ties between users where none are explicitly stated by looking at patterns of "coincidences" or common off-network co-occurrences. Gross and Acquisti [14] discuss the privacy of early users in the Facebook social network, and how information from multiple sources could be combined to identify pseudonymous network users. Narayanan and Shmatikov [20] de-anonymized the Netflix Prize dataset using information from IMDB[3] that had similar user content, showing that statistical matching between different but related datasets can be used to attack anonymity. Puzis et al. [23] simulated the monitoring of a communications network using strategically-located monitoring nodes. They showed that, using real-world network topologies, a relatively small number of nodes could collaborate to pose a significant threat to anonymity. Korolova et al. [17] studied strategies for efficiently compromising network nodes to maximize link information

---

[3] http://www.imdb.com

observed. Altshuler et al. [1] discussed the increasing dangers of attacks targeting similar types of information, and provided measures of the difficulty of such attacks, on particular networks. All of this work points to the difficulty in maintaining anonymity where network data on user behavior is available, and illustrates how seemingly minor information leaks can be aggregated to pose significant risks. Security researcher Dan Kaminsky independently performed an investigation of some aspects of anonymity in the Bitcoin system, and presented his findings at a security conference [15] shortly after an initial draft of our work was made public. He investigated the 'linking problem' that we analyze and describe in Sect. 4.2. In addition to the analysis we conducted, his work investigated the Bitcoin system from an angle we did not consider – the TCP/IP operation of the underlying peer-to-peer network. Kaminsky's TCP/IP layer findings strengthen the core claims of our work that Bitcoin does not anonymise user activity. We provide a summary of Kaminsky's findings in Sect. 5.2.

3 The Bitcoin System

The following is a simplified description of the Bitcoin system (see Nakamoto [19] for a more thorough treatment). Bitcoin is an electronic currency with no central authority or issuer. There is no central bank or fractional reserve system controlling the supply of Bitcoins. Instead, they are generated at a predictable rate such that the eventual total number will be 21 million. There is no requirement for a trusted third-party when making transactions. Suppose Alice wishes to 'send' a number of Bitcoins to Bob. Alice uses a Bitcoin client to join the Bitcoin peer-to-peer network. She then makes a public transaction or declaration stating that one or more identities that she controls (which can be verified using public-key cryptography), and which previously had a number of Bitcoins assigned to them, wishes to re-assign those Bitcoins to one or more other identities, at least one of which is controlled by Bob. The participants of the peer-to-peer network form a collective consensus regarding the validity of this transaction by appending it to the public history of previously agreed-upon transactions (the *block-chain*). This process involves the repeated computation of a cryptographic hash function so that the digest of the transaction, along with other pending transactions, and an arbitrary nonce, has a specific form. This process is designed to require considerable computational effort, from which the security of the Bitcoin mechanism is derived. To encourage users to pay this computational cost, the process is incentivized using newly generated Bitcoins and/or transaction fees, and so this whole process is known as *mining*.

In this chapter, three features of the Bitcoin system are of particular interest. First, the entire history of Bitcoin transactions is publicly available. This is necessary in order to validate transactions and to prevent double-spending in the absence of a central authority. The only way to confirm the absence of a previous transaction is to be aware of all previous transactions. The second feature of interest is that a transaction can have multiple inputs and multiple outputs. An input to a transaction is either the output of a previous transaction or a sum of newly generated Bitcoins and transaction fees. A transaction frequently has either a single input from a previous larger transaction or multiple inputs from previous smaller transactions. Also, a transaction frequently has two outputs: one sending payment and one returning change. Third, the payer and payee(s) of a transaction are identified through public-keys from public-private key-pairs. However, a user can have multiple public-keys. In fact, it is considered good practice for a payee to generate a new public-private key-pair for every transaction. Furthermore, a user can take the following steps to better protect their identity: they can avoid revealing any identifying information in connection with their public-keys; they can repeatedly send varying fractions of their Bitcoins to themselves using multiple (newly generated) public-keys; and/or they can use a trusted third-party mixer or laundry. However, these practices are not universally applied.

The three aforementioned features, namely the public availability of Bitcoin transactions, the input-output relationship between transactions and the re-use and co-use of public-keys, provide a basis for two distinct network structures: the *transaction network* and the *user network*. The transaction network represents the flow of Bitcoins between *transactions* over time. Each vertex represents a transaction, and each directed edge between a source and a target represents an output of the transaction corresponding to a source that is an input to the transaction corresponding to the target. Each directed edge also includes a value in Bitcoins and a timestamp. The user network represents the flow of Bitcoins between *users* over time. Each vertex represents a user, and each directed edge between a source and a target represents an input-output pair of a single transaction wherein the input's public-key belongs to the user corresponding to the source and the output's public-key belongs to the user corresponding to the target. Each directed edge also includes a value in Bitcoins and a timestamp.

We gathered the entire history of Bitcoin transactions from the first transaction on January 3, 2009 up to and including the last transaction that occurred on July 12, 2011. We gathered the dataset using the Bitcoin client[4] and a modified version of Gavin Andresen's `bitcointools` project.[5] The dataset comprises 1,019,486 transactions between 1,253,054 unique public-keys. We describe the construction of the corresponding transaction and user networks, and their analyses, in the following sections. We will show that the two networks are complex, have non-trivial topological structure, provide complementary views of the Bitcoin system, and have implications for the anonymity of users.

---

[4] http://www.bitcoin.org
[5] http://github.com/gavinandresen/bitcointools

4 The Transaction and User Networks

4.1 The Transaction Network

The transaction network T represents the flow of Bitcoins between *transactions* over time. Each vertex represents a transaction and each directed edge between a source and a target represents an output of the transaction corresponding to the source that is an input to the transaction corresponding to the target. Each directed edge also includes a value in Bitcoins and a timestamp. It is straight-forward to construct T from our dataset.

Figure 2 shows an example sub-network of T. t_1 is a transaction with one input and two outputs.[6] It was added to the block-chain on May 1, 2011. One of its outputs assigned 1.2 Bitcoins (BTC) to a user identified by the public-key pk_1.[7] The public-keys are not shown in Fig. 2. Similarly, t_2 is a transaction with two inputs and two outputs.[8] It was accepted on May 5, 2011. One of its outputs sent 0.12 BTC to a user identified by a different public-key, pk_2.[9] t_3 is a transaction with two inputs and one output.[10] It was accepted on May 5, 2011. Both of its inputs are connected to the two aforementioned outputs of t_1 and t_2. The only output of t_3 was redeemed by t_4.[11]

T has 974,520 vertices and 1,558,854 directed edges. The number of vertices is less than the total number of transactions in the dataset because we omit transactions that are not connected to at least one other transaction. The omitted transactions correspond to newly generated Bitcoins and transaction fees that are not yet redeemed. The network has neither multi-edges (multiple edges between the same pair of vertices in the same direction) nor loops. It is a directed acyclic graph (DAG) since the output of a transaction can never be an input (either directly or indirectly) to the same transaction.

Figure 3a shows a log–log plot of the cumulative degree distributions: the solid red curve is the cumulative degree distribution (in-degree and out-degree); the dashed green curve is the cumulative in-degree distribution; and the dotted blue curve is the cumulative out-degree distribution. We fitted power-law distributions of the form $p(x) \sim x^{-\alpha}$ for $x > x_{min}$ to the three distributions by estimating the parameters α and x_{min} using a goodness-of-fit (GoF) method [8]. Table 1 shows the estimates along

---

[6] The transactions and public-keys used in our examples exist in our dataset. The unique identifier for the transaction t_1 is 09441d3c52fa0018365fcd2949925182f6307322138773d52c201f5cc2 bb5976. You can query the details of a transaction or public-key by examining Bitcoin's block-chain using, for example, the Bitcoin Block Explorer (http://www.blockexplorer.com).

[7] 13eBhR3oHFD5wkE4oGtrLdbdi2PvK3ijMC

[8] 0c4d41d0f5d2aff14d449daa550c7d9b0eaaf35d81ee5e6e77f8948b14d62378

[9] 19smBSUoRGmbH13vif1Nu17S63Tnmg7h9n

[10] 0c034fb964257ecbf4eb953e2362e165dea9c1d008032bc9ece5cebbc7cd4697

[11] f16ece066f6e4cf92d9a72eb1359d8401602a23990990cb84498cdbb93026402

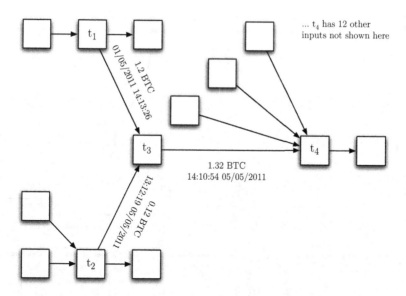

Fig. 2 An example sub-network from the transaction network. Each rectangular vertex represents a transaction and each directed edge represents a flow of Bitcoins from an output of one transaction to an input of another

with the corresponding Kolmogorov–Smirnov GoF statistics and p-values. We note that no distributions for which the empirically-best scaling region is non-trivial has a power-law as a plausible hypothesis ($p > 0.1$). This is probably due to the fact that there is no preferential attachment [5, 25]: new vertices are joined to existing vertices whose corresponding transactions are not yet fully redeemed.

There are 1,949 (maximal weakly) connected components in the network. Figure 3b shows a log–log plot of the cumulative component size distribution. There are 948,287 vertices (97.31%) in the giant component. This component also contains a giant biconnected component with 716,354 vertices (75.54% of the vertices in the giant component).

We also performed a rudimentary dynamic analysis of the network. Figure 3c–e show the edge number, density and average path length of the transaction network on a monthly basis, respectively. These measurements are not cumulative. The network's growth and sparsification are evident. We also note some anomalies in the average path length during July and November of 2010.

4.2 The User Network

The user network $\mathcal{U}$ represents the flow of Bitcoins between *users* over time. Each vertex represents a user. Each directed edge between a source and a target represents an input-output pair of a single transaction wherein the input's public-key

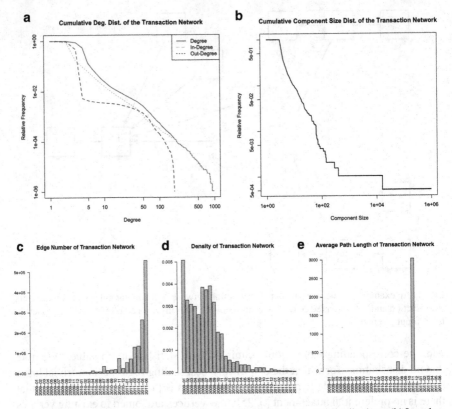

Fig. 3 Transaction network. (**a**) Log–log plot of the cumulative degree distributions. (**b**) Log–log plot of the cumulative component size distribution. (**c**) Temporal histogram showing the number of edges per month. (**d**) Temporal histogram showing the density per month. (**e**) Temporal histogram showing the average path length per month

Table 1 The degree, in-degree and out-degree distributions of $\mathcal{T}$

Variable	$\tilde{x}$	$\bar{x}$	s	α	x_{min}	GoF	p-val.
Degree	3	3.20	6.20	3.24	50	0.02	0.05
In-degree	1	1.60	5.31	2.50	4	0.01	0.00
Out-degree	1	1.60	3.17	3.50	51	0.05	0.00

belongs to the user corresponding to the source and the output's public-key belongs to the user corresponding to the target. Each directed edge also includes a value in Bitcoins and a timestamp.

We must perform a preprocessing step before $\mathcal{U}$ can be constructed from our dataset. Suppose $\mathcal{U}$ is, at first, incomplete in the sense that each vertex represents a single public-key rather than a user and that each directed edge between a source and a target represents an input-output pair of a single transaction. In this case the input's public-key corresponds to the source and the output's public-key corresponds to the target. In order to perfect this network, we need to contract each subset of vertices whose corresponding public-keys belong to a single user. The difficulty is that public-keys are Bitcoin's mechanism for ensuring anonymity: "the public can see that someone (identified by a public-key) is sending an amount to someone else (identified by another public-key), but without information linking the transaction to anyone." [19]. In fact, it is considered good practice for a payee to generate a new public-private key-pair for every transaction to keep transactions from being linked to a common owner. Therefore, it is impossible to completely perfect the network using our dataset alone. However, as noted by Nakamoto [19],

> Some linking is still unavoidable with multi-input transactions, which necessarily reveal that their inputs were owned by the same owner. The risk is that if the owner of a key is revealed, linking could reveal other transactions that belonged to the same owner.

We will use this property of transactions with multiple inputs to contract subsets of vertices in the incomplete network. We constructed an ancillary network in which each vertex represents a public-key. We connected pairs of vertices with undirected edges where each edge joins a pair of public-keys that are both inputs to the same transaction and are thus controlled by the same user. From our dataset, this ancillary network has 1,253,054 vertices (unique public-keys) and 4,929,950 edges. More importantly, it has 86,641 non-trivial maximal connected components. Each maximal connected component in this graph corresponds to a user, and each component's constituent vertices correspond to that user's public-keys.

Figure 4 shows an example sub-network of the incomplete network overlaid onto the example sub-network of T from Fig. 2. The outputs of t_1 and t_2 that were eventually redeemed by t_3 were sent to a user whose public-key was pk_1 and a user whose public-key was pk_2 respectively. Figure 5 shows an example sub-network of the user network overlaid onto the example sub-network of the incomplete network from Fig. 4. pk_1 and pk_2 are contracted into a single vertex u_1 since they correspond to a pair inputs of a single transaction. In other words, they are in the same maximal connected component of the ancillary network (see the vertices representing pk_1 and pk_2 in the dashed grey box in Fig. 5). A single user owns both public-keys. We note that the maximal connected component in this case is not simply a clique; it has a diameter of length four indicating that there are at least two public-keys belonging to that same user that are connected indirectly via three transactions. The 16 inputs to transaction t_4 result in the contraction of 16 additional public-keys into a single vertex u_2. The value and timestamp of the flow of Bitcoins from u_1 to u_2 is derived from the transaction network.

After the preprocessing step, $\mathcal{U}$ has 881,678 vertices (86,641 non-trivial maximal connected components and 795,037 isolated vertices in the ancillary network) and 1,961,636 directed edges. The network is still incomplete. We have not contracted all possible vertices but this approximation will suffice for our present analysis. Unlike T, $\mathcal{U}$ has multi-edges, loops and directed cycles.

Figure 6a shows a log–log plot of the network's cumulative degree distributions. We fitted power-law distributions to the three distributions and calculated their GoF

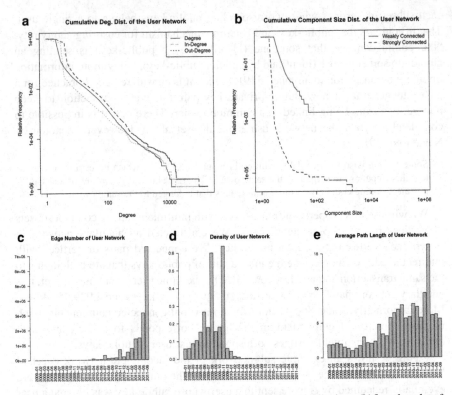

Fig. 4 User network. (**a**) Log–log plot of the cumulative degree distributions. (**b**) Log–log plot of the cumulative component size distribution. (**c**) Temporal histogram showing the number of edges per month. (**d**) Temporal histogram showing the density per month. (**e**) Temporal histogram showing the average path length per month

and statistical significance as in the previous section. Table 2 shows the results. We note that none of the distributions have a power-law as a plausible hypothesis.

There are 604 (maximal) weakly connected components and 579,355 (maximal) strongly connected components in the network; Fig. 6b shows a log–log plot of the cumulative component size distribution for both variations. There are 879,859 vertices (99.79%) in the giant weakly connected component. This component also contains a giant weakly biconnected component with 652,892 vertices (74.20% of the vertices in the giant component).

Our dynamic analysis of the user network mirrors that of the transaction network in the previous subsection. Figure 6c–e show the edge number, density and average path length of the user network on a monthly basis, respectively. These measurements are not cumulative. The network's growth and sparsification are evident. We note that even though our dynamic analysis of the user network was on a monthly basis, the preprocessing step was performed using the ancillary network of the entire incomplete network. This enables us to resolve public-keys to a single user irrespective of the month in which the linking transactions occur.

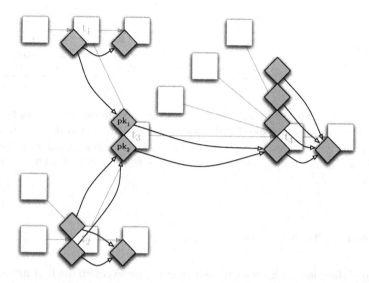

Fig. 5 An example sub-network from the incomplete network. Each diamond vertex represents a public-key and each directed edge between diamond vertices represents a flow of Bitcoins from one public-key to another

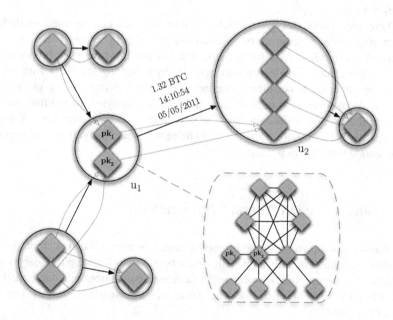

Fig. 6 An example sub-network from the user network. Each circular vertex represents a user and each directed edge between circular vertices represents a flow of Bitcoins from one user to another. The maximal connected component from the ancillary network that corresponds to the vertex u_1 is shown within the *dashed grey box*

Table 2 The degree,
in-degree and out-degree
distributions of $\mathcal{U}$

Variable	$\tilde{x}$	$\bar{x}$	s	α	x_{min}	GoF	p-val.
Degree	3	4.45	218.10	2.38	66	0.02	0.00
In-degree	1	2.22	86.40	2.45	57	0.05	0.00
Out-degree	2	2.22	183.91	2.03	10	0.22	0.00

The contraction of public-keys into users, while incomplete, generates a network that is in many ways a proxy for the social network of Bitcoin users. The edges represent financial transactions between pairs of users. For example, it may be possible to identify communities, central users and hoarders within this social network.

5   Anonymity Analysis

Prior to performing the aforementioned analysis, we expected the user network to be largely composed of trees representing Bitcoin flows between one-time public-keys that were not linked to other public-keys. However, our analysis reveals that the user network has considerable cyclic structure. We now consider the implications of this structure, coupled with other aspects of the Bitcoin system, on anonymity.

There are several ways in which the user network can be used to deduce information about Bitcoin users. We can use global network properties, such as degree distribution, to identify outliers. We can use local network properties to examine the context in which a user operates by observing the users with whom he or she interacts, either directly or indirectly. The dynamic nature of the user network also enables us to perform flow and temporal analyses. In addition, we can examine the significant Bitcoin flows between groups of users over time. We will now discuss each of these possibilities in more detail and provide a case study to demonstrate their use in practice.

5.1   Integrating Off-Network Information

There is no user directory for the Bitcoin system. However, we can attempt to build a partial user directory associating Bitcoin users (and their known public-keys) with off-network information. If we can make sufficient associations and combine them with the previously described network structures, a potentially serious threat to anonymity emerges.

Many organizations and services (such as on-line stores) that accept Bitcoins, exchanges, laundry services and mixers have access to identifying information regarding their users; e.g. e-mail addresses, shipping addresses, credit card and bank account details, IP addresses, etc. If any of this information is publicly

a   b

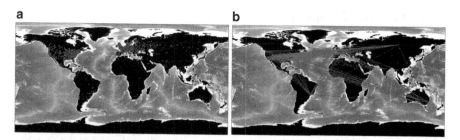

Fig. 7 The Bitcoin Faucet can be used to map users to geolocated IP addresses. (**a**) A map of geolocated IP addresses associated with users receiving Bitcoins from the Bitcoin Faucet during a 1-week period. (**b**) A map of a sample of the geolocated IP addresses in (**a**) connected by edges where the corresponding users are connected by a path of length at most three in the user network that does not include the vertex representing the Bitcoin Faucet

available, or accessible by, for example, law enforcement agencies, then the identities of users involved in related transactions may also be at risk. To illustrate this point, we consider a number of publicly available data sources and integrate their information with the user network.

5.1.1 The Bitcoin Faucet

The Bitcoin Faucet[12] is a website where users can donate Bitcoins to be redistributed in small amounts to other users. In order to prevent abuse of this service, a history of recent give-aways are published along with the IP addresses of the recipients. When the Bitcoin Faucet does not batch the re-distribution, it is possible to associate the IP addresses with the recipients' public-keys. This page can be scraped over time to produce a time-stamped mapping of IP addresses to Bitcoin users.

We found that the public-keys associated with many of the IP addresses that received Bitcoins were contracted with other public-keys in the ancillary network, thus revealing IP addresses that are related to previous transactions. Figure 7a shows a map of geolocated IP addresses belonging to users who received Bitcoins over a period of 1 week. Figure 7b overlays the user network onto a sample of those users. An edge between two geolocated IP addresses indicates that the corresponding users are linked by an undirected path with a length of at most three in the user network (after we exclude paths containing the Bitcoin Faucet itself).

These figures serve as a proof-of-concept from a small publicly available data source. We note that large centralized Bitcoin service providers are capable of producing much more detailed maps.

---

[12] http://freebitcoins.appspot.com

5.1.2 Voluntary Disclosures

Another source of identifying information is the voluntary disclosure of public-keys by users, for example when posting to the Bitcoin forums.[13] Bitcoin public-keys are typically represented as strings approximately 33 characters in length and starting with the digit one. They are well indexed by popular search engines. We identified many high-degree vertices with external information, using a search engine alone. We scraped the Bitcoin Forums in which users frequently attach a public-key to their signatures. We also gathered public-keys from Twitter streams and user-generated public directories. It is important to note that in many cases we are able to resolve the 'public' public-keys with other public-keys belonging to the same user, using the ancillary network. We also note that large centralized Bitcoin service providers can do the same with their user information.

5.2 TCP/IP Layer Information

Security researcher Dan Kaminsky performed an analysis of the Bitcoin system, and investigated identity leakage at the TCP/IP layer. He found that by opening a connection to all public peers in the network simultaneously, he could map IP addresses to Bitcoin public-keys, working from the assumption that "the first node to inform you of a transaction is the source of it...[this is] more or less true, and absolutely over time" [15]. Using this approach it is possible to map public-keys to IP addresses unless users are using an anonymising proxy technology such as TOR.

5.3 Egocentric Analysis and Visualization

For any particular user, we can directly derive several pieces of information from the user network. We can compute the balance held by a single public-key. We can also aggregate the balances belonging to public-keys that are controlled by a particular user. For example, Fig. 8a, b show the receipts and payments to and from WikiLeaks' public-key in terms of Bitcoins, and the number of transactions, respectively. The donations are relatively small and are forwarded to other public-keys periodically. There was also a noticeable spike in donations when the facility was first announced. Figure 8c shows the receipts and payments to and from the creator of a popular Bitcoin trading website aggregated over a number of public-keys that are linked through the ancillary network.

An important advantage of deriving network structures from the Bitcoin trans-action history is the ability to use network visualization and analysis tools to investigate the flow of Bitcoins. For example, Fig. 9 shows the network structure

---

[13] http://forum.bitcoin.org

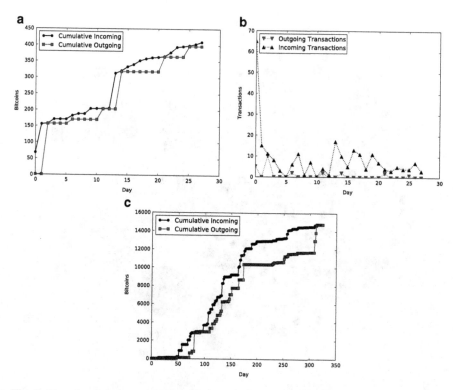

Fig. 8 Plot of cumulative receipts and payments to and from Bitcoin public-keys and users. (a) The receipts and payments to and from WikiLeaks' public-key over time. (b) The number of transactions involving WikiLeaks' public-key over time. (c) The receipts and payments to and from the creator of a popular Bitcoin trading website aggregated over a number of public-keys

surrounding the WikiLeaks public-key in the incomplete user network. Our tools resolve several of the vertices with identifying information described in Sect. 5.1. These users can be linked either directly or indirectly to their donations.

5.4 Context Discovery

Given a number of public-keys or users of interest, we can use network structure and context to better understand the flow of Bitcoins between them. For example, we can examine all shortest paths between a set of vertices, or consider the maximum number of Bitcoins that can flow from a source to a destination given the transactions and their 'capacities' in time-window of interest. For example, Fig. 10 shows all shortest paths between vertices representing the users we identified using off-network information in

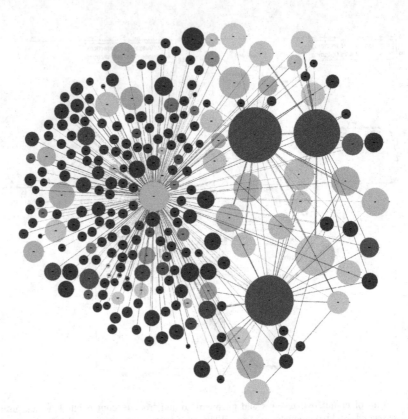

Fig. 9 An egocentric visualization of the vertex representing the WikiLeaks public-key in the incomplete user network. The size of a vertex corresponds to its degree in the entire incomplete user network. The *color* denotes the volume of Bitcoins – lighter colors have larger volumes flowing through them

Sect. 5.1, and the vertex that represents the MyBitcoin service[14] in the user network. We can identify more than 60% of the users in this visualization and deduce many direct and indirect relationships between them.

Case study-Part I :   We analyzed an alleged theft of 25,000 BTC reported in the Bitcoin Forums[15] by a user known as allinvain. The victim reported that a large portion of his Bitcoins were sent to pk_{red}[16] on June 13, 2011 at 16:52:23 UTC. The theft occurred shortly after somebody broke into the victim's Slush pool account[17] and changed the payout address to pk_{blue}.[18] The Bitcoins rightfully belonged to

---

[14] http://www.mybitcoin.com

[15] http://forum.bitcoin.org/index.php?topic=16457.0

[16] 1KPTdMb6p7H3YCwsyFqrEmKGmsHqe1Q3jg

[17] http://mining.bitcoin.cz

[18] 15iUDqk6nLmav3B1xUHPQivDpfMruVsu9f

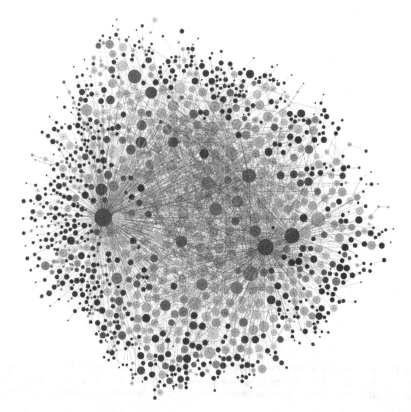

Fig. 10 A visualisation of all users identified in Sect. 5.1 and all shortest paths between the *vertices* representing those users and the *vertex* representing the MyBitcoin service in the user network

pk_{green}.[19] At the time of the theft, the stolen Bitcoins had a market value of approximately US$500,000. This case study illustrates potential risks to the anonymity of a user (the thief) who has good reason to remain anonymous.

We considered the incomplete user network before any contractions. We restricted our analysis to the egocentric network surrounding the thief: we include every vertex reachable by a path of length at most two, ignoring directionality and all edges induced by these vertices. To avoid clutter, we also removed all loops, multiple edges, and edges that were not contained in some biconnected component. In Fig. 11, the red vertex represents the thief who owns the public-key pk_{red} and the green vertex represents the victim who owns the public-key pk_{green}. The theft is represented by a green edge joining the victim to the thief.

Interestingly, the victim and thief are joined by paths (ignoring directionality) other than the green edge representing the theft. For example, consider the

---

[19] 1J18yk7D353z3gRVcdbS7PV5Q8h5w6oWWG

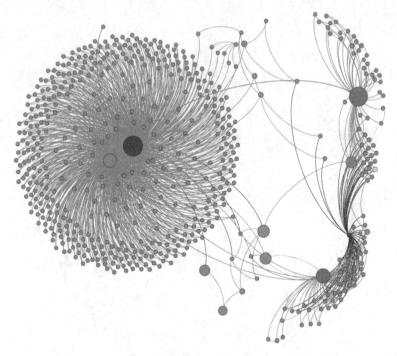

Fig. 11 An egocentric visualization of the thief in the incomplete user network. For this visualization, vertices are colored according to the text, edges are colored according to the color of their sources and the size of each vertex is proportional to its edge-betweenness within the egocentric network

sub-network shown in Fig. 12 induced by the red, green, purple, yellow and orange vertices. This sub-network is a cycle. We contract all vertices whose corresponding public-keys belong to the same user. This allows us to attach values in Bitcoins and timestamps to the directed edges. We can make a number of observations. First, we note that the theft of 25,000 BTC was preceded by a smaller theft of 1 BTC. This was later reported by the victim using the Bitcoin forums. Second, using off-network data, we identified some of the other colored vertices: the purple vertex represents the main Slush pool account, and the orange vertex represents the computer hacker group known as LulzSec.[20] We note that there has been at least one attempt to associate the thief with LulzSec.[21] This was a fake; it was created after the theft. However, the identification of the orange vertex with LulzSec is genuine and was established before the theft. We observe that the thief sent 0.31337 BTC to LulzSec shortly after the theft but we cannot otherwise associate him with the group. The main Slush pool account sent a total of 441.83 BTC to the victim

---

[20] http://twitter.com/LulzSec/status/76388576832651265

[21] http://pastebin.com/88nGp508

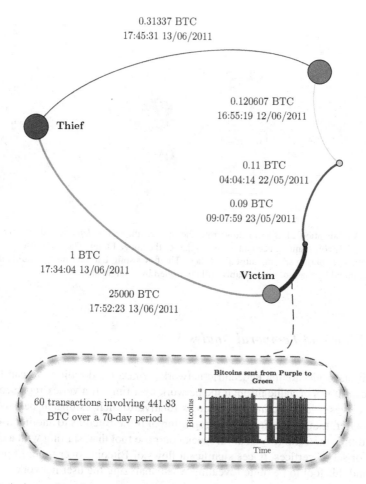

Fig. 12 An interesting sub-network induced by the thief, the victim, and three other vertices. The notation is the same as in Fig. 11

over a 70-day period. It also sent a total of 0.2 BTC to the yellow vertex over a 2 day period. One day before the theft, the yellow vertex also sent 0.120607 BTC to LulzSec.

The yellow vertex represents a user who is the owner of at least five public-keys.[22] Like the victim, he is a member of the Slush pool, and like the thief, he is a one-time donator to LulzSec. This donation, the day before the theft, is his last known activity using these public-keys.

---

[22] 1MUpbAY7rjWxvLtUwLkARViqSdzypMgVW413tst9ukW294Q7f6zRJr3VmLq6zp1C68EK1 DcQvXMD87MaYcFZqHzDZyH3sAv8R5hMZe1AEW9ToWWwKoLFYSsLkPqDyHeS2feDVs VZ1EWASKF9DLU CgEFqfgrNaHzp3q4oEgjTsF

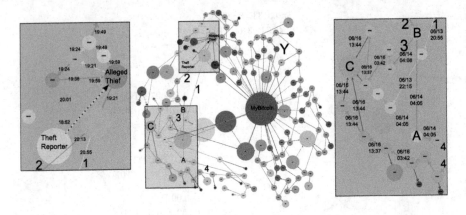

Fig. 13 Visualization of Bitcoin flow from the alleged theft. The *left* inset shows the initial shuffling of Bitcoins among accounts close to that of the alleged thief. The *right* inset shows the flow of Bitcoins during several subsequent days. The flows split, but later merge, validating that the flows found by the tool are probably still controlled by a single user

5.5 Flow and Temporal Analyses

In addition to visualizing egocentric networks with a fixed radius, we can follow significant flows of value through the network over time. If a vertex representing a user receives a large volume of Bitcoins relative to their estimated balance and, shortly after, transfers a significant proportion of those Bitcoins to another user, we deemed this interesting. We built a special purpose tool that, starting with a chosen vertex or set of vertices, traces significant flows of Bitcoins over time. In practice we found this tool to be quite revealing when analyzing the user network.

Case Study – Part II: To demonstrate this tool, we re-considered the Bitcoin theft described previously. We note that the victim developed their own tool to generate an exhaustive list of public-keys that received some portion of the stolen Bitcoins after the theft.[23] However, this list grows very quickly and, at the time of writing, contained more than 34,100 public-keys. Figure 13 shows an annotated visualization produced using our tool. We note several interesting flows in the aftermath of the theft. The initial theft of a small volume of 1 BTC was immediately followed by the theft of 25,000 BTC. This is represented as a dotted black line between the relevant vertices, magnified in the left inset of the figure.

In the left inset, we note that the Bitcoins were shuffled between a small number of accounts and then transferred back to the initial account. After this shuffling step,

---

[23] http://folk.uio.no/vegardno/allinvain-addresses.txt

we identified four significant outflows of Bitcoins that began at 19:49, 20:01, 20:13 and 20:55. Of particular interest are the outflows that began at 20:55 (labeled as "1" in both insets) and 20:13 (labeled as "2" in both insets). These outflows pass through several subsequent accounts over a period of several hours. Flow 1 splits at the vertex labeled A in the right inset at 04:05 on the day after the theft. Some of its Bitcoins rejoin Flow 2 at the vertex labeled B. This new combined flow is labeled as "3" in the right inset. The remaining Bitcoins from Flow 1 pass through several additional vertices in the next 2 days. This flow is labeled as "4" in the right inset.

A surprising event occurs on June 16, 2011 at approximately 13:37. A small number of Bitcoins were transferred from Flow 3 to a heretofore unseen public-key pk_1.[24] Approximately 7 min later, a small number of Bitcoins were transferred from Flow 3 to another heretofore unseen public-key pk_2.[25] Finally, there were two simultaneous transfers from Flow 4 to two more heretofore unseen public-keys: pk_3[26] and pk_4.[27] We have determined that these four public-keys, pk_1, pk_2, pk_3 and pk_4 – which received Bitcoins from two separate flows that split from each other 2 days previously – were all contracted to the same user in our ancillary network. This user is represented as C in Fig. 13.

There are several other examples of interesting flow. The flow labeled Y involves the movement of Bitcoins through 30 unique public-keys in a very short period of time. At each step, a small number of Bitcoins (typically 30 BTC which had a market value of approximately US$500 at the time of the transactions) were siphoned off. The public-keys that received the small number of Bitcoins are typically represented by small blue vertices due to their low volume and degree. On June 20, 2011 at 12:35, each of these public-keys made a transfer to a public-key operated by the MyBitcoin service.[28] Curiously, this public-key was previously involved in a separate Bitcoin theft.[29]

We also observe that the Bitcoins in many of the aforementioned flows were transferred between public-keys very quickly. Figure 14 shows two flows in particular wherein the intermediate parties waited for very few confirmations before re-sending the Bitcoins to other public-keys.

Much of this analysis is circumstantial. We cannot say for certain whether or not these flows imply a shared agency in both incidents. However, our analysis does illustrate the power of our tool when tracing the flow of Bitcoins and generating hypotheses. It also suggests that a centralized service may have additional details on the user(s) in control of the implicated public-keys.

[24] 1FKFiCYJSFqxT3zkZntHjfU47SvAzauZXN

[25] 1FhYawPhWDvkZCJVBrDfQoo2qC3EuKtb94

[26] 1MJZZmmSrQZ9NzeQt3hYP76oFC5dWAf2nD

[27] 12dJo17jcR78Uk1Ak5wfgyXtciU62MzcEc

[28] 1MAazCWMydsQB5ynYXqSGQDjNQMN3HFmEu

[29] http://forum.bitcoin.org/index.php?topic=20427.0

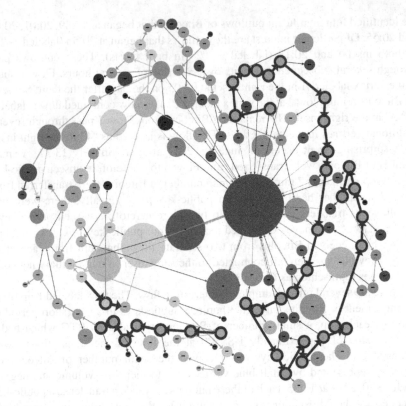

Fig. 14 Bitcoins are transferred very quickly, between the public-keys on the highlighted paths

5.6 Other Forms of Analysis

Many other forms of analysis could be applied to de-anonymize the workings of the Bitcoin system:

- Many transactions have two outputs, where one is the payment from a payer to a payee and the other is the return of change to the payer. If we assume that a transaction was created using a particular client implementation and we have access to the client's source code, then we might be able to distinguish, in some cases, between the payment and the change. We can then map the public-key that the change was assigned to, back to the user who created the transaction.
- Order books for Bitcoin exchanges are typically available to support trading tools. As orders are often placed in Bitcoin values converted from other currencies, they have a precise decimal value with eight significant digits. It might be possible to find transactions with corresponding amounts and thus map public-keys and transactions to the exchanges.
- Over an extended time period, several public-keys, if used at similar times, might belong to the same user. It might be possible to construct and cluster a co-occurrence network to help deduce mappings between public-keys and users.

- Finally, there are far more sophisticated forms of attack wherein the attacker actively participates in the network; for example, using marked Bitcoins or operating a laundry service.

5.7 Mitigation Strategies

In addition to educating users about the limits of anonymity in the Bitcoin system, some risks to privacy could potentially be mitigated by making changes to the system. A patch to the official Bitcoin client has been developed[30] that allows users to prevent the linking of public-keys by making the user aware of potential links within the Bitcoin client user-interface. It is also possible for the client to automatically proxy Bitcoins through dummy public-keys. This would come at the cost of increased transaction fees but would increase deniability and obfuscate the chain of transaction histories. Finally, if a future version of the protocol supported protocol-level mixing of Bitcoins, then the difficulty for a passive third-party to track individual user histories would increase.

6 Conclusions

For the past half-century futurists have heralded the advent of a cash-less society [2]. Many of their predictions have been realized, e.g. the 'on-line real-time' payment system and bank-maintained 'central information files' described by Anderson et al. [2]. However, cash is still a competitive and relatively anonymous means of payment. Bitcoin is an electronic analog of cash in the online world. It is decentralized: there is no central authority responsible for the issuance of Bitcoins and there is no need to involve a trusted third-party when making online transfers. However, this flexibility comes at a price: the entire history of Bitcoin transactions is publicly available. In this chapter we described the results of our investigation of the structure of two networks derived from this dataset, and their implications for user anonymity.

Using an appropriate network representation, it is possible to associate many public-keys with each other, and with external identifying information. With appropriate tools, the activity of known users can be observed in detail. This can be performed using a passive analysis only. Active analyses, by which an interested party can potentially deploy 'marked' Bitcoins and collaborate with other users can be used to discover even more information. We also believe that large centralized services (such as the exchanges and wallet services) are capable of identifying and tracking considerable subsets of user activity.

---

[30] http://coderr.wordpress.com/2011/06/30/patching-the-bitcoin-client-to-make-it-more-anonymous – Retrieved 2011-11-04.

Technical members of the Bitcoin community have cautioned that strong anonymity is not a primary design goal of the Bitcoin system. However, casual users need to be aware of this, especially when sending Bitcoins to users and organizations with whom they would prefer not to be publicly associated.

Acknowledgements This research was supported by Science Foundation Ireland (SFI) Grant number 08/SRC/I1407: Clique: Graph and Network Analysis Cluster. The authors gratefully acknowledge this support. Both authors contributed equally to this work, which was performed independently of any industrial partnership or collaboration of the Clique Cluster.

References

1. Altshuler Y, Aharony N, Elovici Y, Pentland A, Cebrian M (2011) Stealing reality: when criminals become data scientists (or vice versa). IEEE Int Syst 26(6):22–30
2. Anderson A, Cannell D, Gibbons T, Grote G, Henn J, Kennedy J, Muir M, Potter N, Whitby R (1966) An electronic cash and credit system. American Management Association, New York
3. Back A (2002) Hashcash – a denial of service counter-measure. http://www.hashcash.org/papers/hashcash.pdf, Retrieved 12 Nov 2011
4. Backstrom L, Dwork C, Kleinberg J (2007) Wherefore art thou r3579x?: anonymized social networks, hidden patterns, and structural steganography. In: Proceedings of the 16th International Conference on World Wide Web, Banff. ACM, New York, pp 181–190
5. Barabási A, Albert R (1999) Emergence of scaling in random networks. Science 286(5439):509–512
6. Brockmann D, Hufnagel L, Geisel T (2006) The scaling laws of human travel. Nature 439(26):462–465
7. Cavusoglu H, Cavusoglu H, Raghunathan S (2005) Emerging issues in responsible vulnerability disclosure. In: Proceedings of the 4th Annual Workshop on Economics of Information Security (WEIS'05), Cambridge
8. Clauset A, Shalizi C, Newman M (2009) Power-law distributions in empirical data. SIAM Rev 51(4):661–703
9. Crandall D, Backstrom L, Cosley D, Suri S, Huttenlocher D, Kleinberg J (2010) Inferring social ties from geographic coincidences. Proc Natl Acad Sci U S A 107(52):22436
10. Dai W (1998) B-money proposal, http://www.weidai.com/bmoney.txt, Retrieved 12 Nov 2011
11. Dwork C, Naor M (1992) Pricing via processing or combatting junk mail. In: Proceedings of the 12th Annual International Cryptology Conference on Advances in Cryptology (CRYPTO'92), Santa Barbara. Springer, pp 139–147
12. Fugger R (2004) Money as IOUs in social trust networks a proposal for a decentralized currency network protocol, http://ripple-project.org/decentralizedcurrency.pdf, Retrieved 12 Nov 2011
13. Grinberg R (2011) Bitcoin: an innovative alternative digital currency. Hastings Sci Tech Law J 4:159–208
14. Gross R, Acquisti A (2005) Information revelation and privacy in online social networks. In: Proceedings of the 2005 ACM Workshop on Privacy in the Electronic Society, Alexandria. ACM, New York, pp 71–80
15. Kaminsky D (2011) Black ops of TCP/IP presentation. Black Hat, Chaos Communication Camp
16. Kichiji N, Nishibe M (2008) Network analyses of the circulation flow of community currency. Evol Inst Econ Rev 4(2):267–300

17. Korolova A, Motwani R, Nabar S, Xu Y (2008) Link privacy in social networks. In: Proceedings of the 17th ACM Conference on Information and Knowledge Management, Napa Valley. ACM, New York, pp 289–298
18. Lewis K, Kaufman J, Gonzalez M, Wimmer A, Christakis N (2008) Tastes, ties, and time: a new social network dataset using {F}acebook.com. Soc Netw 30:330–342
19. Nakamoto S (2008) Bitcoin: a peer-to-peer electronic cash system, http://bitcoin.org/bitcoin.pdf, Retrieved 12 Nov 2011
20. Narayanan A, Shmatikov V (2008) Robust de-anonymization of large sparse datasets. In: Proceedings of the 29th Symposium on Security and Privacy, Oakland. IEEE, pp 111–125
21. Narayanan A, Shmatikov V (2009) De-anonymizing social networks. In: Proceedings of the 30th Symposium on Security and Privacy, Oakland. IEEE, pp 173–187
22. Nishibe M (2004) Chiiki Tuka No Susume (in Japanese). Hokkaido Shokoukai Rengou
23. Puzis R, Yagil D, Elovici Y, Braha D (2009) Collaborative attack on internet users' anonymity. Internet Res 19(1):60–77
24. Saito K (2006) i-WAT: the internet WAT system – an architecture for maintaining trust and facilitating peer-to-peer barter relationships. Ph.D. thesis, Keio University
25. Simon H (1955) On a class of skew distribution functions. Biometrika 42:425–440
26. Stalder F (2002) Failures and successes: notes on the development of electronic cash. Inf Soc 18(3):209–219
27. The Economist (2011) Digital currencies – bits and bob, http://www.economist.com/node/18836780, Retrieved 12 Nov 2011
28. Vishnumurthy V, Chandrakumar S, Sirer E (2003) KARMA: a secure economic framework for peer-to-peer resource sharing. In: Proceedings of the 1st Workshop on Economics of Peer-to-Peer Systems, Berkeley, California
29. Where's George? http://www.wheresgeorge.com, Retrieved 12 Nov 2011
30. Yang B, Garcia-Molin H (2003) PPay: micropayments for peer-to-peer systems. In: Atluri V, Liu P (eds) Proceedings of the 10th ACM Conference on Computer and Communication Security (CCS'03), Fairfax. ACM Press, New York, pp 300–310

Privacy-Preserving Data Integration Using Decoupled Data

Hye-Chung Kum, Stanley Ahalt, and Darshana Pathak

Abstract Data from social network websites are an excellent source of information for studying human behavior and interactions. Typically, when analyzing such data, the default mode of access is de-identified data, which provides a level of privacy protection. However, due to its inability to link to other data, de-identified data has limitations with regard to answering broad and critically important questions about our complex society. In this study, we investigate the properties of information related to privacy, and we present a novel model of data access called decoupled data access for studying personal data using these properties. "Decoupling" refers to separating out the identifying information from the sensitive data that needs protection. We suggest that decoupled data access can provide flexible data integration with error management while providing the same level of privacy protection as de-identified data. We further test the ability of different mechanisms to hinder inference of identity when names are revealed for data integration. Our results show that through chaffing, not specifying the universe around the data, and revealing names in isolation, the real identities of names for both common and rare names can be protected.

H.-C. Kum (✉)
Department of Computer Science, School of Social Work, University of North Carolina (UNC-CH), Chapel Hill, NC, USA
e-mail: kum@email.unc.edu

S. Ahalt
Renaissance Computing Institute (RENCI), Department of Computer Science, University of North Carolina (UNC-CH), Chapel Hill, NC, USA
e-mail: ahalt@renci.org

D. Pathak
Department of Computer Science, University of North Carolina (UNC-CH), Chapel Hill, NC, USA
e-mail: dpathak@cs.unc.edu

Y. Altshuler et al. (eds.), *Security and Privacy in Social Networks*,
DOI 10.1007/978-1-4614-4139-7_11, © Springer Science+Business Media New York 2013

Keywords Privacy-preserving data integration • Decoupled data • De-identified data • Computational social science • Record linkage • Entity resolution

1 Introduction

Data from social network websites are an excellent source of information for studying human behavior and interactions. However, there are limitations in addressing broad questions about our complex society using only data from social network websites. A model capable of integrating online social network data with other sources of data could present a much broader picture.

Integrating data from disparate sources requires the ability to identify linkages across different datasets with no established common identifiers. In addition, data integration is made even more difficult by diverse formatting standards, missing data, and erroneous data. The main difficulty is that data are often expressed differently (e.g., nicknames), change over time (e.g., last names), are not unique attributes (e.g., John Smith), are missing (e.g., social security numbers are often missing), or are incorrectly entered. Many models for record linkage under such uncertainty factors have been investigated since they were first proposed in 1959 by Newcombe [1]. All such models for approximate record linkage require careful management of errors that are introduced during the linkage process and manual resolution of ambiguous links. It is important that these errors are noted and passed on to the next phase of analytics in order to analyze the merged data accurately. As shown in a variety of papers in the statistical literature [2-4], properly accounting for linkage errors during the analysis of a merged data can have a significant impact on the accuracy of research projects using merged data from multiple sources.

Applications that merge personal data, such as data from various social network websites, are becoming more common. Indeed, the increase in these linkage activities has resulted in growing concerns about the privacy of the individuals being linked [5, 6]. In 2001, the United States Government Accountability Office (US GAO) published a report on record linkage and privacy [6]. This report discussed the use of record linkage for national statistics and research, privacy and data stewardship issues, and current technologies (e.g. third-party linkage, list inflation, grouped linkage, secure data centers, signed consent forms, and techniques to perturb data) that help address privacy protection in federally-funded projects that require record linkage.

Ten years after this report was published, privacy-preserving data integration is still a largely unresolved issue. We observe that there are still only two modes of access to individual level micro-data for research:

- *De-identified mode*: Data is de-identified by stripping personally identifiable information (PII) from the data to make the data more anonymous. Note that stripping PII does not make the data fully anonymous for everyone in the data due to quasi-identifiers such as race [7]. PII is explicitly identifiable information such as name, social security number, and sometimes birth date. Exactly which fields are considered PII is not always clear. Many Institutional Review Boards (IRBs) include IP addresses as PII [8]. De-identified data has limited value in research due to the inability to link such data to other data sources.

- *Trust mode*: For compelling research, we trust government agencies or social scientists to properly guard the PII entrusted to them and use it strictly for IRB-approved purposes only.

Both modes of access have significant problems when applied to the study of broad research questions that require integrated data. First, de-identified data has limited use in data integration. Second, the trust mode provides little privacy protection and questionable accuracy in data integration. Under the trust mode, PII is exposed to approved personnel with little protection against insider attacks. When social scientists are trusted with PII, they can create the linkage themselves. However, individual project principal investigators and social scientists are responsible for maintaining a highly secure IT system that can store and protect the PII. It is unrealistic to expect investigators leading individual social science projects to be able to maintain such highly secure systems. In reality, such systems depend on the social scientist keeping the research team in compliance with the IRB, and rely on basic security technology for protection in compelling research projects with reasonably secure systems. It is no wonder that the bar for compelling research is quite high. The most common case for linkage, when required, is for government agencies (e.g., state health statistics divisions or the United States Census Bureau) that have access to highly secure systems to perform the data integration for the scientist. Resources are limited in government agencies to carry out such tasks, so very few researchers are able to find such collaborations. More importantly, when government agencies perform data integration for the scientist, error management in the linkage process becomes problematic. As discussed in Sect. 3, record linkage is a complex iterative process that requires careful management of errors. However, when data integration is done by government staff, social scientists have no control over the process and thus cannot manage the level of error in the integrated data. Consequently, propagating the measurement errors of the linkage process into the statistical analysis step is also difficult. Furthermore, this process provides no protection against insider attacks by government staff, who have access to many types of private information such as social security numbers on the system.

To the best of our knowledge, no privacy-preserving data integration system has been modeled for use with real world problems. The only models of privacy in record linkage are research papers on private record linkage; these define the research goal as computing a set of linked records and then outputting them to the two private parties without revealing any information about the non-linked records. One of the assumptions of private record linkage is that the two parties each have private data that should not be revealed to the other party unless it is necessary as a result of the linking process. This formulation of the problem inherently prevents effective human intervention during the linkage process that could resolve ambiguities that occurred during linkage. Consequently, a major challenge remaining for all methods in private record linkage for real applications is a lack of discussion on how the model parameters will be estimated, and how the ambiguous links will be resolved without human intervention [9].

We emphasize that we do not formulate the privacy-preserving record linkage as is done in private record linkage. We believe that as a general framework, human intervention is necessary to guide good data analysis; this requires that data be revealed. In fact, our innovative approach to protecting individual privacy focuses on revealing information rather than hiding it. Our approach is to understand the minimum information required for acceptable linkage, and then to design protocols to reveal, in a secure manner, only that information.

The main use case in this study was designed for scientists who already have access to multiple de-identified data sets. Our goal is to build a privacy-preserving data integration model that can provide the same level of protection as de-identified data, but with the ability to integrate data to support broad research in computational social sciences [10-13].

We present a novel mode of access for research – the decoupled mode – that falls between the de-identified mode and the trust mode. Decoupling refers to separating out the identifying information from the sensitive data that needs protection. Compared to de-identified data (which cannot be linked), decoupled data is much more powerful while still providing the required privacy. Privacy is not an issue for non-unique isolated information. If the name John cannot be linked to any sensitive information, there is little danger in exposing just the name. The decoupled mode can allow social scientists to perform the linkage themselves and to manage the errors in the linkage process while still preserving privacy. In essence, decoupled data access can lower the bar for doing linkage for research. This is because with proper protocols in place, all de-identified data could be released as decoupled data to these secure systems, thereby enabling flexible record linkage. Compared to the trust mode, much less information is revealed under strictly controlled environments. Therefore, high-level security clearance would no longer be needed for those working on record linkage. Instead of high clearance government staff, graduate students with IRB approval who sign data use agreements would be able to access the controlled information required to perform record linkage without compromising privacy. The protocols of accessing decoupled data need not be different than the protocols for accessing sensitive de-identified data. However, the system requires good security protocols for controlling the information being revealed as well as good audit systems to closely monitor use.

The remainder of this chapter is organized as follows. Section 2 details the use case for privacy-preserving record linkage and describes the main threat models in the use case. Section 3 gives a short overview of related work in record linkage and privacy-preserving computation. In Section 4, important properties of information related to privacy are described. Section 5 presents our proposed decoupled data access model using these properties. Section 6 describes our experiment, and presents findings on how people perceive identity. We conclude with a discussion of future work in Section 7.

2   Use Case and the Threat Model

2.1   Use Case for Private Record Linkage

The use case for private record linkage involves two private parties, each with full information for each of their systems and each in need of some information from the other system. This commonly occurs when two separate parties need to share data. Such use cases are common in government agencies, but are not as common for social network data. For example, if a child welfare agency is trying to investigate educational outcomes for children in foster care, the child welfare agency would have full information about the children on welfare whereas the education agency would have all information about educational outcomes of all children. The goal of private record linkage is to link and share the data on outcomes of children in foster care such that the child welfare agency does not gain any information about the education data for children not in the child welfare system. The opposite is true for the education agency. If a trusted third party is used, the third party should not have access to any information from the education data or the child welfare data. This set up makes it very difficult to manage errors or resolve ambiguities during the record linkage process. Furthermore, theoretically, the third party model is often discussed as a privacy protection mechanism in research papers; however, most projects will not bear the extra cost of involving a non-related third party. In practice, it is often the case that one party will send all identifying information to the other party who then performs the linkage and sends the merged information back. The extra financial cost of using a third party, as well as the additional exposure of PII, is not practical in real applications. In this example, the child welfare agency would send all PII for the children in the child welfare system to a trusted staff member at the education agency. The education staff member will make the best effort to merge the two systems and return the educational outcomes data for the children in foster care back to the child welfare agency. In the process, the education agency staff has access to a full list of children in the child welfare system, opening the door for potential privacy violations.

2.2   Use Case for Privacy-Preserving Record Linkage

The use case for the privacy-preserving record linkage modeled in this study involves computational social science research wherein the scientist already has access to multiple de-identified datasets. Let us assume that a researcher is studying the relationship of Twitter posts and Facebook posts. Under the model of de-identified data access, the scientist can gain access to de-identified data from both social network sites without detailed identifying information for the actual accounts in each social network. However, it would be difficult to accurately answer questions about the relationship between the posts in the two sites without being able to link up the accounts. Our goal is to build a privacy-preserving data integration model that can provide levels of protection similar to de-identified data, but with the ability to allow the social scientist to flexibly merge different information and carefully manage errors to support broad research in computational social sciences [10-13].

Large research databases of personal information usually require strict protection in secure settings, even for de-identified data that is not fully anonymous. Our use case for supporting research in computational social science assumes a data infrastructure with these secure controlled access settings, wherein the kinds of operations carried out on the data and access to the data are strictly controlled [5, 14-16]. Access to all data would require appropriate IRB approval, with data available for analysis only on secure servers and only for approved purposes. It will be easy to control and monitor analysis performed on the data under these conditions. This assumption of controlled access realistically reduces the threat model significantly without much loss in usefulness in real applications. Under these assumptions, most sophisticated cryptographic attacks or link attacks for re-identification would be very difficult due to high security and 24/7 monitoring.

2.3 Threat Model for Privacy-Preserving Record Linkage

For a large data collection containing extensive private information, the most common threat model is an attack to gain unauthorized information from the data. An example of a potential attack of this kind for private health data would be a health insurance company that gains access to unauthorized health information about a potential customer from a research data source, then illegally denies that customer an insurance policy based on unauthorized use of the information.

There are two kinds of attack for an unauthorized access to information. First, an unauthorized user of the system can hack into the data collection. These are users who do not have a login to the system. For these attacks, most data collections rely on well-established security measures such as login authentication, requirements for routinely changing passwords, and 24/7 monitoring of the system. Second, an insider attack might be initiated from an authorized user who hacks into parts of the data collection that they are not authorized to access. These attacks are by users with valid logins who bypass the access rights established on the system. Again, protection from these threats relies on well-established security protocols such as 24/7 monitoring of the system. Protection from these threat models requires that all micro-level research data be stored under well-maintained and monitored secure systems with strict, fine grain access control.

The most difficult attacks to protect against are insider attacks by authorized users for unauthorized purposes. Access is granted to most personal data for research via IRB approvals that clearly state the authorized uses for the data. It is very difficult to protect against insider attacks by users who violate the IRB and access the data for unauthorized purposes. For this reason, almost all social science research data is de-identified to protect against this type of attack. We present a new decoupled model that can protect private data from these attacks through a computerized third party model. Using encryption, chaffing, shuffling, and privacy protocols for processing PII, the proposed decoupled mode can provide levels of protection similar to de-identified data access for this kind of attack. In the decoupled data system, a social scientist has access to the same de-identified sensitive data. What the scientist gains by using the decoupled system is access to computerized third-party software that can access the PII in order to merge the de-identified data. The scientist can ask the computer to merge two de-identified tables, after which the computerized third party takes control and carries out the linkage. In this process, the software actively interacts with the scientist as needed for guidance on parameter settings and resolving ambiguities.

There is one more important threat model for the research data use case: a threat from someone who wants to manipulate the study results by falsifying information on the system. Fortunately, similar to protection against unauthorized read access, these unauthorized write access threats can be stopped by the aforementioned standard and well-established security protocols. However, we acknowledge that there is no good protection against insider attacks from the scientist conducting the research.

3 Related Works

3.1 Record Linkage

Integrating multiple data from disparate sources requires the ability to identify the same entity across different tables with no common unique identifiers. Identifying the same real world entities and linking records from different tables for the same entity is called record linkage or entity resolution. The same technology is used for de-duplicating one table by linking the table to itself and linking multiple tables for integration. The main difficulty in entity resolution is that data are often expressed differently (e.g., nicknames), change over time (e.g., last names), do not have unique attributes (e.g., John Smith), are missing (e.g., social security numbers (SSNs) are often missing), or are erroneous. Let us consider an example where a SSN, first name, last name, and birth date are available. If we merged only on the SSN, issues arise from missing and erroneous numbers. If we merge using all four attributes on an exact match, many true matches will be missed. How many of the true matches are missed with an exact match depends on the quality and the similarity of the data systems. Typically, linkages across government administrative data systems using exact matches give poor results. Approximate matching methods can easily identify 50% more links than the exact methods. As a rule of thumb, when merging government records, exact matching methods identify roughly 60–70% of the identifiable links using approximate matching methods [17]. We suspect that data collected from social network websites might have lower levels of error but higher levels of missing data because the integrity of the data set relies primarily on users entering the data correctly with little verification. Social network data is also likely to have more occurrences of nicknames, which introduce variations in the data that also result in difficulty with entity resolution.

The goal of the different approaches to approximating record linkages is to identify as many of the false negatives missed using the strictest rule while introducing as few false positives as possible. Typically, all approaches will perform approximate matching and produce three categories: "match," "uncertain," and "unmatch." The objective is to minimize the uncertain region, which generally requires manual review by a person to resolve the ambiguous links.

The most difficult links to resolve involve twins. In this case, much of the identifying information is validly the same or very similar [17]. Often, SSNs are only one digit off, and one system might have assigned the SSN in one way, while another system has it assigned in the other way. These types of data errors make it almost impossible to automatically resolve entities without human intervention. Multiple birth rates have been rising in the United States, with twin birth rates at 29.3 per 1,000 births in 2000 [18]. That is approximately six twins in every 103 children born, not including triplets and higher-order births. These are substantial numbers that need to be considered when performing record linkage on people-level data. In one system of education data that performs record linkage on a regular basis, we have seen a twin field being regularly collected to differentiate data errors from real twins.

A record linkage model of personal data given such uncertainty was first proposed in 1959 by Newcombe [1], and the mathematical foundations were established by Fellegi and Sunter [19]. Since then, several approaches to entity resolution have been proposed [20–25]. The most straightforward methods are rule-based approaches, called deterministic record linkage, in which a set of reasonable rules are specified [17]. Typically, people build the rules incrementally by examining the most similar unlinked records and adding good rules to capture a greater number of false negatives. It is easy to see why manually building a full set of rules with small uncertainty regions is a labor intensive and iterative process.

Consequently, the most popular method is probabilistic record linkage based on calculating the probability of two records being a match [1, 19, 20, 25]. A blocking step is used to reduce the search space from N*N by grouping similar records in one quick pass (e.g., blocks of records with the same last names). The records that are blocked together are scored to determine the match. To avoid missing matches that were not blocked together, it is typical to perform several block/score passes. The probability of a match can be calculated by estimating an agreement weight for each attribute and combining them into one score. The user specifies two thresholds in the match score that determine the match, uncertain, and unmatch regions. The agreement weight can be estimated based on a model trained using the naive Bayes method or other machine learning techniques [22]. The main drawbacks for use with probabilistic record linkage are the difficulty in training the model, and in estimating the two thresholds for match and unmatch. Again, human intervention is required during the linkage process to estimate the parameters and resolve the uncertainty region.

3.2 Privacy-Preserving Computation

Although different from our use case, private record linkage is one model of privacy-protected record linkage. The goal of private record linkage is to compute the set of linked records and then output them to the two private parties without revealing anything about the non-linked records [9, 26]. There are three main approaches to private record linkage. First, secure set intersection methods deal with exact matching and are too expensive to be applied to large databases [27, 28]. Second, there are methods that attempt to mask the identifying information so as not to reveal the actual identifying data, but to reliably link using the masked data [29-32]. These methods will often use a third party to perform the match to avoid sophisticated cryptographic attacks. There are also hybrid methods [33]. One major challenge for these private record linking methods in real applications is the lack of discussion on how the threshold parameters for match and unmatch will be estimated, and how the uncertainty region will be resolved without human intervention. A comprehensive survey of private record linkage can be found in [9].

Another closely related area is a more general problem in privacy-preserving data mining [34] that focuses on performing useful data analysis without revealing private information. Protocols that can securely merge the data, perform analysis on the merged data, and only output the results of the regression without revealing any of the data are examples of privacy-preserving data mining. Sanitizing methods that perturb the quasi-identifiers to obscure individual identity [35-37] and differential privacy [38] are recent advancements in the area. These methods often involve privacy metrics to control the tradeoff between accuracy and privacy. A higher level of protection is provided by higher levels of sanitization that come at the cost of accuracy.

4 Information and Privacy

For many people, privacy protection in data means making the data anonymous to prevent identification. This generally agreed upon understanding of privacy protection has been used to propose privacy preservation mechanisms that allow data to be released for statistical research. However, preventing identification for privacy protection will never allow for good record linkage. This is because in entity resolution, the goal is to exactly identify the entity represented by the data in each table being linked so that the tables can be accurately merged. It is important to be able to accurately differentiate between two twins in the data so that in the analysis, two twins are not treated as a data error of one person. We need a more in-depth understanding of privacy and information in order to model privacy-preserving record linkage for research. In this section, we present important properties of information relating to privacy.

Table 1 HEW code of fair information practices [41]

Openness	There must be no personal data record keeping systems whose very existence is secret
Access	There must be a way for an individual to find out what information about him is in a record and how it is used
Control	There must be a way for an individual to prevent information about him that was obtained for one purpose from being used or made available for other purposes without his consent
Integrity	There must be a way for an individual to correct or amend a record of identifiable information about him
Security	Any organization creating, maintaining, using, or disseminating records of identifiable personal data must assure the reliability of the data for their intended use and must take precautions to prevent misuse of the data

4.1 Understanding Privacy and Security

Webster's dictionary defines privacy as *the state of being free from observation.* Privacy in regard to personal information has been defined as the right or desire of individuals to control the release of information about themselves [39]. In other words, it is the right of individuals to selectively reveal sensitive information about themselves to others. We note that the desire for privacy usually relates to controlling the use of sensitive information, not identifying information. Controlling the release and use of digitized personal data is particularly challenging because of the ease of sharing digitized data via remote access and replication.

Privacy protection is a social construct rather than a technical construct that is often defined via privacy laws. Most modern information privacy laws around the world, including The Privacy Act adopted in 1974, are based on what are known as Fair Information Practices (FIPs) [40]. FIPs were first published in a report issued by the Advisory Committee on Automated Personal Data systems of the U.S. Department of Health, Education and Welfare (HEW) in 1973 [41]. The five principles are (1) openness of the data system, (2) access to one's personal data, (3) integrity of one's personal data, (4) control of the use of data, and (5) security safeguards on the data (Table 1).

From a technical standpoint, these privacy standards result in policy requirements on digital data about (1) who has access to which data, (2) for what purpose, and (3) how the data should be maintained. Security technology tools are often used to implement these privacy policies in an information system.

4.2 Privacy in Social Network Websites

Privacy issues in social network sites primarily arise from *control of the use of data, and security safeguards on the data*. Privacy is an actively researched topic in social network sites because the revealing of personal information in social network sites, which often occurs voluntarily by users, can lead to serious privacy implications. These risks include exposure to various physical and cyber risks including identity theft and link privacy attacks [42-44]. Many users freely reveal surprisingly large amounts of personal data including names, phone numbers, and birth dates on social network sites with little control of how this information might be used. Furthermore, limiting the visibility of the revealed information through privacy settings is rarely used. Users often have a poor understanding of how such personal information can be misused, and social network websites do little to prevent misuse [42]. In addition, more care is needed to protect seemingly benign information such as group membership information and link information in social network sites as they can inadvertently leak private information as well [43, 44]. In fact, the boundaries blur between personal information published intentionally, either conditionally (i.e. for specific audience) or not, and information over which the users have no control. Such ambiguities make issues of personal privacy on social network sites even more complex [45].

Even in anonymized social networks, where names are replaced with meaningless unique identifiers, it is possible to trace the user information based on connections, usage patterns, and related context. So even if name is unavailable, the information about the universe around the name is also potentially risky in revealing private data [46]. These findings reiterate the notion that de-identification, stripping some designated list of information, cannot provide good privacy protection on data. Instead, data needs to be understood in a continuum where any data reveals some information, which has a potential for privacy violation. Some data just have more potential for violation than others. We discuss these continuums in the next section.

Given that all data have some potential to violate privacy, it is crucial that we better understand how to control the use of information on social network websites to provide protection. FlyByNight is a prototype system for mitigating the privacy risks to users using encryption techniques to protect sensitive data. It uses proxy cryptography to ensure that sensitive data is always encrypted when transmitted on the network and before reaching the servers, thereby raising the cost of attacks and providing better legal protection for privacy [47]. Privacy-by-proxy hides user identity and sensitive data behind special markup tags to implement better access controls for such data. While displaying such data, special permission check is done by the proxy server, and only retrieved and displayed to users with appropriate privileges. This approach can better protect user data exposure to third party developers who use social networking APIs [48].

4.3 Sensitivity and Identifiability

There are two dimensions of information that are important in understanding privacy: the sensitivity of information and the identifiability of information.

Definition 1 (The Sensitivity of Information). The **sensitivity of information** is defined as how private the information is. The lower the sensitivity, the more public the information, and the higher the sensitivity, the more private the information. For privacy protection in computational research, we use the potential risk of harm to the individual when information is leaked as a measure of information sensitivity. Thus, information is designated as sensitive by the researcher and approved by the IRB committee.

In the real world, sensitivity of information is individual-dependent as well as time-dependent. However, modeling privacy protection with such dependencies is very difficult. Thus, for the purposes of privacy-preserving computation for research, we use the potential risk of harm to the individual when information is leaked as a measure of information sensitivity. For example, if the release of a particular piece of data could mean that individuals might lose their job, health insurance, or reputation, then the information is considered highly sensitive. The IRB committee makes the final determination on the potential harm of leaked information based on the proposal made by the scientist. Note that IRB members are obligated to review all research activities and to ensure that all research subjects are protected.

Definition 2 (Identifiability of Information). The **identifiability of information** is defined as the extent to which the information can uniquely identify the entity represented by the data. The lower the identifiability of the information, the more difficult it is to uniquely identify the entity by releasing that information. The highest possible identifying information is something that can uniquely identify all entities; for example, social security numbers. In the literature, highly identifying information is often called explicitly identifying information or personally identifiable information (PII).

Identifying information is universe-dependent and thus may be indirectly time-dependent if the universe is dynamic. For example, the identifiability of a name depends on the universe in which the name is used, such as the region. The indirect time dependence of the identifiability of names results from people dying and being born in that region, and from migration.

Figure 1 depicts the two important properties of information related to privacy on a two-dimensional graph. The two properties are continuous, and all forms of information, either single fields or a combination of multiple fields, have some level of sensitivity and identifiability. Privacy protection is most needed for information in the upper right corner where information is highly sensitive and highly identifiable (HSHI). As information moves downward in either dimension, it can be shared with more people with fewer restrictions because either it is not sensitive (low sensitivity, high identifiability – LSHI), the sensitive information is difficult to associate with a real world entity (HSLI), or both (LSLI).

We can model privacy in terms of these two dimensions. A dimension that correlates highly to the sensitivity of information is the level of detail in the information. Typically, more detailed information is more sensitive, although not

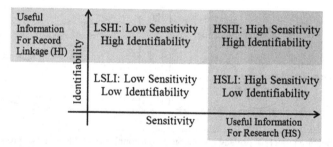

Fig. 1 Sensitivity and Identifiability of Information

always. The level of detail in information is important to understand because for information to be used in social science research, a high level of detail is required. In Fig. 1, we show this correlation and designate high sensitivity (HS) as the region of information most useful for social science research. For flexible record linkage with error management, high identifiability (HI) is required, as shown in Fig. 1.

Definition 3 (Privacy-Preserving Information in Universe *U*). When no highly sensitive information that is designated by the researcher and approved by the IRB committee can be uniquely associated with an entity in universe U, the data is said to be **privacy-preserving information in universe *U*.** The level of privacy protection provided can be quantified by "anonymity," which is the minimum number of entities that the information can be associated with in the universe.

The de-identified model of privacy-preserving data is shown in Fig. 2(a). De-identification, the most commonly accepted form of privacy protection in social sciences, transforms HSHI (high sensitivity, high identifiability) information into HSMI (high sensitivity, medium identifiability) information, which has better levels of privacy protection. However, by using medium identifying information, sometimes called quasi-identifiers, HSMI information becomes vulnerable to linkage attacks in which openly available LSHI (low sensitivity, high identifiability) information, such as voter registration, is linked to HSMI information to recreate the HSHI information. Recent advancements in privacy protection for de-identified data, including *k*-anonymity [37], *ℓ*-diversity [36], and t-closeness [35], transform HSMI information into MSLI (medium sensitivity, low identifiability) information using generalization and suppression to protect against such linkage attacks. The level of privacy protection is enhanced from the de-identified data by reducing the identifiability of the sensitive information. By generalizing and suppressing quasi-identifiers, there is some reduction in the level of detail in the information. This loss of detail effectively lowers the identifying power in the information, but often this loss of detail also reduces the usefulness of the information.

For most statistical computing where the purpose is to learn general characteristics about the data, moving HSHI information to the low or medium identifying regions is not much of an issue, as long as the sensitivity and usefulness level is mostly maintained. However, as seen in Fig. 2(a), when HSHI data is moved to a low identifying region, record linkage becomes impossible.

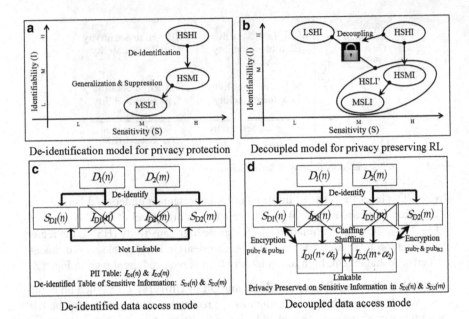

Fig. 2 Models for record linkage (RL)

Definition 4 (Privacy-Preserving Research Information System). A **privacy preserving research information system** is an information system that has the required security protocols in place for researchers to access one or more privacy-preserving information in universe U, as defined above, for research.

The U.S. Census Bureau and the Center for Disease Control (CDC) Research Data Centers (RDC) [14, 16] offer good examples of privacy-preserving research information systems. The RDC is an information system wherein researchers can gain access to micro-level de-identified data under restricted access control for approved research with many security protocols in place for the highest level of privacy protection required by government agencies. Restricted access is the strictest level of access wherein researchers are required to use designated computers in physical locations, and all releases of information are fully monitored.

5 A Model for Privacy-Preserving Record Linkage

5.1 Decoupled Data Access Model

Let U be a universe with multiple entities that have multiple attributes. Then let D (n) be a table with n rows collecting data on x attributes from universe U, where each row represents an entity in universe U and each column represents an attribute. $D[i]$ denotes row i in table D. Thus, row $D[i]$ represents attributes of an entity in universe U. We note that the entity represented by $D[i]$ may not be uniquely mapped from $D[i]$ to the entity in universe U. For example, let table $D(n)$ be a one-attribute table of gender. Then, $D[i] = male$ represents all entities that are male in universe U.

Definition 5 (PII Table and De-identified Table). Given a table D(n), the **PII table** for D(n) is denoted by I_D(n) where table I_D(n) is composed of attributes that can explicitly identify the entity in universe U. Note that "explicitly identify" does not necessarily mean uniquely identify. S_D(n) denotes the **de-identified table** composed of columns in D(n) that are not in table I_D(n). Then, D(n) = I_D(n) + S_D(n).

$I_D(n)$ is typically the entity that is stripped and discarded from the full table $D(n)$ to create the de-identified table $S_D(n)$ consisting of only the sensitive data. So, $D(n)$ is a HSHI table, $I_D(n)$ is a LSHI table, and $S_D(n)$ is a HSLI' table as depicted in Fig. 2(b). Figure 2(c) is the model for de-identified data access from which the de-identified table $S_D(n)$ is released for research.

Definition 6 (Decoupled Table). Let there be a mapping function recordID() such that recordID(I_D[i]) = recordID(S_D[j]) iff I_D[i] and S_D[j] consist solely of values originating from the same row in table D(n). A **Decoupled table** is defined as the PII table I_D(n') and the de-identified table S_D(n) such that n' > n and there exists a pair of encryption and decryption functions, En_R(M, $pub_{R(D)}$) and De_R(M, $priv_{R(D)}$), such that

En_R(recordID(I_D[i]), $pub_{R(D)}$) = EnRecordID(I_D[i]) and
De_R(EnRecordID(I_D[i]), $priv_{R(D)}$) = recordID(I_D[i]) = recordID(S_D[j]).

Basically, a decoupled table is produced when a PII table and a de-identified table have been separated, and the PII table has been shuffled and inflated with fake data to block row association between the PII table and the de-identified table. The asymmetric encryption function $En_R()$ ensures that only holders of the private key, $priv_{R(D)}$, can gain access to the row association between the PII table and the de-identified table. Each decoupled table has its own set of keys as denoted by the subscript D in $pub_{R(D)}$ and $priv_{R(D)}$. Furthermore, extra rows are built into the table I_D (n') through chaffing such that $I_D(n')$ has more rows than the originating table D(n) and the de-identified table $S_D(n)$.

Definition 7 (Decoupled Data Access System). Let there be a mapping function tableID() such that tableID(I_D) = tableID(S_D) = D. A **decoupled data access system** is a database system that has one or more decoupled tables such that there exists a pair of encryption and decryption functions, En_T (M, pub_T) and De_T(M, $priv_T$), such that

En_T (tableID(I_D), pub_T) = EnTableID(I_D) and
De_T (EnTableID(I_D), $priv_T$) = tableID(I_D) = tableID(S_D).

In a decoupled data access system, the association information of matching the PII table $I_D(n')$ to the attribute table $S_D(n)$ is only available to those with the private table key, $priv_T$. RSA is a well-established secure method of public key encryption that can be used for encrypting both the row association and table association information [49]. Encryption of the row and table association information provides the same level of protection to the de-identified data in the decoupled system as the plain de-identified data. Thus, the privacy protection in the decoupled data access system relies on the encryption technology used in the system. Figure 2(d) shows the model of the decoupled data access system.

Definition 8 (Duplicate). If two rows D[i] and D[j] represent the same entity in universe U, then the table D(n) is said to have **duplicates**.

Definition 9 (Record Linkage). If row i from table D_1 (n) and row j from table D_2 (m) represent the same entity in universe U, then the mapping of EnRecordID $(I_{D1}[i]) = EnRecordID(I_{D2}[j])$ is called a **record linkage**. Tables D_1 and D_2 are said to be linked when all common entities in table D_1 and table D_2 have been mapped. Note that the mapping between table D_1 and table D_2 is often an N-to-N mapping in reality since many tables have some duplicates.

Property 1 (k-anonymous in universe U). Given a universe U from which the data D(n) is collected, a PII table $I_D(n)$ is said to be **k-anonymous in universe** U iff for all rows in I_D (n) there exist at least k entities in U represented by the row.

Note that when all entities in universe U are not known, then k entities do not need to explicitly exist in universe U; rather, merely the possibility of k entities in the universe U is sufficient. We further discuss the importance of creating an intractable universe U' through chaffing in Sect. 5.3.

Definition 10 (Privacy-Preserving Record Linkage). Given two tables D_1 and D_2, a **privacy-preserving record linkage** is defined as linking the two PII tables, $I_{D1}(n)$ and $I_{D2}(m)$, using the decoupled data access system, and both the PII tables I_{D1} (n) and I_{D2} (m) are k-anonymous in universe U.

Figure 2(b) depicts the privacy-preserving record linkage model in terms of the sensitivity and identifiability of information. Given no breach of the security protocols for association of HSLI' with the LSHI information, privacy-preserving record linkage has an identical level of protection for the original HSHI information $D(n)$ as the commonly used de-identified data access model. However, flexible linkage with error management is now possible using the LSHI information in the decoupled system. Thus, the problem of privacy-preserving record linkage is now effectively a problem of designing security protocols to prevent leaking the association of HSLI' information with the LSHI information.

5.2 Social Security Numbers

The advantage of modeling privacy-preserving record linkage using the sensitivity and identifiability of information comes from the relationship between them as seen in real data. In reality, most attributes either have high identifiability or high sensitivity because most attributes that can explicitly identify all entities in the

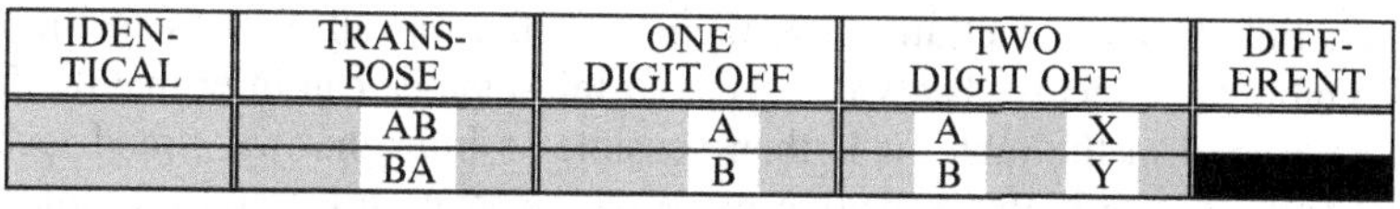

IDEN-TICAL	TRANS-POSE	ONE DIGIT OFF	TWO DIGIT OFF		DIFF-ERENT
	AB	A	A	X	
	BA	B	B	Y	

Fig. 3 SSN similarity information

universe are public information. A name, address, and phone number is commonly accepted as an explicitly identifying information that has low sensitivity. This type of information has a very low potential of harming the individual when leaked. By comparison, highly sensitive data, such as HIV status, usually have low identifiability. The dichotomous nature of most real information having either high sensitivity or high identifiability but not both makes it fairly easy to transform HSHI data into HSLI data because the highly identifying data can be dropped without dropping the useful highly sensitive data.

The one exception is the social security number. The most powerful types of identifying information in a country are its national identification numbers, which in the U.S. are social security numbers. The identifiability is usually highest when there are no errors or missing data. These data are also highly sensitive data, since leaked SSNs can lead to identity theft and cause serious harm to the individual. Fortunately, although the SSN is highly sensitive data, it is not useful for research. Thus, for the purposes of privacy-preserving computation for research, we can group the SSN with the other LSHI information. However, special security measures are required to protect SSNs during linkage, so that the actual SSN is never leaked. In the record linkage process, the actual SSN does not need to be revealed to the scientist. The only information the scientist needs is the difference between two SSNs. This information can be conveyed as the number of digits that are different and the number of transposes, without ever revealing the SSN. Figure 3 shows a simple scheme to convey the similarity of two SSNs.

5.3   Need for Chaffing

In a decoupled data access system, enough information can be revealed during linkage for some entities in the PII table to be exposed, thereby allowing a scientist to uniquely identify the entity in universe U. For example, if the scientist saw a row with a friend's name and birthday, the identity of the friend could be revealed. The probability of this record representing the friend will depend on the possibility of other entities in the universe that share both of these attributes. The rarer the name and the smaller the geographical region of the universe, the more likely the friend's identity has been revealed. Fortunately, even when the identity is revealed, given that the scientist cannot associate the particular row with any row in the de-identified data, none of the sensitive data would be exposed and privacy of the information would be maintained. However, any tautology for table D being linked would hold true for the scientist's friend. For example, if the research involved linking child welfare data, then by definition all entities in the child welfare table have received services. Thus, if the scientist can infer that the friend was represented in the table, it is then possible to infer that the friend received welfare services – a highly sensitive piece of information that would violate the privacy of the friend.

Thus, strict decoupling via encryption is not sufficient to protect privacy when identities can be revealed during the linkage process. We need to employ chaffing to enforce the property of k-anonymity in universe U to prevent potential inferences that might be made from the PII tables while the scientist is working on the linkage. k-anonymity in universe U will ensure that the scientist cannot infer guaranteed unique identification from the PII table. In the preceding example, if the data covered all child welfare services in a large state, the scientist would not be able to infer the identity of the row. Even though the scientist might suspect it, there would be no way to know how many people share the same name and birthday with the friend in the state. Such uncertain information is not as useful for most attackers who want unauthorized information. Most importantly, referring back to our operational definition of sensitive information based on potential harm, little harm can come from uncertain information because it is difficult to take action based on such information.

Clearly, universe U is very important in privacy protection. The uncertainties of universe U can provide a cover for the revealed PII data and prevent action that might harm the individual. Adding false data to the PII table effectively enlarges the universe to an infinite intractable universe. Thus, effective chaffing can prevent any guaranteed inferences that might violate privacy.

We note that some names are more anonymous than others, but few are strictly unique, even when paired with a birth date. More importantly, there is no guarantee that any name and birth date pair refers to a particular person. Even when there is only one entity in the universe with a particular pair of name and birth date, there is no guarantee of unique identification because it is very difficult to know the full universe. The uncertainties of U provide the required protection. This inherent property of non-unique identification by name is what makes the entity resolution problem extremely difficult, requiring extensive computation and careful management of errors.

In comparison, addresses and phone numbers can closely identify most people in universe U. Attributes such as these that can uniquely identify most entities require close monitoring and careful handling. Physical location information such as zip code or city can also be used to effectively narrow down the universe. Thus, if physical location information needs to be used for linkage, chaffing becomes critical to enlarging universe U for protection.

5.4 Computer-Based Third Party Model

A decoupled data access information system is essentially a computerized third party that strictly controls information. Although trusted human third parties are not used in practice, the trusted third party mechanism to protect privacy is well understood.

Two very important advantages are gained by implementing a computer-based third party. Most importantly, unlike human third parties with which interaction is costly and thus limited, it is very easy to interact with a computerized third party through properly designed software. With a computerized third party acting as an oracle, a person can interact frequently with information held by the computer third party at the smallest level in order to manage errors in the linkage. The scientist can ask detailed questions, such as how similar are two encrypted SSNs. In addition, a computerized third party model of privacy protection is a realistic way to implement the secure third party model in practice. The software should function like a bank vault with security deposit boxes that have well-developed security protocols for importing and accessing datasets in the system. Access to each dataset is given only to those who have the appropriate decryption key. Even the software itself is not able to decrypt without the user-presented key. Furthermore, access to different parts of the dataset, the PII table, and the de-identified table requires different clearance levels with virtually no person having the clearance to view the full table together.

6 Experimental Results

In this study, we considered how privacy could be preserved in entity resolution by better understanding the sensitivity and identifiability of information. Revealing names without distortion is important for accurate entity resolution, and we suggest that privacy can still be maintained, even when names are revealed due to the non-uniqueness of names and uncertainty in the universe around the data. There is no way to know how many people named John exist in the universe of the data, especially if the universe is unknown. To better understand how people infer identity from names, we conducted an experiment to measure the perceived identifiability of names under various circumstances. Our goal was to test the effectiveness of the different methods in obscuring the actual identity of names, given that the names are revealed to the researcher. In this experiment, we measured (1) the impact of the universe around the data, (2) the effect of chaffing, and (3) the identifiability of three different identifying information characteristics; namely, the common name, the common name and date of birth, and the rare name.

6.1 Survey Design

Our basic experiment included performing an online survey to measure how confident people are when inferring identity under different conditions. The full survey had 18 questions; however, we will discuss only the eight questions most relevant to this chapter. Using a Likert scale, we asked participants to state their confidence level in identifying a person from a list given different identifying

Table 2 Basic survey question format

Scenario 1. Q1. Meet George Brown, a student at Meadowgreen High School

Using only the information on this screen, how likely is it that the George Brown introduced above
is the same person listed on the honor roll provided here?

	Meadowgreen HS Honor Roll
	Brian Richards
1. Highly likely to be the same person	Amanda Ward
2. Moderately likely to be the same person	Edward Jones
3. Slightly likely to be the same person	Hilary Ford
4. I don't know if they are the same person or not	George Brown
5. Slightly likely to be two different people	Susan Miller
6. Moderately likely to be different people	David Green
7. Highly likely to be two different people	Alexander Parker
	Daniel Parker
	Alex Parker

Scenario 1. Q2. *Repeat Q1 above but change the honor roll list to be for an unspecified school, titled*
A High School Honor Roll

Scenario 2. Meet Susan Miller (date of birth 4/17/1994), a student at Meadowgreen High School

Using only the information provided here, how likely is it that the Susan Miller introduced above is
the same person listed on the honor roll provided here?

Modify honor roll lists to include a column for dob

Scenario 3 and 4. Meet Rahul Ghosh, a student at Meadowgreen High School

Using only the information provided here, how likely is it that the Rahul Ghosh introduced above,
has made the honor roll at his school?

The lists for scenarios 3 and 4 were modified to include more rare names such as Viswanath Sastry,
Jie Lee, and Juan Lopez. The scale was also adjusted to [Highly – Moderately – Slightly] likely
to have [NOT] made the honor roll

information and a universe. We used a seven-point scale to measure the confidence
level. The participant could choose between three levels of yes, three levels of no,
or "I don't know." We presented the participants with certain identifying information for a target student and an honor roll list that included the same identifying
information. We then asked the participants to measure their confidence level as to
the likelihood that the two are the same person. Table 2 shows the basic setup of all
questions. We used the high school honor roll scenario because it was a relatively
neutral list, and participants would not have emotional or biased assumptions about
the list. There were four scenarios. Each scenario had two separate questions.

First, we measured the difference in confidence level when the universe around
the data was specified versus when it was not specified. We did this by giving an
honor roll from the same high school that the target student attends (known universe), versus an honor roll from an unspecified high school (unknown universe).
General instructions were given at the beginning. The instructions clearly stated that
the unspecified school may or may not be the same school that the target students
attended. For each target student, we asked the question two times: first with the
honor roll from the specific high school, followed by the same question with an
honor roll from an unspecified school, to measure the change in confidence level.

Table 3 Instructions given to measure the effect of chaffing

We did not tell you this before, but the tables used in the previous questions contained a few pieces of false data. Those tables included students who were *NOT* actually on the honor roll. It's too late to go back and change your answers for those questions, but we'll give you another chance here. *Knowing that these honor rolls are not fully correct*, answer the questions again as to how likely is it that the Rahul Ghosh made the honor roll at his school

As seen in Table 2, we highlighted the source of the list so that the participants would pay attention to the changes in the universe in different questions. Then, we went through multiple sets of the two questions, changing the identifying information given for the target student. We used four scenarios: (1) a target student with a common name (George Brown), (2) a target student with a common name and date of birth (Susan Miller, born on 4/17/1994), (3) a target student with a rare name (Rahul Ghosh), and (4) a target student with a rare name (Rahul Ghosh) with a list that included false names of students not on the honor roll. For the second scenario (in which we included dates of birth for identifying information), we also added a column of birth dates to the honor roll lists.

The fourth scenario measured the effect of chaffing on how people infer identity. We first used a target student with a rare name, Rahul Ghosh, as the base question and asked the two questions. This was scenario three. For these questions, we also changed both lists to include more rare names such as Viswanath Sastry, Jie Lee, and Juan Lopez. In addition, we changed the question slightly to ask how likely it is that the target student had made the honor roll at his school. The scale wording was also adjusted to indicate the confidence of having made the honor roll. We changed the question slightly so that we could ask the participants to answer the same question one more time, knowing that the honor roll included some false data of students who did not make the honor roll. This is the fourth scenario, wherein we tested a given rare name as the identifying information on a chaffed list. The exact instructions given just before the fourth scenario are shown in Table 3. The four scenarios used to ask two questions each gave us a total of eight questions.

6.2 Method

.The main goal of this study was to quantify the impact of different mechanisms that hinder inference of identity when a name is revealed to graduate students and researchers in the course of entity resolution. Thus, we recruited participants by sending out e-mails to various mailing lists on different campuses targeting graduate students and researchers in both the social sciences and computational sciences. The social science students were mostly in public health and social work, whereas computational science students were mostly in computer science, statistics, and operational research. We targeted graduate students and researchers because they are most likely to use the decoupled data system for record linkage with error management. Thus, understanding how this population infers identity from names was important.

Table 4 Demographics of participants (total participants = 59)

	Demographics					
Student	Yes	50 (84.75%)	No	9 (15.25%)		
Education	Bachelors	25 (42.37%)	Masters	26 (44.07%)	Ph.D.	8 (13.56%)
Department	Social science	26 (44.07%)	Computational science	31 (52.54%)	Missing	2 (3.39%)
Race	White	44 (74.58%)	Asian	9 (15.25%)	Other	6 (10.17%)
Gender	Female	27 (45.76%)	Male	32 (54.24%)		

Table 5 Data experiences of participants (total participants = 59)

	Experience with data			
Record linkage experience	Experience	25 (42.37%)	No experience	34 (57.63%)
Secondary data analysis	Yes	23 (38.98%)	No	36 (61.02%)
Large data that is de-identified	Yes	23 (38.98%)	No	36 (61.02%)
Large data that is NOT de-identified	Yes	19 (32.20%)	No	40 (67.80%)
No experience with data	Experience	53 (89.83%)	No experience	6 (10.17%)

We received 59 responses. Tables 4 and 5 show the basic demographics and data experiences of the respondents. To gather information on the participants' experiences with data, we asked the participants to check all that apply on a list of descriptions. Although we made no attempt to recruit from students with experience in data analysis, we obtained a good mix of participants with various experiences in data. This is probably a reflection on the general experience of a broad range of graduate students; all but six had some experience with data. Approximately 40% had experience in record linkage, secondary data analysis, and large data analysis using de-identified data. 32% of the participants had experience with large data that was not de-identified. Therefore, about one in three of the participants had some experience in accessing data under the trust mode with little privacy protection. This was a larger number than we expected in the general academic community, suggesting the need for this work on decoupled data systems. Data integration is the primary reason for researchers to have access to data that is not de-identified. The decoupled data system could provide better privacy protection in these circumstances while still allowing for the data integration.

We tested the change in the confidence level of identity by comparing responses to different questions using the Wilcoxon signed rank test, a non-parametric t-test. The Wilcoxon signed rank test considers the statistical difference in the median of measured ordinal variables such as the Likert scale [50].

6.3 Results

Figure 4 shows our experimental results as stacked bar charts. Each of the eight questions corresponds to one stacked bar. *HS name* refers to the question that was asked with the high school specified on the honor roll, and the *No HS name* refers to

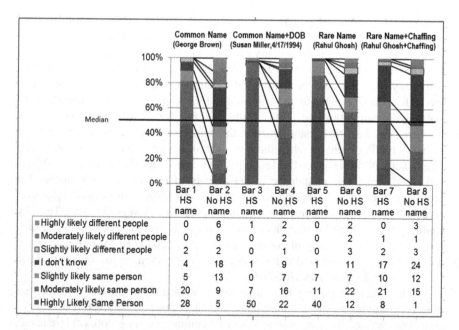

Fig. 4 Experimental results

the question that was asked with the unspecified high school honor roll. The bar chart is shown as a percentage of participants, and the table below shows the counts of participants. The experiment had three important findings.

First, the results showed that in all four scenarios when the universe around the data was not specified (Bars 2, 4, 6, and 8), the level of confidence that people had on the identity of the target student dropped significantly compared to the case in which the universe was specified (Bars 1, 3, 5, and 7). For example, when presented with just a common name for identifying information (George Brown), of the 28 participants who were highly confident that the target student was also the same student on the honor roll for Meadowgreen high school, only 5 (18%) remained highly confident when we told them the list came from an unspecified school. Overall, the median level of confidence dropped by two levels, from *moderately likely to be the same person* when the high school was properly specified to *I don't know* when the school was not specified. The non- parametric t-test revealed that the drop in confidence when the school name was not specified was statistically significant at the .005 level in all four scenarios. The implication is that in general, in the decoupled data system, making the universe of the list unknown has significant impact in reducing the inference power of any given name. Specifically, even if a researcher encounters familiar names during the linkage process, they are significantly less confident in the real identity of the name when the universe around the data is unknown.

Second, we found that chaffing is effective in reducing identifiability for rare names to levels lower than those of simple common names. The participants who were highly confident of the identity of Rahul Ghosh after being given a list from the same school dropped by 54%, from 68% (40/59) to 14% (8/59) (Bar 5 vs. Bar 7), when they were told that the list had false data. Overall, the median dropped two levels, from *highly confident* to *slightly confident*, with the t-test showing a statistically significant difference in the median at the .005 level (Bar 5 vs. Bar 7). Furthermore, the t-test result between the common name scenario and the rare name + chaffing scenario when the high school was specified is also statistically significantly different at the .005 level (Bar 1 vs. Bar 7). In other words, our subjects had significantly less confidence in the identity of rare names on a chaffed list compared to common names on an accurate list. The distributions of the responses given in Fig. 4 clearly support this drop in the confidence level of identity. Thus, by chaffing the list, the identifiability of rare names were reduced to similar or lower levels of the identifiability of common names. Note that even for rare names, the median dropped further to ideal levels of *I don't know* when the list was chaffed and the high school was not specified (Bar 8).

Finally, when comparing the four scenarios, we found that the test subjects were most confident in identity when the name and date of birth were given. The order of confidence of identity from high to low is (1) common name + dob, (2) rare name, (3) common name, and (4) rare name + chaffing. The least confidence in identity given only a common name is expected. The more interesting finding was that people tended to have more confidence in inferring identity when a pair of common name + dob was given compared to when a rare name was given. This finding suggests that even though objectively a given pair of name and date of birth might not be uniquely identifying information, subjectively people might think otherwise. This could lead to wrong conclusions about the identity of a familiar name and birth date pair. In entity resolution, dates can be used in a scheme similar to the SSN (Fig. 3) for depicting the distance between two dates using elements of dates (namely, day + month + year) without actually revealing the dates. Thus, we suggest not revealing dates of birth in decoupled data systems.

6.4 Implications

Our experiment found that if (1) a name is shown in isolation with respect to other identifying information, (2) the universe around the data is not specified, and (3) chaffing is performed on the list to protect against high identifiability of rare names, then more than 50% of the participants responded that they could not infer the identity when given a rare or common name (Bar 2 and Bar 8). These are promising results for a privacy-preserving record linkage system via decoupling. The most difficult but important data to use for entity resolution without revealing the true identity are names (e.g., the names of people, companies, or streets) because nicknames and abbreviations are difficult to capture once the name space is distorted. Our experimental results support the proposal that there are ways to lower the identifiability of names even when they are revealed without distortion. For other numeric-based data elements that can be broken out into meaningful units, such as digits or elements of dates, there are simple methods that can calculate and reveal only the distance without the actual values being revealed. It is sufficient to only share the results of the distance calculation with the researcher for entity resolution. A well-combined scheme of revealing names and distance metrics of other data can lead to an accurate privacy-preserving record linkage system.

7   Conclusion and Future Work

In this chapter, we presented a new mode of data access for research that falls between the de-identified mode and the trust mode. The general mode of access for social science research, the de-identified mode, is too limiting for data integration. On the other hand, the trust mode of access reveals too much private information to the scientist and requires very high levels of security. Such levels of security often lead to government agencies performing the data integration for the scientist. This separation of the data integration process and data analysis of the merged data produce questionable results due to measurement errors introduced during linkage that were not properly accounted for in the analysis. The typical kinds of errors often found in data entered by people result in the need to manage errors during linkage. The proposed decoupled mode of access will allow for flexible linkage with error management while protecting privacy by implementing a secure computer-based third party using encryption, chaffing, and shuffling. Our experimental results show that chaffing is an effective mechanism for privacy protection, and a well-combined scheme of revealing names and distance metrics of other data can lead to an accurate privacy-preserving record linkage system. With such a system, a social scientist can gain access to diverse existing databases to build a high-quality network of social relationships such as families, friends, and neighbors without compromising individual privacy.

Research in decoupled data access has only begun, and there is much work remaining. Below are some directions for future research.

- Chaffing: What kind of false data, and how much of it, is required to prevent inferences without interfering with decision making during entity resolution?
- Encryption: What is the best encryption technology to enforce strict decoupling? How do we implement a scheme in which authorized users are given a key that is required to decrypt the information?
- Record linkage: What information should be revealed to allow high quality linkage while protecting privacy? How can we use attributes that can uniquely identify the majority of the entities in the universe for record linkage? We briefly discussed SSNs, but there are other attributes such as a phone number and address. These highly unique attributes are excellent for record linkage but pose a great danger to privacy protection.

- Visual analytics: What visual analytic techniques can be used to effectively convey highly identifying information while still protecting privacy?
- Security system: How can we build an overall secure computer-based third party system to manage the PII tables, the de-identified tables, and the information flow between them for accurate record linkage and data cleaning?
- Audit system: What privacy audits should be performed on the decoupled data access system? What logs should be kept for the privacy audits? Can we design anomaly detection algorithms to automatically detect major threats?
- IRB process: All research involving human subjects requires approval from the IRB in the US. This includes research involving human subject data, and the standards around IRB approvals for human subject data need to be updated if we are to use the decoupled system. What should the IRB process look for when using data in a decoupled data system? What training should be required for researchers using the system?
- Identity inference: Our experiment was a small study on limited identifying information with only one rare name. It would be interesting to study the impact of context and the types of names on how people infer identity. Do people infer more or less about more emotional lists such as cancer status? How much bias do people have toward the ethnicity of names?
- Record linkage is an important problem for industry. Can commercial infrastructure be upgraded to build in privacy-preserving record linkage?
- Understanding the types and nature of errors in data is important for entity resolution. Research on the quality of data in social network sites and on selection bias for users of social network sites will be important for the application of data to broad computational social science.

Finally, we note that recent progress in privacy has shown that de-identified data is still open to re-identification, making the de-identified data access dangerous. Such link attacks are very difficult under the controlled data access assumption. More importantly, any new technology to improve privacy on de-identified data can be applied to decoupled data as well. Therefore, we note that the focus of this study is on the problem of making de-identified data linkable under the same privacy protection, rather than on the problem of making de-identified data safer.

There is no silver bullet for privacy-preserving computation. Developing an effective model for privacy-preserving linkage with sensitive data for research requires a well-orchestrated system with strong fine-grained access control, regular privacy audits, and good IRB approval guidelines [8]. Our proposed decoupled data access system can be a blueprint for such privacy-preserving linkage systems for broad-based applications in computational social sciences.

Acknowledgement We thank everyone who participated in the survey. We also thank Mike Reiter and Fred Brooks for their insightful comments, and Gautam Sanka, Ian Sang-Jun Kim, and Ren Bauer for their assistance with the experiment. This research was supported in part by funding from the NC Department of Health and Human Services and by NSF award no. CNS-0915364. The authors gratefully acknowledge their support.

References

1. Newcombe H, Kennedy J, Axford S, James A (1959) Automatic linkage of vital records. Science 130:954–959
2. Baldi I, Ponti A, Zanetti R, Ciccone G, Merletti F, Gregori D (2010) The impact of record-linakge bias in the Cox model. J Eval Clin Prac 16:92–96
3. Lahiri P, Larsen M (2005) Regression analysis with linked data. J Am Stat Assoc 100 (469):222–230
4. Scheuren F, Winkler W (1997) Regression analysis of data files that are computer matched, Part II. Surv Meth 23:157–165
5. Lane J, Schur C (2010) Balancing access to health data and privacy: a review of the issues and approaches for the future. Health Serv Res 45:1456–1467
6. U.S. General Accounting Office (GAO) (2001) Record linkage and privacy: issues in creating new federal research and statistical information. In: GA0-01-126SP, April 2001, GAO: U.S. General Accounting Office, Washington, DC 20013
7. Sweeney L (1997) Weaving technology and policy together to maintain confidentiality. J Law Med Ethics 25(2–3):98–110
8. Narayanan A, Shmatikov V (2010) Myths and fallacies of personally identifiable information. Commun ACM 53:24–26
9. Hall R, Fienberg S (2011) Privacy-preserving record linkage. In: Privacy in statistical databases 2010: LNCS 2011, vol 6344/2011, pp 269–283, Privacy in statistical databases, 2010, Corfu, Greece.
10. Cook K, King G, Laitin D (2010) Providing the Web of social science knowledge for the future: a network of social science data collaboratories. NSF-SBE white paper, Oct 2010
11. King G (2011) Ensuring the data-rich future of the social sciences. Science 331:719–721
12. Kum HC, Ahalt S, Carsey T (2011) Dealing with data: governments records. Science 332:1263
13. Lazer D, Pentland A, Adamic L, Aral S, Barabasi A, Brewer D, Christakis N, Contractor N, Fowler J, Gutmann M, Jebara T, King G, Macy M, Roy D, Van Alstyne M (2009) Computational social science. Science 323:721–723
14. Center for Disease Control and Prevention (CDC), NCHS Research Data Center (RDC). http://www.cdc.gov/rdc/
15. Lane J, Heus P, Mulcahy T (2008) Data access in a cyber-world: making use of cyberinfrastructure. Trans Data Privacy 1:2–16
16. U.S. Census Bureau, CES Research Data Center (RDC). http://www.census.gov/ces/rdcresearch/index.html
17. Kum HC, Duncan D, Bowers H, Cambridge D (2009) Linking across multiple databases with less than perfect data. In: NRC-CWDT, June 2009
18. Reynolds MA, Schieve LA, Martin JA, Jeng G, Macaluso M (2003) Trends in multiple births conceived using assisted reproductive technology, United States, 19972000. Pediatrics 111 (Supp 1):1159–1162
19. Fellegi P, Sunter AB (1969) A theory for record linkage. J Am Stat Assoc 64(328):1183–1210, American Statistical Association, Alexandria, VA 22314–3415
20. Elmagarmid K, Panagiotis GI, Verykios SV (2007) Duplicate record detection: a survey. IEEE Trans Knowl Data Eng 19:1–16, American Statistical Association, 1429 Duke St. Alexandria, VA 22314-3415
21. Guo S, Dong X, Srivastava D, Zajac R (2010) Record linkage with uniqueness constraints and erroneous values. Proc VLDB Endowment 3(1):417–428, VLDB 2010: Singapore
22. Sarawagi S, Bhamidipaty A (2002) Interactive deduplication using active learning. In: Proceedings of the 8th ACM SIGKDD international conference on knowledge discovery and data mining (KDD '02), ACM, New York, pp 269–278, 10.1145/775047.775087
23. Whang SE, Benjelloun O, Garcia-Molina H (2009) Generic entity resolution with negative rules. VLDB J 18:1261–1277

24. Whang SE, Garcia-Molina H (2010) Entity resolution with evolving rules. Proc VLDB Endowment 3(1):1326–1337
25. Winkler WE (1999) The state of record linkage and current research problems. In: Technical report, U.S. Bureau of the Census
26. Yakout M, Atallah MJ, Elmagarmid AK (2009) Efficient private record linkage. In: ICDE IEEE, 2009, pp 1283–1286, ICDE, 2009: Shanghai, China
27. Agrawal R, Evfimievski A, Srikant R (2003) Information sharing across private databases. In: SIGMOD '03, New York, pp 86–97
28. Freedman MJ, Nissim K, Pinkas B (2004) Efficient private matching and set intersection. In: Proceedings of EUROCRYPT 2004, Heidelberg
29. Churches T, Christen P (2004) Blind data linkage using n-gram similarity comparisons. In: PAKDD, Lecture notes in computer science, vol 3056. Springer, pp 121–126
30. Churches T, Christen P (2004) Some methods for blindfolded record linkage. BMC Med Inform Decis Mak 4(1):9
31. Scannapieco M, Figotin I, Bertino E, Elmagarmid AK (2007) Privacy preserving schema and data matching. In: SIGMOD conference, pp 653–664, SIGMOD, 2007: Beijing, China
32. Schnell R, Bachteler T, Reiher J (2009) Privacy-preserving record linkage using bloomfilters. BMC Med Inform Decis Mak 9(1):41
33. Inan A, Kantarcioglu M, Bertino E, Scannapieco M (2008) A hybrid approach to private record linkage. In: Data engineering, 2008. ICDE 2008. IEEE 24th international conference, ICDE 2008, Cancún, México.
34. Vaidya J, Zhu Y, Clifton C (2005) Privacy preserving data mining. Advances in information security. Springer, New York
35. Li N, Li T, Venkatasubramanian S (2007) t-Closeness: privacy beyond k-anonymity and l-diversity. In: 2007. ICDE 2007. IEEE 23rd International Conference on data engineering, Piscataway, pp 106–115, 15–20, April 2007
36. Machanavajjhala A, Kifer D, Gehrke J, Venkitasubramaniam M (2007) L-diversity: privacy beyond k-anonymity. ACM Trans Knowl Discov Data 1(1), Article 3
37. Sweeney L (2002) k-anonymity: a model for protecting privacy. Int J Uncertain Fuzz Knowl-Based Syst 10(5):557–570
38. Dwork C (2008) Differential privacy: a survey of results. In: Theory and applications of models of computation: lecture notes in computer science, vol 4978/2008, pp 1–19, LCNS 2008, Springer-Verlag, Berlin Heidelberg
39. Rindfleisch TC (1997) Privacy, information technology, and health care. Commun ACM 40 (8):92–100. doi:10.1145/257874.257896
40. Privacy Protection Study Commission. Personal Privacy in an Information Society, July 1977. http://epic.org/privacy/ppsc1977report/
41. U.S. Department of Health, Education and Welfare (HEW) (1973) Report of the secretary's advisory committee on automated personal data systems: records, computers and the rights of citizens
42. Gross R, Acquisti A (2005) Information revelation and privacy in online social networks. In: Pre-proceedings version. ACM workshop on privacy in the electronic society (WPES), Alexandria
43. Korolova A, Motwani R, Nabar SU, Ying Xu (2008) Link privacy in social networks. In: CIKM '08, Oct 2008
44. Zheleva E, Getoor L (2009) To join or not to join: the illusion of privacy in social networks with mixed public and private user profiles. In: WWW 2009 MADRID, WWW 2009 Madrid, Spain
45. O'Hara K, Shadbolt N (2010) Privacy on the data Web. Commun ACM 53:39–41
46. Backstrom L, Dwork C, Kleinberg J (2011) Where fore art thou R3579X ?: anonymized social networks, hidden patterns, and structural steganography. Commun ACM 54(12):133–141
47. Lucas M, Borisov N (2008) flyByNight: mitigating the privacy risks of social networking. In: WPES '08, Alexandria

48. Felt A, Evans D (2008) Privacy protection for social networking APIs. In: Workshop on Web 2.0 Security and Privacy (W2SP), W2SP 2008, Oakland, California
49. Rivest R, Shamir A, Adleman L (1978) A method for obtaining digital signatures and public-key cryptosystems. Commun ACM 21(2):120–126
50. Corder GW, Foreman DI (2011) Nonparametric statistics for non-statisticians: a step-by-step approach. Wiley, New Jersey, May 2009